THE POLITICS OF
NONFORMAL EDUCATION
IN LATIN AMERICA

THE POLITICS OF NONFORMAL EDUCATION IN LATIN AMERICA

Carlos Alberto Torres

Foreword by
MARTIN CARNOY

PRAEGER

New York
Westport, Connecticut
London

Library of Congress Cataloging-in-Publication Data

Torres, Carlos Alberto.
    The politics of nonformal education in Latin America / Carlos
Alberto Torres.
       p.   cm.
    Includes bibliographical references.
    ISBN 0-275-93419-5 (alk. paper)
    1. Adult education—Latin America. 2. Non-formal education—Latin
America. 3. Education and state—Latin America. 4. Educational
sociology—Latin America. I. Title.
LC5255.A2T67   1990
374'.98—dc20   89-36651

Library of Congress Catalog Card Number: 89-36651
ISBN: 0-275-93419-5

First published in 1990

Praeger Publishers, One Madison Avenue, New York, NY 10010
A division of Greenwood Press, Inc.

Printed in the United States of America

The paper used in this book complies with the
Permanent Paper Standard issued by the National
Information Standards Organization (Z39.48-1984).

10 9 8 7 6 5 4 3 2 1

CONTENTS

TABLES AND FIGURES

FOREWORD: HOW SHOULD WE STUDY ADULT EDUCATION?

Martin Carnoy

Education can be a fundamental instrument of social change. Simultaneously, the way it expands reflects political conflicts and compromises in the "modernization" of conditioned capitalist societies or the transition from conditioned capitalism to some vision of socialist social organization. Educational reform also represents both the dominant (often changing) definition of knowledge and how the society intends to re-create individuals and reintegrate them into the state and the people-nation.

It is logical that the form and content of education should be a fundamental issue during the process of economic development and social change. This is true both in capitalist societies, where ideological formation and politics are significantly shaped by social relations outside the state in capitalist production, and in revolutionary societies, where the dynamic of social change is crystallized in the state itself. Particularly in the latter case, the educational system, as a principal ideological apparatus of the state and the definition of knowledge on which that system is based, necessarily reveals the shape of social relations and social change.

Adult education is a significant component of the educational effort in many developing countries (and with increasing unemployment and worker retraining, in the highly industrialized countries as well). To some extent, the rationale for such education is the same in all societies, independent of social organization or structure (capitalist or in transition to some noncapitalist political form). Both capitalist and revolutionary states seek to increase productive skills through literacy and other forms of adult training. States also attempt to use adult education to redefine the relationship that adults have with the state (and the production system). This is more than simply an effort to use education to legitimize the training that is now such an important part of adult education; it is also an attempt to redefine the individual adult in the society, to incorporate him or her into a particular definition of nation and a particular role in production.

But there are also crucial differences in what adult education attempts to do and can do in different social-political structures. Ultimately, these differences depend heavily on the possibilities and limits of the state, since it is the state that defines adult education and is the principal beneficiary of its effective implementation. These possibilities and limits of the state are, then, a key issue in understanding the form and content of adult education.

Literacy training, for example, appears similar in different societies, but in practice produces very different results, not only in the degree of coverage of the program (in conditioned capitalist countries, coverage is much smaller than in revolutionary societies) but also in the way the program incorporates adults of different social classes into the society.

How do we explain these similarities and differences? And once we have reached a reasonable explanation, what does it tell us about policymaking for adult education in different kinds of societies? These are precisely the issues that Carlos Torres addresses in this book. Torres aims to understand what drives adult education, how that education relates to a nation's political and social structure, and what policy options are available in various historical-structural conjunctures.

Torres' essays are necessarily comparative, across theoretical perspectives, across nations with different social-political structures, and across nations with similar social-political structures that are developing and implementing different policies on adult education. This comparative approach yields a rich harvest, not only in terms of understanding the possibilities and limits of adult education but also in developing a research agenda.

THE STATE AND ADULT EDUCATION

Most conditioned capitalist states have difficulty integrating and standardizing the individual successfully into a class-based hierarchy of knowledge for two principal reasons: (1) the state is often unwilling or unable to mobilize enough resources to make public education (state-defined knowledge) generally available; and (2) even if education is made generally available, the private production sector and the state are often unable to provide sufficient wage employment to absorb those with average education—this tends to make the average level of public schooling (and therefore the average level of knowledge) insufficient for integration into the regularly employed labor force.

The other side of this coin is that in highly class-structured societies, when public education is relatively scarce, it cannot disguise its class nature. Individuals are differentially schooled, but differential access and success are rather evidently associated with rural/urban location, social class, and region. The hierarchy of knowledge in that education-scarce situation cannot be separated from the unequal social relations in civil society and, hence, the class nature of the state.

Education and knowledge in conditioned capitalist societies, as in industrialized capitalism, represent mobility and social and political democratization. Education as a symbol of mobility is even more accentuated, we will argue, in conditioned societies. But unlike the metropole state, most conditioned states generally make education and knowledge accessible to the mass of the population only on a limited basis. They do not re-create a "meritocratized" individual, and fail to incorporate the separated worker into a state that can use expertise as the basis for its reproduction. Obviously, there are a number of counterexamples, such as Argentina, the Philippines, Peru, South Korea, Taiwan, Venezuela, and Mexico. But even in some of those countries, the average education of the labor force remains very low, and a large fraction of the population is bound by traditional and personalistic social and economic relations. In most conditioned societies, the masses are so little incorporated into the capitalist knowledge hierarchy (a high percentage has a maximum of a few years of primary school) that they are not subject to the manipulation of "expertise" in the same way that a highly schooled society might be.

We have suggested elsewhere (Carnoy and Levin, 1985) that the tension in capitalist societies between mass education as a democratizing force (social mobility, the equalizing experience of public education, the democratic ideal taught in school) and education as a reproducer of capitalist inequalities (the class, race, or gender division of labor, unequal access to knowledge, the re-creation of the "separated" individual as a citizen identifying with the inequalities of the capitalist people-nation) underlies the expansion and reform of the education system and the system of knowledge production in those societies. Education as a democratizing force results in the expansion of mass education and more equal access to (the democratization of) knowledge. Education as a reproductive force requires controls on access and limits educational expansion.

In conditioned capitalism the tension between these two forces is exacerbated both from the supply side (limits on state expansion of public schooling) and the demand side (demand for schooling exaggerated by greater material and political inequalities between schooled and unschooled).

On the supply side, the conditioned state is constrained in increasing state social spending (hence in expanding and universalizing public education) by difficulties of private and state capital accumulation (Carnoy, 1984: ch. 7) and by the nature of the conditioned state itself, which (a) wastes limited state revenues by converting them into the increased consumption of individual bureaucrats, their relatives, and their friends, and (b) relies on particularistic political relations to reproduce itself, allocating jobs on the basis of patronage rather than competence. The impact on education of inefficiency and corruption in public bureaucracies (in addition to more limited funding than in the metropoles) cannot be underestimated. Since ministries of education at all levels (federal, state, local) are the largest single public employer in conditioned

capitalist economies, these elements are particularly present in public education and limit its expansion. In prerevolutionary Cuba, corruption in the Ministry of Education was so great that the average amount of schooling per young
person fell in the 1950s while budget allocations per pupil rose significantly.
The World Bank reported that these increased budget allocations were ending
up in the pockets of bureaucrats.

Supply-side constraints also result in the provision of such low-quality education to the mass of children that few can hope to reach the higher grades. Rural
and marginal urban schools in many conditioned capitalist countries have no
textbooks and teachers who have completed only primary schooling. Furthermore, what the bureaucracy defines as knowledge (the basis of the meritocracy)
is metropole-centered, and hence far from the experience of the average peasant or worker. This knowledge is, in turn, the basis of the primary and secondary school curriculum. The bureaucracy and the local bourgeoisie therefore
systematically convey a message of impossibility and distance between the
knowledge needed for material success and what the masses can learn in their
schools. It is probably no surprise to peasants and to the urban poor (themselves
only recently peasants or landless agricultural labor) that they fail in school,
even though in many countries, marginal (rural and urban) communities have
shown enormous commitment to their children's education despite such barri-
ers. But failing in schools where very few succeed helps to pacify claims for increased access to resources and political power, since such claims are restricted
to those of proven merit.

The growing commitment to education of those with little chance of success
reflects the exacerbation of the tension in conditioned society from the demand
side. The stakes of success or failure in school are much higher than in the
metropole. Schooling was provided by the conditioned state initially to produce
the modern skills required by the state bureaucracy (to mediate its relationship
with the metropole) and to politically incorporate a small middle class into the
conditioned people-nation by giving its children access to the university and the
liberal professions. This made schooling into a very important symbol of escape
from marginality, powerlessness, and poverty.

But, more important, the unequal distribution of consumption in conditioned
societies accentuates the importance of this symbol. Not only are the highest
positions in the society associated with university training (often in foreign universities), but the income and wealth associated with these positions are extremely high compared with that of the average worker or peasant. The relative
value of the prize awarded for attaining higher levels of schooling is therefore
much greater than in industrialized capitalist societies. And schooling appears—
much more than in the metropoles—to be the only way to achieve high income
and status, especially because such a large fraction of university graduates are
state bureaucrats, and the state bureaucracy is an acknowledged road to riches.
At the other extreme, the cost of doing poorly in school is usually denial of access to meaningful political participation and to full membership in the people-

nation. Thus, formal education and literacy come to represent the authenticity of membership in the modern nation, precisely what the metropole offers to its workers to re-create them as citizen-individual participants in the capitalist state.

This inability or unwillingness to incorporate the individual into a newly defined standardization of differences through schooling has the perverse effect (for the conditioned state) of creating an "excessive" demand for schooling services and a political conflict with the conditioned state over the lack of such services. The state makes years of formal schooling (as a proxy for merit or potential productivity) a condition of material success, but does not sufficiently democratize access to schooling to obscure its class role. The importance of education as a symbol of social mobility is accentuated, but so is the reality of its role as a reproducer of great social inequality.

Partly in response to such "excess demand" and a newfound rationale (human capital theory) for investing in education for economic growth, the United States and multilateral agencies in the 1960s and 1970s put enormous emphasis on increased schooling in low-income countries as a way of combating poverty and ignorance. It has moved a number of conditioned states to democratize educational access (for example, Costa Rica, which already had relatively high levels of schooling in the early 1960s, Kenya, Mexico, and Venezuela) through rapid expansion. Yet even with expansion, conditioned capitalist economies have had difficulty incorporating the educated into jobs requiring this education. Expansion reaches into rural and marginal urban areas last, assuring that the mass of youth in these countries will have lower levels of schooling and much poorer education than their urban middle- and working-class counterparts. The failure rates at the primary level in rural and marginal urban areas are high, requiring several grade repetitions and resulting in high dropout rates. And, in the absence of a policy to equalize income distribution and economic opportunity, increased access to schooling through expansion has only a minor effect on overall social equality.

School expansion does, however, make public education available to more people and tends to increase belief in meritocracy. In the absence of expansion (and often, even with expansion), the children of peasants, agricultural workers, marginal urban traders, and low-level service workers are excluded from all but a few, often painful, years in low-quality primary schools. The bureaucrats of the conditioned state remain distant from this vast majority of pupils and their parents.

By denying these children a new identification, the self-serving bureaucrats inadvertently help a revolutionary movement organize enough of that distanced majority to overthrow the state. Thus, although the conditioned state is often able to reproduce itself through the systematic manipulation of the least-schooled members of the society, the disintegration of the particularistic political relations that form the basis of that manipulation may turn the illiterate and low-schooled against the state. They are in no way responsible for the state, nor engaged in it, so they feel little compulsion to halt its disintegration.

The importance of scarce education as a symbol of social mobility in conditioned capitalistic society and the role of education in the formation of the revolution itself have made the expansion of education a fundamental tenet of revolutionary policy. The overthrow of the conditioned capitalist state does not mean the destruction of its symbols, especially those symbols which for generations have come to represent social self-authenticity. Formal education is one of these symbols. Universally, but particularly in societies marked by large differences in material consumption and social status, acquiring formal schooling represents possibilities for individual social mobility, even though relatively few actually achieve such mobility. At an ideological level, capitalist states have promoted the concept that a society with more schooling will be marked by greater income equality and more democracy, even though, empirically, the link between expanded schooling and income equality, while positive, is rather weak. Thus, at both the individual and the societal level, the promise of education for greater equality is strong symbolically despite the absence of a conforming, supportive reality.

This symbolic role is not lost on revolutionary movements. They incorporate the symbol of self-authenticity through education near the top of revolutionary reforms. Literacy becomes a revolutionary symbol of equality, and "authentic" knowledge—knowledge rooted in the history and culture of the society itself—is posed as a counterforce to the distant, foreign-rooted, metropole knowledge represented in the political and material symbols of the conditioned state. "Authentic" knowledge is both revolutionary and inclusive, and in that sense is simultaneously part of a new definition of the people-nation. The revolutionary movement, in turn, defines itself in terms of educating the mass of peasants and workers into an "authentic" self-definition that includes worker- and peasant-based knowledge, literacy, participation, and skill development. In China, Cuba, Mozambique, and Nicaragua, revolutionary guerrilla training included formal adult and youth schooling. In areas that came under guerrilla control, these various movements set up schools for villagers as part of their definition of "liberated territory."

Revolutionary education obviously has ideological aims. The revolution brings people into schools in order to reach the population with the revolutionary message. But not only must the revolutionary message have some appeal in order to bring people into these schools, the schooling must represent a response to an existing demand for knowledge, precisely the knowledge denied peasants and workers in conditioned capitalist society. By delivering literacy and math skills, revolutionary movements confer a self-identification in terms that had already been partly defined by the preceding capitalist society. School-learned skills are a response to educational demands exacerbated by the gross inequalities of conditioned capitalism.

At the same time, however, there is an attempt to achieve a new self-

identification within the context of a new, revolutionary authenticity and definition of the people-nation—within what Gramsci called "counterhegemony" and
what Che Guevara called the "new man." Whether this counterhegemony or new
person is indeed created in the countries analyzed is open to question. One of
the many problems we raise is whether schools can carry out this mission if political and economic institutions are not themselves sufficiently transformed
both to reflect and to create a new consciousness and new social relations, and,
in turn, whether in a world still dominated by powerful capitalist economies and
capitalist values, it is possible to build a work and social ethic that is based on
collective goals rather than the aims of individual consumption.

ADULT EDUCATION AS SOCIAL POLICY

It is in the context of these very different conditions that adult education takes
place in developing countries. In both contexts, adult education has taken on increased importance as education itself has been increasingly viewed as a human
right and as an integral part of access to political power and participation.

Yet, as we have tried to show, and as Torres makes clear in a systematic way,
adult education is not just literacy training or human capital formation. It is part
and parcel of a political strategy—and it is shaped by that strategy. At the same
time, however, the rise in importance of adult education suggests that popular
demands—even implicit demands—are gradually being responded to and are
themselves shaping political strategy.

It is this dialectical interaction between structure and history—between the
attempt by the state to impose a history on workers and peasants and the struggle by those groups to make history—that forms the basis of this book and that
produces a framework for developing a research agenda on adult education.

Perhaps most interesting is to what extent the research agenda is similar in
conditioned capitalist and revolutionary societies despite the major differences
in the context of the implementation of adult education programs. For no matter
how limited adult education may be in conditioned capitalist societies, it may
very well serve as a source of significant political change; and no matter how extensive adult education has become in revolutionary societies, it may very well
have to be reformed to act as a source of political change.

In summary, this book is an important contribution to the study of adult education as public policy. Carlos Alberto Torres provides us with an analytical
framework and a research agenda that are highly inspiring to develop empirical
and theoretical research in this field.

PREFACE: A POLITICAL SOCIOLOGY OF NONFORMAL EDUCATION IN LATIN AMERICA

The notion of political sociology suggests the study of power and relations of authority as structured in the various levels of social organization. It suggests an analytical approach concerned with the connections among religion, kinship relations, social classes, interest groups (of the most diverse type), and the political culture (ideology, value system, weltanschauung) of actors and social groups in the determination of political decisions, and in the constitution of social consensus—or, failing that, a confrontation or distancing—of actors and social classes with respect to the legitimation of public policy (Washburn, 1982: 126–27).

Obviously, any study in political sociology has to consider questions of bureaucracy and rationalization, power, influence, authority, and the constitutive aspects of such social interactions (clients and political and social actors, their perceptions of the fundamental questions of political conflict, and the alternative programs that derive from these). Similarly, at the heart of a political sociology are the connections between civil and political society, as well as the complex interactions among individual subjects, collective subjects, and social practices.

A political sociology of education implies considering all of these topics, theoretical questions, and problematics in a specific program of investigation to understand why a given educational policy is created; how it is planned, constructed, and implemented; who are the most relevant actors in its formulation and operationalization; what are the repercussions of such policy for both its clienteles and its social questions; and what are the fundamental, systemic, and organizational processes involved from its origins to the implementation and evaluation of the policy.

Though a political sociology of education has intimate connections with a sociology of education in the conventional sense (with questions of equity, efficiency, equality, mobility, etc.), its center of attention is an emphasis on questions of power, influence, and authority; its goal is to explain the process of decision making and educational planning at several levels (individual, institutional, organizational, and governmental) (Pescador and Torres, 1985).

It is useful to note that a political sociology of education is more an "interdisciplinary hybrid" (Sartori, 1969) than a new subdiscipline in the social sciences. Its connections with political science, anthropology (and ethnographic studies), political economy, and history are evident and require no further justification. Perhaps it is appropriate to emphasize that a political sociology of education that seeks to overcome the weaknesses of the Anglo-Saxon tradition—reflected, for example, in the classic political sociology of electoral behavior in the United States—and offer significant responses for our understanding of the formation of educational policy—must be distinctly interdisciplinary, historical-structural, comparative, and macroscopic (Dale, 1983; Washburn, 1982; Eisenstadt, 1971).

This book as a whole reflects my interest in discussing theoretically and explaining the formulation of adult educational policy in Latin America by focusing on few salient cases. Chapter 1 attempts to sensitize the reader to some of the basic problematics of illiteracy and adult education in Latin America, and offers a conceptual framework and a typology of the main approaches to nonformal education. Following La Belle, nonformal education is defined in this book as "any organized, systematic educational activity carried on outside the framework of the formal system to provide selected types of learning to particular subgroups of the population. . . ." (La Belle, 1986: 2). Within the overall framework of nonformal education, the notions of adult education and popular education are contrasted as alternative strategies for adult education policy and planning.

Chapter 2 offers a succinct discussion of the relations between the state and education, and sets the stage for the overall theoretical discussion in the following chapters. The relationship between state and education is central to a political sociology of education. It is also fundamental to understanding the reproductive character of adult education and its emancipatory possibilities.

Chapter 3 analyzes the political economy of adult education in Latin America. It discusses the relationships among models of development, educational ideologies, and adult education reform. Similarly, it points out the relationship between adult education as a welfare policy and the legitimation of political regimes. It was originally published in *Canadian and International Education*, Vol. 13, No. 2 (1984): 22–36. Reprinted with permission.

Chapter 4 offers a discussion of the political implications of adult education and literacy training. A concrete analysis of the national system of adult education in Mexico during the late 1970s and early 1980s (the foundation for the present system based on the National Institute of Adult Education) is presented.

Chapter 5, written with Daniel Schugurensky, analyzes adult education reform in socialist-oriented experiences in Latin America. Cuba, Nicaragua, and Grenada are placed in comparative perspective by contrasting the pre- and postrevolutionary situations in adult education, and lessons from the three experiences are drawn.

Chapters 6 and 7 present a theoretical and methodological perspective for the study of adult education policy formation, and a new agenda for research inspired by the political sociology of education. Chapter 8 offers a summary of the book and some indications for further metatheoretical and theoretical research.

I am deeply indebted to the University of Alberta for giving me the time and the resources through a Killam Postdoctoral Fellowship and a Central Research Grant, and for providing me with the unique intellectual environment of the department of educational foundations to complete this book. In this regard, I should recognize the help provided by Robert J. Carney and M. Kazim Bacchus, as chairpersons, friends, and enlightening colleagues.

Overall, this book has benefited from comments made by many colleagues and students over the years, and I have become indebted to so many that it will be impossible to list all of them here—I have noted the specific contributions of several colleagues in several chapters. I would like, however, specially to recognize the contribution of a few good friends and colleagues, including Raymond Morrow, who translated some of the materials that were originally written in Spanish; José Angel Pescador; Martin Carnoy; Raj Pannu; and Pablo Latapí. Paulo Freire's writings and personal advice through many conversations held over the years have always been inspirational to me, beyond and above any measure or qualification.

The contributions of my graduate students at several seminars held at the Latin American Faculty of Social Science (FLACSO) in Mexico City during 1984–1986, and courses that I have taught at the Graduate School of Education of UCLA in the spring of 1986, at World College West in California during the fall of 1986, and at the department of educational foundations, University of Alberta, Canada since 1986, have to be highlighted here. Their challenging criticisms, and their willingness to engage in the act of knowing as a mutual, shared experience, have contributed enormously to my own thinking and pedagogical practice. Daniel Schugurensky, a graduate student in the department of educational foundations at the University of Alberta, and coauthor of Chapter 5, deserves a very special mention for his diligent, imaginative, and hardworking contribution to this book. In spite of the quality of the contributions of so many scholars, friends, and colleagues, I remain solely responsible for the many limitations and shortcomings of this book.

I dedicate this book to the loving memory of my father, Domingo Roberto. His life taught me the meaning of honesty, decency, creativity, and struggle. His death taught me so many things that cannot be captured in a sentence.

THE POLITICS OF
NONFORMAL EDUCATION
IN LATIN AMERICA

1

PARADIGMS OF NONFORMAL EDUCATION

ASSUMPTIONS AND LIMITATIONS OF THE ANALYSIS

The task of this chapter is to sketch, in a preliminary form, a classification of the alternative approaches to adult education and nonformal education. In classifying and explaining the foundations, arguments, and methodologies of the alternative approaches to the topic, an effort will be made to contribute to the evaluation of strategies and programs of adult education and nonformal education, to the extent that such policies and programs are oriented toward a specific rationality.

The first assumption of this analysis is that every sketch of educational policies, plans, and programs, in whatever field of educational activity, is governed—explicitly or implicitly—by principles, presuppositions, and hypotheses that can be called a theoretical rationality.

The second assumption is that in educational practice there is a complex set of theoretical-methodological controversies that arise from and possess their own context in a specific field of educational practice; nevertheless, it is still possible to detect and trace their parentage, in one manner or other, to distant relations in different educational camps.

The third assumption is that, despite the variety of topics, discussions, or rationalities endemic to the field of education, it is possible to discern the parameters of constants that can be classified. In this chapter an effort has been made to isolate a number of approaches for each of the theoretical rationalities involved.

The fourth assumption is that in the last instance these approaches are not internally articulated—in the daily practice of the formulation and application of educational policy—in an organic, systematic, and functional form. On the contrary, there is a constant struggle between alternative rationalities. This struggle reflects a persistent conflict whose fundamental basis, situated at the level of civil society, is not conveyed to the state as a by-product but finds in the public arena a propitious context for the unfolding of specific contradictions. In some cases these are the origin of new sources of conflict. In other words, the theoretical rationalities, in their controversies and disagreements, express a level of conflict and struggle with origins in the basic sources of social practice.

The fifth assumption will therefore be that this effort to classify these approaches in a preliminary form, referring uniquely to the field of adult education, will necessarily remain limited: it will indicate only one of the aspects of the conflict (the ideological, rational, theoretical), using as empirical material the arguments codified and crystallized historically. Hence the level of analysis sought is primarily theoretical and not historical; nevertheless, the historical reality will appear indirectly in the concepts and arguments, as well as in the form of authors, topics of investigation, and formalization of education policies.

The sixth assumption makes reference to the context of analysis—adult education—which is perhaps more class-oriented than any other type of education. Far from directing itself to the totality of individuals in civil society (as, for example, in the case of elementary education), it directs itself to a sector of classes and social categories that we could characterize as socially subordinated sectors or, using terminology now in vogue, "popular" sectors.

Finally, a critical assumption of this study is that it is possible to capture the universe of processes that are expressed in state educational policy at a micro level (for example, at the level of adult education), where the texture and dynamics of general tendencies become visible. It is very important to stress that the alternative approaches referred to later represent fertile soil for the discussion at the level of the state. This is not due to the particular character of adult education, but to the fact that in the twentieth century education has become primarily and increasingly a function of the state. As a final observation before entering into the present theme, it should be noted that the classification of approaches that follows constitutes a preliminary typological effort whose utility is simply heuristic and not analytic. In no way is it suggested that the approaches indicated constitute ideal types for analyzing phenomena empirically observed in reality. These approaches cannot be used to classify mechanically different educational policy formulations. This typology, however, may serve as an aid for the study of theoretical rationalities underlying programs and not, as is often the case in the use of typologies, for using these instead of the concrete analysis of historical situations.

RATIONALITIES AND EDUCATIONAL PRACTICES

When we classify approaches, we refer to explicit rationalities in some way present or operative in educational practice. Nevertheless, there is an important difference between rationality and practice. While one may systematize a group of propositions and (rational) predictions for a particular practice, it is not always—even the majority of the time—to shape educational practice in the image and ideals of these rationalities. Educational practices, like social practices, must be seen not as effects or reflections of rationalities and structures, but as fundamental elements and irreducible to the social dynamic. In other words, the relation between rationalities (approaches) and practice is analogous to the relation between language and conversation: the language structures the conversation in terms of syntax and grammar, but exercises only a partial control over the contents of the communication (Bowles and Gintis, 1981).

Following this analogy in attempting to systematize the general rationalities underlying educational practice requires referring explicitly to "language" and not to the content of the communication expressed through the conversation. To simplify the analysis, a matrix of theoretical rationalities will be distinguished; from these, referring to different historical situations, diverse approaches emerge. In contemporary education this matrix may be organized in two broad visions of education: an incremental and a structuralist. The incremental vision has been often associated with the social sciences of North American origin, especially with the sociology and economics of education. This vision has been, and continues to be, the dominant one in the educational scene of that continent. In a strict sense, the incremental perspectives do not question the roots in the socioeconomic system where education takes shape; on the contrary, the grounding nucleus of this rationality can be expressed in these terms: to make educational processes a functional variable in the structural and systemic complex of the capitalist economy and society.

This notion of functionality and dysfunctionality is linked with a liberal pluralist perception of the state in which the latter is conceived as representing the general interests of individuals or, in its most critical version, as the neutral arbiter of the struggles between groups and social classes in civil society. Referring to education, this is a vision that puts its greatest confidence in educational planning and administration, in the techniques of decision making, in the techniques of administration and evaluation, in the techniques of resource optimization (e.g., in the production-function analysis). That is to say, it is "technocratic" in the sense that it puts greater stress on the technical and technological aspects of education than on the social and political aspects.

From this perspective, the principal role of educational planners and administrators is to improve the efficiency of the system by means of rational planning and administration, as well as through research, experimentation with new projects, or, in general, the formation of educational policies by experts. This role must be performed in isolation from political and social pressures, without giving effective participation to other social agencies, since the experts possess the autonomy and scientific legitimacy for this purpose. This approach argues that educational reforms must contribute to the specialization and structural differentiation of society, particularly to improving the skills of the labor force. In this manner, education appears as one of the most important determinants of the objective of equity and social well-being, contributing to the vertical mobility of individuals. Equally, as a result of its political functions, modern education contributes to the strengthening of liberal democracy (symbol of the most rational form of organizing power and government). Finally, with respect to production, the incremental perspective stresses that educational investment contributes to the improvement of the productivity of the labor force, thus improving its income, with subsequent repercussions at the macrosocial level: the creation of more wealth and social and economic development. The implications of this perspective at the level of educational policy include the claim that an increase in the level of education of the population will increase the productivity, as well as the remuneration, of the labor force and contribute, ultimately, to reducing social inequality.

Among those authors who traditionally defend an education that contributes to the development of human potential as well as social growth is John Dewey, who enormously influenced Latin American pedagogical circles. This idealist and pragmatic perspective[1] has been strengthened by those theoretical currents which consider education as an act of socializing individuals for social competence. In this second approach, which is slightly different from the first, one of the most important representatives is the American sociologist Alex Inkeles (Inkeles and Smith, 1974; Schuman, Inkeles, and Smith, 1967).

The structuralist perspective, in contrast, is based on historical-structural analysis of the process of economic, social, and political development. Education is considered a social phenomenon that plays an important role in capitalist growth, very often regulating the flows of the labor force. This labor force, as a result of formal and systematic educational processes, becomes better qualified (dexterity, skills, knowledge) as well as being socialized in certain norms and values that, in many cases, contribute to the reinforcement of social control and the existing hegemony, even if in other cases it becomes a source of contradiction and conflict.

From this perspective, the state is intimately linked with the constitution and reproduction of the capitalist system, protecting it from potential menaces and guiding its transformation. The state is not understood as an autonomous political institution that operates beyond the system of production and the structure of social classes; on the contrary, it is an arena where the contradictions of the production system and the contradictory dynamic of the conflict between social classes are manifested in public policies.

Hence, unlike the incremental perspective, the relation between education and the labor process is revised along nonpluralist lines. It is argued that there is a gap between the labor market dynamics and education's output that is reflected in three basic tendencies: (1) a maladjustment in the structure of the curriculum, that is, the persistence of a relatively homogeneous curriculum in face of the demands of an increasingly heterogeneous productive system; (2) a maladjustment between the production of graduates at all levels and the demand for them in previously established work positions, as is evident in the systematic fall in the rate of private and social return for graduates in advanced, as well as peripheral, capitalism; (3) the problem of the overqualification of the labor force employed in some industrial areas and the service sector, which results in an increasing dissatisfaction with work and the waste of resources, with its corollary in the inadequate production of scientific and technical knowledge. Closely related to this is a second body of work that is indicated by this perspective in analyzing the contradictory tendencies in both spheres. On the one hand, public education continues expanding, becomes more massive and diverse, and increases educational offerings, and also raises the level of education of the population; on the other hand, the dynamic of contraction in specific labor markets has the opposite effect, demanding personnel with increasingly lower levels of training to reduce the costs of production, enhance the control of workers, and facilitate the mobility of labor through this substitution; to improve the mobility of capital through new organizational techniques; and to avoid state control all at the same time (Braverman, 1974; Van Wass, 1981).

The structuralist perspective contains two contradictory macro perspectives: one does not question the capitalist basis of society, whereas the other, which is derived from the Marxist tradition, strongly attacks those capitalist foundations and envisions an alternative society. This radical perspective, in contrast with the incremental perspective, points out that educational policies rarely constitute a basic and effective factor in democratization and social equalization, since they continue to operate within the logic dominating society as a whole: the maximization of capital accumulation. As an alternative perspective, radical structuralism focuses its perception of the "educational problem" more on the social, political, and economic aspects than on the technical determinants of the formation of educational policy. The capitalist-oriented structuralist perspective, in contrast, uses technical rationality to reinforce tendencies to order and continuity in the sociopolitical system where education takes place. It would be a "systems" perspective on educational practice.

ALTERNATIVE APPROACHES IN ADULT EDUCATION

Along with the rationalities operating in education, it is necessary to consider the historical experience of Latin American societies. Even at the risk of forcing an excessively simplistic interpretation of social processes, it is possible to argue that the social atmosphere of the mobilization and participation of social classes, communities, groups, and individuals in educational questions constitutes a decisive variable for the formulation, implementation, and evaluation of policies in adult education. That is, any effort to characterize educational programs has to make reference to the social circumstances in which these programs take place and, especially, the social dynamic. In this respect, it is possible to distinguish two basic short-term situations (relegating large-scale organic-historical movements to another type of analysis): (1) a social conjuncture of political and participative activation of citizenry that corresponds—with the

Table 1.1
Alternative Approaches to Adult Education

Policy-Planning Modes		
Political Participation	Incrementalism	Structuralism
Political Activation and Participation	Modernization-Human Capital	Pedagogy of the Oppressed-Popular Education
Political Control, limited participation	Pragmatic-Idealism	Social Engineering-(Corporatism)

conceptual license of the case—to a historical situation where the dynamic of social transition overcomes the forces of order (or the latter at least have been eroded in a significant way); (2) a social conjuncture in which social and political order is reinforced by means of political control and limited participation of the citizenry. Now we are in a position to define the four dominant approaches to adult education.

The Modernization-Human Capital Approach

The modernization approach considers education in general, and adult education in particular, as a variable intimately linked to the processes of socioeconomic development. Development, in turn, is conceived as growth of the social product, taking as models the advanced Western capitalist societies. But why have these societies become developed while the countries of the Third World remain stagnant? The response for this approach is simple: because individuals in advanced societies enjoy a basic social personality that possesses standard values opposed to those in underdeveloped societies. Individuals in industrial advanced capitalism cultivate the attitude of achievement, a universalistic perspective, and a specialized and functional division of labor, while underdeveloped societies struggle helplessly with an orientation toward ascriptive statuses, a particularistic perspective on the world, and a nonspecialized division of labor.

These characteristics render difficult the passage from economic backwardness to economic development. Knowing the points of departure and arrival of the process of development, this approach indicates the necessity of identifying the mechanisms through which this passage can be realized in different situations. Literacy and basic education count among the privileged mechanisms for increasing contacts with modern societies (and their products), disorganizing traditional cultures (often of oral origin) that are considered an element of backwardness, and permitting development of social heterogeneity in the adoption of innovations.

Mark Blaug and others have noted that literacy and the basic education of adults in general contribute to economic development in distinct forms, by (1) increasing the productivity of the newly literate; (2) increasing the productivity of those who work with the newly literate; (3) expanding the diffusion of the general knowledge of individuals (training in health and infant nutrition) and generally reducing the cost of transmitting practical information; (4) stimulating the demand for technical training and vocational education; (5) acting as an instrument for selecting the most valuable elements of the population and enhancing their occupational mobility; (6) strengthening economic incentives, that is, the tendency of people to respond positively to an increment of compensation for their efforts (Blaug, 1966). In these terms, political scientists like Karl Deutsch point to literacy as one of the most important elements in the process of modernization and the development of nations undergoing industrialization. In some cases it has been suggested that an illiteracy rate between 30% and 45% is a precondition for obtaining average per capita incomes between $200 and $300 (UNESCO, 1968a, 1968b).

Diverse investigations have indicated a significant correlation between the percentage of illiterates and income per capita (.84), as well as between illiteracy and industrialization (.87). Further, the coefficient of multiple correlation for 54 countries among literacy, urbanization, recognition of the value of information, and political participation was .91 (Lerner, 1958). In fact, George Psacharopoulos has argued from a human capital approach that

> economists have established the link between increases in the educational level of the labour force and economic growth. Similarly, they have documented a direct link between increases in the level of schooling in the population and distributional equity. Sociologists have established the relationship between education and upward social mobility. Historians have documented the link between early rises in literacy and the economic take-off of nations. And a variety of other disciplines have established the relationship between education and further developmental outcomes like health, sanitation and fertility. (Psacharopoulos, 1988: 1)

Furthermore, regarding basic education, Marin and Psacharopoulos have argued (1976) that it has been found in Mexico that giving primary education to 10% of those who lack it would reduce a measure of income inequality by 10%.

A second line of argument stresses that the social psychological level of modernization entails a fundamental change in values, attitudes, and expectations; for the latter, changes in adult education are very relevant. Daniel Lerner suggests that (1) literacy is the skill that underlies the whole process of modernization; (2) that with literacy come benefits beyond reading and writing. This is one of the principal interests of the study of Howard Schuman, Alex Inkeles, and David S. Smith, (1967), which argues that the rates of literacy are strongly associated with a broad range of variables that are the cause or result of development. Thus, for Daniel Lerner, literacy and the basic education of adults permit the anticipation of social psychological changes that are a substantial part of the theory of modernization, which is understood as

> a complex but coherent group of psychological dispositions manifested in general qualities such as the sense of efficiency, orientation toward new experiences, interest in planning, all of which are linked, in turn, with a certain willingness to participate in institutional relations such as being an active citizen, giving science a high value, and maintaining autonomy in kinship relations. (Lerner, 1958: 63–64)

Finally, adult education and literacy are considered essential factors in the process of social mobilization. Huntington claims that one of the most relevant aspects in the process of political modernization is the change in attitudes, values, and expectations, changes that are a direct consequence of literacy, education, increases in communications, exposure to mass media, and urbanization (Huntington, 1971).

The Pedagogy of the Oppressed and Popular Education

For this approach the principal problems of adult education are not pedagogical or methodological, but political. Programs of adult education are explicitly designed as mechanisms or instruments of pedagogical and political collaboration with subordinate social sectors. It is a pedagogy for social transition, and hence defines its educational activity as "cultural action" whose central objective can be summed up in the term "conscientization." In its most radical version, the specificity of conscientization resides in the development of critical consciousness as class knowledge and practice, that is, it appears as part of the "subjective conditions" of the process of social transformation (C. Torres, 1982b).

In strictly educational terms, its intention is a nonauthoritarian pedagogy. Teachers and students are simultaneously students and teachers, with similar status, and are linked through a pedagogical dialogue characterized by a horizontal relation (Jarvis, 1985; C. Torres, 1982b; Shor and Freire, 1987). The educational agenda does not take place in the classroom but in a "cultural circle." The transmission of ideas, values, and knowledge is second relative to the notion of the sharing of experience. Among the principal characteristics of this approach is its resistance to links with the apparatus of the (capitalist) state and the bureaucratic organization of educational practice. To the extent that the state and the school represent sites of social mediation and repression, it advocates, in contrast, the creation of nonacademic, nonstate alternatives inserted into the heart of civil society. As a consequence, many of the representatives of this pedagogy work politically and professionally very close to political parties, universities, and centers of research, as well as the grassroots organizations of churches.

The link between this theoretical approach and adult education is natural and logical. As personalized in the figure of Paulo Freire, this pedagogy was developed first in Brazil, then in Chile, and has implemented or influenced literacy campaigns in Tanzania, Guinea-Bissau, Grenada, Nicaragua, and Mexico. The use of the so-called psychosocial method of adult literacy training has a clear practical and experimental basis in this pedagogical approach, though its application within, for example, primary education remains a subject of heated discussion. The political implications of adult education exceed those of school education—for example, the idea of using the necessities of communities as the primary material for vocabulary development in literacy programs.

Adult education, from the perspective of this philosophy, is more closely linked to the needs of communities and responds more easily to the demands of communities than does the system of formal education. In addition, adult education possesses the curricular and organizational flexibility that more bureaucratized and rigid formal systems lack. The results of adult education are more immediate than those of formal education. It is not necessary to wait through 10 to 15 years of formal training before the "graduate" can be incorporated into the labor markets or political activity, as would be the case with children. The demands for this type of education—especially in peripheral capitalism—are made by socially oppressed sectors; hence, illiteracy, far from being a social problem, is the result of a determinate structure and dynamic of classes, a consequence of the capitalist organization of production. Accordingly, the clientele of adult education constitutes, in its own right, a contradictory sector as well as a source of social change.

Finally, adult education has proved to be of great importance as an instrument of mobilization and the development of political consciousness in diverse experiments in the transition to socialism, as was the case in Cuba and is at present the case in Nicaragua. In every sense the pedagogy of the oppressed represents a liberating and progressive pedagogy.

Popular education's models spring from the original Freirean pedagogy of the oppressed developed in the early 1960s. The common features of popular education projects have been described by many analysts (García-Huidobro, 1985; Latapí, 1984; Rodriguez Brandão, 1984). First, they arise from a political and social analysis of the living conditions of the poor and their outstanding problems (such as unemployment, malnourishment, poor health), and attempt to engage the poor in individual and collective awareness of those conditions. Second, they base their educational practices on collective and individual previous experiences (as previous knowledge), and they work in groups rather than on an individual basis. Third, the notion of education provided by these projects is related to the concrete skills or abilities that they try to instill in the poor (i.e., literacy or numeracy), and these projects strive to arouse pride, a sense of dignity, personal confidence, and self-reliance among the participants. Finally, these projects can be originated by governments, as in Colombia and Dominican Republic, with projects related to integrated rural development (García-Huidobro, 1985; La Belle, 1986) or, as in Nicaragua, with the collectives of popular education

(Arnove, 1986); and they may be directed toward adults as well as children (La Belle, 1986).

Several types of popular education projects have been undertaken in the region. In a very well documented book, Thomas La Belle has identified three dominant paradigms of nonformal education in Latin America. La Belle's analytical approach is built on three dimensions: (1) the relationships between premises and outcomes of theoretical paradigms when confronted with their practical applications, (2) the relationships between rhetoric and reality in the programs, and (3) the issue of who sponsors and who controls nonformal education (La Belle, 1986). Using this model, La Belle has identified the following paradigms in the region: "human resource training" (which has been described above under modernization-human capital approaches), "popular education," and "guerrilla warfare." Popular education, according to La Belle, attempts to provide the more disadvantaged classes of society with skills that are considered necessary for their survival or will help them to live more productively within the existing social order and, eventually, to challenge it. "Revolutionary guerrilla warfare" is the definition that La Belle gives to "popular education" implemented in societies in social transition or in the so-called liberated zones of societies undergoing civil war in Latin America, such as El Salvador today, or Nicaragua and Cuba earlier (La Belle, 1986).

Considering only the paradigms related to popular education, and by focusing on their interpretation of social structure and the degree of people's involvement in the educational projects, García-Huidobro (1985) has distinguished (a) projects concerned with native, indigenous populations that focus on issues of language, multiculturalism, the retention, revaluation, and revival of self-identity among certain ethnic groups, and their resistance to assimilation into the dominant culture; (b) projects connected with participatory action research, which attempt to restore the collective memory of the people, drawing from popular knowledge the appropriate technology and the cultural elements to resist, challenge, and reappropriate the power that is usurped by the dominant groups through their manipulation of information, their control of ideological apparatuses, and, in the last analysis, their reliance on coercion and force (Latapí, 1988); (c) projects based on community participation in detecting common educational problems that could be solved through a network of horizontal relationships established among parents, teachers, and children (Ochoa and Garcia-Huidobro, 1982); (d) popular education projects connected with attempts to improve the utilization of the land (and land reforms) as well as with rural education oriented toward strengthening the negotiating power of the people (Muñoz Izquierdo, 1982a, 1982b), especially the small rural producers, and their managerial and technical skills (these are more incrementalist in nature than many other popular education projects); and (e) strictly political projects that strive to use educational resources and activities (i.e., literacy training or educational needs of marginalized classes) for organizing and mobilizing the socially subordinate population to challenge the established social structures and the state's power.

Pragmatic Idealism

The approach that has been termed "pragmatic idealism" has its roots in various pedagogical schemes, all of which are closely related with respect to premises, central objectives, strategies of reform, and operation of educational systems. Among the principal sources of this approach is the philosophy of education of John Dewey, the contributions of the Swiss educator Pierre Furter, the view of permanent education that inspired the report of the Faure Commission (*Learning to Be*), and the general orientations included under the rubric of andragogy (Knowles, 1980).

Dewey, who without doubt has been the most important educator of liberal inspiration, and one of the most influential in the context of Latin American education, was the mentor of the North American educational reform movement (1920–1950) that was projected onto Latin America. According to this philosophy, every person possesses unlimited potential that must be explored for the benefit of both the individual and society. The primary tool of this process is education, which is considered as fundamentally moral education in creating a future society based on individual development within the framework of a liberal democracy (Dewey, 1899, 1926).

It is fundamental for Dewey's position that education give internal compensation to the student and that it stop being a rational exercise and become an experiential one. This approach does not question the society where education takes place; on the contrary, it presupposes that industrial (capitalist) society allows the advance of science and technology, and the expansion of education—all of which, in the opinion of Dewey, are desirable in themselves and not subject to criticism. A second aspect that is completely glossed over by this perspective is the social processes and forces that have formed the educational process. In general terms, education is disconnected from the social system, which is taken as a given and necessary value (i.e., not contradictory). The final theme that is totally neglected is the labor-production-education relation; in other words, there is no concern whatever with the social effects of educational activity on the labor sphere.

The operationalization of this educational program has the following characteristics: (1) education is a good that people cannot renounce, so adult education takes on the character of a moral imperative for all of those marginalized within a culture; (2) it is thus a question of a "compensatory" or "remedial" type of approach that offers new educational opportunities to those who left the system or never had the opportunity to be incorporated into it; (3) in general terms, there are no substantial differences between teaching children and adults, and as a consequence the didactic materials designed for primary education can be used practically without modification for adult education; (4) illiteracy is a social problem, a "noxious weed" that must be exterminated; (5) even if the social determinants of illiteracy are recognized, one of the central themes of this orientation is the lack of will and motivation of adults to educate themselves, so most of the responsibility for illiteracy lies with the illiterate, who are lazy and stubborn when faced with educational efforts; (6) this orientation tends to underestimate informal and nonformal education, giving priority to academic forms, so that the mechanism of teaching/apprenticeship for adults resembles the classic night school with a teacher imparting lessons and the pupils sitting passively in classes; (7) although the massive campaigns for adult education constitute in themselves a pedagogical experiment without greater social repercussions, the institutionalizing tendencies of this pedagogy give greater value to stable, systematic, and selective services than to mass experiments; (8) the accreditation of knowledge, despite the stress put on experience, continues to be the center of educational practice.

The concept of continuing education points out that education does not have to be conceived as a period of life at the end of which a person is sufficiently formed to live in society. As an approach it has its origin in the preoccupations of the Faure Commission (and the book *Learning to Be*), an effort supported by UNESCO and other international organizations in order to respond to the problem outlined in the widely circulated book by Phillips Coombs, *The World Educational Crisis* (Coombs, 1968). To envision the future steps in the evolution of education, this approach distinguishes between extended education (the prolongation of academic education during the adult years) and continuing or permanent education (education distributed through life, and not necessarily academic) (Furter, 1966a, 1966b). From this perspective there should be (a) a spatial continuity (not limited to the physical space of the school, but including all possible locations, e.g., clubs, trade unions, cultural circles); (b) a continuity in learning, which means engendering attitudes and aptitudes for learning; (c) an organic-structural continuity in the form of the integration of the academic and the nonacademic; (d) a vital continuity such that there is not a hiatus between what is learned in life and in the school; (e) a continuity in communication where education does not limit itself to a single medium but is provided by radio, television, film, the press, and so on.

A reading of the UNESCO documents that have appeared from approximately the mid–1970s to the present—in particular the work of Pierre Furter in Brazil and Venezuela (Furter, 1966a, 1966b, 1970)—allows us to systematize this theoretical perspective in the following manner. First, permanent education must be considered as a continuous process of individual development. This encompasses (a) the constant increase in the knowledge thought to be necessary for an activity (the "knowledge explosion"); (b) the accelerated renewal of the knowledge acquired (to avoid the obsolescence of what is learned); (c) the structural modifications provoked by technological advance (reeducation and adaptation to new technologies and scientific logics); (d) the confrontation of the differences between the level of educational expectations and the capacity of the current system for satisfying them; (e) the facilitation of the extension of leisure time (as a result of cybernetics and mechanization); and (f) the facilitation of the growing participation of the population in programs to generate cultural integration. Second, permanent education must be considered as the principle of a general system of education. From the perspective of an emergent world culture, permanent education must simultaneously transcend academic education, integrating it into a general process of education; contribute to the creation of an "educational city" where the maximum output (technological, cultural, educational) can be incorporated, irrespective of the origin of the innovation or its underlying values (considered as rational and, therefore, utilitarian); and transform indigenous cultures, valid in themselves but limited in the face of the process of global integration, particularly through satellite communications and the increase in world commercial contacts. Third, permanent education must appear as a cultural strategy within a process of integral development (Furter, 1966a). Only this strategy will allow underdeveloped societies to overcome their limitations, realizing the development pointed out by the andragogical orientation. This approach was very prevalent in certain academic circles in Brazil during the early 1960s and 1970s, following the 1964 coup d'état, which has prompted several sharp criticisms from progressive scholars (Gadotti, 1983: 92–100).

Closely linked with the previous approach, and supported by organizations like the OAS and certain Latin American academic institutions, this approach emphasized that pedagogy must be considered as the science of the apprenticeship of the child, whereas andragogy refers to the science of the education of adults. Associated with a number of existentialist influences, this orientation emphasizes three programmatic dimensions. First, there must be promotion of educational opportunities for all social sectors (where this is understood in merely educational terms). This does not imply advocating economic or political democratization or a greater participation of social sectors subordinated in the system of social power. The focus of action is eminently educational. Second, the central problem of adult education does not reside solely in understanding the processes of adult learning (as distinct from that of children), or even in radically modifying the contents, methods, systems of evaluation, and mechanisms for organizing services; rather, everything derives from a combination for a new general organization of this education along with the necessity to strengthen the agents and instruments involved in the educational process (Cirigliano and Paldao, 1982).

There is an obvious coincidence between this argument and the hypothesis that the principal determinant of educational success is the experience and training of teachers—along with their existence in appropriate numbers; the third programmatic dimension, it emphasizes the necessity of self-learning and self-evaluation to incorporate the qualitative changes and innovations provoked by technological development.

In general terms these three orientations, which have been subsumed under the pragmatic idealist approach, respond to the necessity for the rationalization and justification of educational action by certain transnational institutions and organizations; it presupposes an unlimited confidence in the possibilities of scientific-technical advance for adult education, points to this as a precondition of development, and invites the elites to take into account the task of educating adults as part of cultural development. Independently of the discrepancies that might exist within this approach—from the humanistic radicalism of Dewey to the pragmatism of permanent education or the ingenuous confidence in technology underlying andragogy—they all coincide in one respect: they do not question the form of the organization of production, the effects of social hierarchies, and the form of articulation of power and social domination. They also have points of contact with modernization theory. However, pragmatic idealism, particularly in its contemporary versions, distances itself by considering human capital theory to be too optimistic with respect to the possibilities of economic and social development (confronted with the problems of planning the "world system"), and because the modernization perspective focuses its educational action too much on the school and academic systems. Finally, pragmatic idealism notes that modernization theory, in taking a quantitative perspective on growth and educational development, does not put sufficient emphasis on the new technologies of education and their implications for adult education.

Social Engineering (Corporatism)

This approach, usually related to military dictatorships in Latin America, conceptualizes education primarily as an exercise in social engineering. At the center of this form of thought one finds the presumption that a postindustrial society is emerging that is based on a high level of bureaucratic rationality in which the political and economic differences between social classes will disappear. A technical, professional, and scientific elite will emerge to displace social classes, to transcend, once and for all, ideological differences, imposing a scientific and objective rationality upon social action.

Though this postindustrial society can be clearly perceived in advanced capitalism, the perspective of social engineering—which has points of contact with the immediately preceding approach—would suggest that in Third World countries the mission of the state is to accelerate such development.

The political theory at the heart of this ideology is a normative perspective, an organicist, statist theory that concedes a certain importance to the decentralized political participation of semiautonomous, functional groups. The logic of interactions underlying these corporatively represented groups and the state forms a pyramid centralized in its strategic conception of development, but decentralized in its execution and operationalization of development programs.

The state assumes the role of intermediary in the economy, attempting to distance itself from both the laissez-faire principle of the liberal economy and the "rigid centralism" of centrally planned economies. The underlying economic model proposed is a mixed one in which the state assumes, jointly with private sectors, responsibility for the model of economic development, and the technocratic sectors assume increasing importance in the bureaucracy.

For this orientation, adult education appears as a conjunctural response to the processes of social mobilization and to the expansion of social demand. Among the preferred instruments for educational planning are open systems of education, which are conceived as parallel to academic systems but more economic, thus providing those subjects who will come to constitute the basis of manpower with medium qualifications. Adult education is intensified at those points where the demand for education expands and where it is necessary to compensate the part of the population that has remained marginalized from formal systems. Thus, to a great extent the macro systems of education are subtly designed as mechanisms of recruitment and training that are alternative to traditional political social channels. Social engineering, especially in its corporatist version, consolidates through adult education the experience of a political clientele under technocratic and bureaucratic rules.

Like the theory of modernization, this approach supports an ideology of technical progress in which the function of the educational apparatus appears to be linked to the requirements and imperatives of industry. It is a question of forming human resources as an instrument for economic purposes and includes open acceptance of displacing the social components of education, thus moving away from the more humanistic approach of Dewey or permanent education.

In general terms, social engineering designs an educational policy based on lengthy formal education and high levels of investment and return, and on informal and nonformal systems for those sectors of the population destined to occupy the less desirable social positions.

In strictly methodological terms, social engineering is characterized by the planning and expansion of mass systems of adult education that are generally oriented toward rural and suburban areas without a major preoccupation for the quality of the education imparted or for the continuity with prior education (e.g., systematic mechanisms of postliteracy training and community development). There are two reasons for this: (1) an effort to legitimate the state's image within the popular sectors—especially those not incorporated into processes of state control; and (2) an effort to make the state's presence felt in those areas where there are traditional mechanisms of organization and political control, including those historically supported by the state (e.g., *caciquismo*, or regional bosses).[2] Adult education is thus understood as a mechanism of political clientelism, and the tendencies stemming from pragmatic idealism that suggest increasing autonomous (or semiautonomous) participation by populations and communities are openly combated by social engineering, which proposes participation only through corporate channels of active state intervention.

Given the preceding, as well as the bureaucratic rationality internal to this perspective, it holds in high estimation the objectives of efficiency and efficacy in educational administration—in clear tension with the options of the political clienteles—and, moreover, argues for the rationalization of the educational process by means of the incorporation of teaching machines and advanced methods of planning and administration. What follows is an attempt to show the discrepancies of these two macro views, synthesized as incrementalist versus structuralist, in the realm of literacy training. In this regard, most of the incrementalist perspectives would be classified as national strategies for adult education, while the structuralist perspectives would be classified as national strategies for popular education.

THE CRISIS OF ADULT EDUCATION OR THE RENAISSANCE OF POPULAR EDUCATION?

Illiteracy is still with us: with the sweaty campesino behind the plow; wandering aimlessly with the unemployed in urban areas; sleeping in the same shack with the helpless Indian; in the prematurely aged hands of the young servant girl who immigrated to the city in search of a better life; afflicting the unskilled laborer in any factory in Latin America.

Recent statistical reports indicate that 120 million of the 380 million inhabitants of Latin America live in poverty. Of these, 60 million are indigent, their income not even sufficient for the food necessary for a minimum diet. Can we also infer, therefore, that there are at least 60 million absolute illiterates? Illiteracy, unemployment, and malnutrition are the basic elements of an equation that results from structural poverty.

The census definition suggests that an illiterate is a person who is incapable of reading and writing a simple, brief text about facts relating to everyday life. Perhaps this criterion is acceptable, but the mechanics of collecting this data is not. In the first place, we begin with an induced declaration of the interviewees without any empirical proof of their abilities. Second, phenomenologically, for such evidence to exist, we accept in general the skill to recognize symbols and to express them (or reproduce them graphically), and the possibility of possessing a certain capacity for abstract logic, as signs of participating in the world of literacy.

But are we really capturing the phenomenon we refer to as literacy, or are we simply approximating its most vague and imprecise contours? Let us put aside questions such as the following: What is the adequate level of literate culture for a society? What does it mean to say that a person is "literate" in politics, in civic duties, or in human affairs? How is the oral culture of a society linked with the written (e.g., in the case of pre-Columbian cultures Spanish always appears as an imposed) culture? Pierre Furter is correct when he notes that

> in the Middle Eastern empires of antiquity, the theocratic and centralized regimes which invented, adopted, or introduced the use of writing did so in order to solve the complex problems of accounting and administration posed by an accel-

erated urbanization. Historically, it would seem, writing was not invented for communication or expression, but to control and . . . oppress (Furter, 1972: 318).

Indeed, the introduction of reading and writing could have deleterious consequences in a given culture, as anthropologists such as Lévi-Strauss and others have demonstrated. These issues, however, are not our immediate concern in what follows. This and the concluding section of this chapter attempt to show some of the main elements in looking at illiteracy and adult education from the perspective of public policy, and how, in the final analysis in Latin America, the alternative approaches of adult education seem to boil down to only two dominant strategies for nonformal education policy and planning: adult education and popular education.

In Latin America in 1950 only two countries had a rate of illiteracy less than 15% of the total population, seven countries had a rate between 15% and 29.9%, six countries had between 30% and 49.9%, and eight had a rate higher than 50%. Thirty years later, 13 countries had rates less than 10%, 10 had rates between 10% and 24.9%, and six had rates higher than 25% (only one, Haiti, had a rate higher than 50%).

The disparity with respect to gender has not changed—illiteracy continues to be higher for women than for men. The urban-rural differences continue. In 1970, in 14 countries in the region, the illiterates living in rural areas represented 69% of the population 15 years and older. Hence discrepancies in regional development have not changed significantly: the most developed areas, especially metropolitan urban centers, continue to be the most literate. Ethnic disparities still persist. For example, in Panama, with a national illiteracy rate of 21.7%, the Indian population has a rate of more than 70%.

Finally, confronted with the loss of linguistic skills in the mastery of the mother tongue among the youths in Latin America, how can we be sure that we have put up a dike against illiteracy since the impressive expansion of primary education in the last few decades? Is illiteracy a question of a many-headed Hydra—every time we chop off one head, two grow in its place, even more horrible than the first? In a conversation with primary teachers in Minas Gerais (Brazil), Paulo Freire found that the loss in content and mastery of language is, for the young, clearly one of the greatest challenges currently in education. He added that the reason for this phenomenon must be found in the authoritarianism of parents, teachers, and the state in this civil society (Freire, 1981). To think about the metamorphosis of illiteracy is to anticipate, in a way, new directions and to foresee educational challenges.

Yet there remain two decisive questions to be resolved in discussions of national strategies of literacy development: (1) How are the history of adult education and economic development linked such that illiteracy persists despite the industrial advances in Latin America? (2) When we speak of adult education and popular education, are we speaking of two distinct phenomena or the same objective and theoretical entity? In the following section, only this second question will be addressed.

ADULT EDUCATION OR POPULAR EDUCATION: DILEMMA OR DISJUNCTION OF NATIONAL LITERACY STRATEGIES?

It is indispensable to begin an analysis of national literacy strategies with a clear distinction between popular and adult education. Popular education existed previously as political-pedagogical projects supported by the state. Consider, for example, the educational process driven by "socialist education" in Mexico during the government of General Lázaro Cárdenas (1934–1940). This educational movement contributed greatly to the creation of rural education in Mexico. Given the libertarian and socialist ideology that animated this educational project, the character of the state where it was designed and promoted, the objectives for social change pursued, and, above all, given the high level of popular participation it had, it must be legitimately included among projects of popular education.

Similar considerations would result from studying the literacy and cultural renewal programs led by Lunatcharski and Krupskaya at the dawn of the Russian Revolution (1918–1924), or the antioligarchical peasant education led by the MNR in Bolivia in 1952. In terms of nonstate projects, the education led by the anarchic-syndicalist unions in Argentina during the first two decades of the twentieth century could undoubtedly be considered as working-class initiatives for developing popular education in today's sense of the term (Puiggrós, 1984).

Adult education represents perhaps a more recent concept, without necessarily having the political-pedagogical connotations of popular education. Nor does it imply a radical project of change, radical ideologies of change at the level of the social relations of production, or a specific type of state or a political regime where such projects may take shape. Adult education arose in intimate association with the postwar euphoria when the defeat of fascism released processes of democratic renovation in Western societies. Elections as a device for guaranteeing the functioning of democratic structures and the political education of (adult) citizens constituted the pillars of this social renewal.

Here the activities of UNESCO—in program material and the missions of experts—constituted the key element of the machinery for establishing this educational subdiscipline. With diverse terminological ornaments such as functional literacy, community development, and continuing education, and consolidating itself in world conferences on adult education (from the celebrated one in Helsinki to the one in Paris in 1982), adult education became systematized and incorporated into specific theories—theories of "medium range," to paraphrase the sociologist Robert Merton. In Latin America, it would appear that adult education acquired a new force when, in the middle of the 1960s, the experiments of Freire in Brazil and Chile became publicly known, a process aided by the increase in educational financing in the region. Nevertheless, the efforts of Freire were slowly becoming part of the tradition of the theory of popular education in Latin America, constituting a theoretical and methodological focus anticipated by popular education, problem-posing literacy training, and participative education (Gajardo, 1985; Latapí, 1988).

At the time of the UNESCO declaration in Mexico in December 1979, adult education was strengthened when the agreement between the international organizations and governments of the region was renewed to bring, by the end of the century, reading, writing, and basic calculation skills to the 45 million illiterates of the area.

In sum, a national strategy of literacy training must put itself into one of these theoretical, methodological, and practical camps: the camp of adult education (with whatever of its paradigms is in vogue) or the camp of popular education (with its political orientation). This would define in a conclusive manner the following aspects of literacy development:

1. The delimitation of objectives
2. The compatibility between literacy training and economic development
3. The creation of organizational models and mechanisms of operation for literacy programs
4. The delimitation of the resources and methodologies for literacy training
5. The delimitation of the relations between social organisms (civil society)
6. The generation of standards, instruments, and methods of control (external or internal) of the process of literacy training, as well as its future projections (Flores, 1982).

Obviously these six organizational steps are interpreted according to the theoretical perspective that holds for both adult education and popular education. For purposes of exemplification, Table 1.2 allows a comparison of the fundamentals of both perspectives.

CONCLUSION

It is important to note, as Carlos Rodriguez Brandão does, that adult education in Latin America has not contributed significantly to educational innovations. It has simply used pre-existing practices, routinizing and institutionalizing them while helping to "bury the remains of those considered to be enemy forms" (Rodriguez Brandão, 1984: 28–29). In short, adult education has become an institutionalized practice whose main goal is to reproduce itself, thus leading to attempts from both the left and the right to create alternatives to it. For Rodriguez Brandão, adult education is simply the "memory of the colonizer" represented in a set of institutions that are centralizing and domesticating (Rodriguez Brandão, 1984: 29, 31).

Table 1.2
Adult Education and Popular Education as Alternative Strategies for Policymaking

Parameters of comparison	Strategies of adult education	Strategies of popular education
General orientation	Technocratic or traditional orientation	Politically oriented
Pedagogical-political program	Emphasis on economic development	Emphasis on political development
Style of conception and execution (decision making)	Centrally planned, non participative, antimobilizing	Highly participative and mobilizing
Educational project/society relation	Greater emphasis on the state educational project than on the mobilizing dynamic of the civil society	Greater emphasis on social mobilizaton as a framework for educational mobilization than on educational change per se
Sociological vision	Relatively insensitive to the structure of social forces and their antagonistic contradictions: a relatively segmented vision	Highly sensitive to the structure of political and social forces; the vision of the concrete totality
Usual methods	Generally nonparticipative; open, nonacademic; controlled critical level	Generally participative; open, academic systems; highly critical methods

Important distinctions in studying adult education have been advanced by Bock and Papagiannis (1983), who want to determine who is sponsoring a given program, including government sponsorship (in this case it is important to assess its degree of commitment to social change) and nongovernment sponsorship (in this case we need to identify what degree of congruence to government ideology the nongovernment organizations have); the organization and administration of the programs (i.e., whether they are top-down, bottom-up, or a combination); the pedagogical approach involved (Bock and Papaggiannis distinguished pragmatic, ideological, didactic, and participatory); the main assumptions about development; and the degree of integration with other social institutions. These and other criteria for classification will be addressed theoretically in Chapters 6 and 7 of this book in order to understand policy formation in adult education. Suffice it to mention here that if we consider the classic socialization and social mobility functions, the selection and recruitment process, and the exchange value of adult education (as suggested by Bock and Papaggiannis, 1983: 19), the evaluation of adult education in Latin America will show that the economic and social returns of adult education are very limited. Indeed, such an evaluation will show that adult education has been usually co-opted by the state and employed as an instrument of social legitimation and the extension of state authority, more than as a tool for self-reliance of individuals and communities in the poor segments of the Latin American societies (Bock and Papagiannis, 1983: 339).

The term "popular education" often appears as something different from adult education. While adult education is, by and large, compensatory education, popular education attempts to be a radical departure that originates in the popular classes and may be designed to alter the social order (Rodriguez Brandão, 1984). Although since the 1950s adult education has gone through several permutations and name changes that may have produced the illusion of constant renewal (i.e., functional literacy, selective-intensive functional approaches, fundamental education, lifelong education, permanent education), Rodriguez Brandão contends that it is popular education that grew as a movement of educational innovation in Latin America—in some cases as a clandestine one. According to Rodriguez Brandão, popular education in the 1960s did not pretend to be an advanced form of adult education but a pedagogical movement that rested on the negation of mainstream adult education and the educational system that generates banking learning. That is, Rodriguez Brandão, among others, contends that in the 1960s popular education in Latin America was neither a set of cultural revival practices nor a social movement (as argued by Zachariah, 1986). The distinctive characteristic of popular education today is that it is tied to popular movements. Popular education, then, (1) proposes a new renewing theory of the relationship between human beings-society-culture-education and pedagogy, (2) takes place primarily among the adults of popular classes and becomes defined as political action for popular liberation, (3) seeks to transcend mere ad hoc activities like literacy campaigns or adult basic education (R. M. Torres, 1983; Gerhardt, 1985).

The history of popular education in Latin America is not linear, but has proven to be limited only by the imagination of its advocates and grass-roots practitioners in a dialectical tension with their living, material, and political conditions (Puiggrós et al., 1987). This shows that the coexistence of traditional, hegemonic, and emergent pedagogical forms has been the rule, not the exception. In turn, popular education has produced a confrontation between "official" state-sponsored strategies of adult education and alternative or advanced forms of nonformal education. But this confrontation, as in the emerging paradigm of participatory action or participatory education, has had an impact on the adult education projects that more and more may be incorporating the letter, but not the spirit, of the participatory action research approaches (Rodriguez Brandão, 1984: 33).

Educational research has proven that the decisive features of mainstream adult education are its methodological individualism, its technocratic and economic rationale for policymaking, its case-study or project-by-project approach, its normative and prescriptive emphasis instead of an explanatory and analytical focus, and its ahistorical and antitheoretical biases. A more dynamic approach, popular education, calls for democracy, participation, and economic political reorganization of the poor and greater autonomy for the communities. These premises are indeed a radical departure from mainstream adult education programs. Undoubtedly there are still numerous dilemmas for popular education, but it has moved from being an emergent educational model (Avalos, 1988: 167–69) to become a politically established practice whose point of reference is popular movements.

NOTES

1. Pablo Latapí, in personal correspondence with the author, has criticized the use of the term "idealist-pragmatic" to refer to the three diverse currents represented in Dewey's progressivism, andragogy, and "recurrent education." I shall argue, however, that some of the naive assumptions embedded in them about the relationships between human agency and structure, and their unfounded optimism for the role of technology and adult education in humanization and social change will qualify as idealist. The pragmatic side comes from the refusal to discuss the practical implications of the current organization of production (i.e., constraints imposed by social and economic structures) for a comprehensive reform of nonformal education, and the possibility that adult education could impact on the division of labor and well-being of adults segmented by classes, races, and gender. Stressing an epistemological approach, the pragmatism can be equated with the lack of a critical theory of society to understand the dynamics of transformation of capitalist structures that would impede generation, in Habermas's terms, of massive ideal speech situations.

2. There are obvious differences between civilian corporatist states and military dictatorships, and among military dictatorships. Similarly, there are strong differences between inclusionary and exclusionary forms of corporatism (Stepan, 1978). For instance, while the bloody military dictatorship that ruled Argentina between 1976 and 1983 drastically diminished the provision of adult education, its Brazilian counterpart, after the coup d'état of 1964, created the MOBRAL (Brazilian Movement of Literacy Training) in 1967, (Bhola, 1984; Chapter 4 of this book). The Mexican corporatist state, which because of the radical trends emerging from the Mexican Revolution does not entirely share an organic-statist normative perspective, greatly expanded the provision of mass adult education in the 1980s, though there was not immediate concern with the quality of education provided to adults (Pescador and Torres, 1985; Morales-Gómez and Torres, forthcoming). Finally, while the Brazilian state (1964–1983) and the Mexican state may have oscillated between inclusionary and exclusionary policies, the Argentine experience can be characterized as an exclusionary political reform, a form of corporatism called by O'Donnell a bureaucratic-authoritarian state. There are still important theoretical problems in analyzing corporatist experiences of policymaking in industrial advanced societies, particularly in Western Europe (Therborn, 1988).

2

THE STATE, EDUCATIONAL
POLICY, AND THE POPULAR
SECTORS IN LATIN AMERICA

In this chapter I will discuss some of the theoretical connections between the capitalist state and education. As a point of departure an effort will be made to synthesize in four major hypotheses the Gramscian conception of the relations between the state and education. With his theoretical explorations of education, culture, and superstructures in general, Gramsci provides an obligatory reference point for my analysis. Along with this interpretive synthesis of Gramsci, I propose to make some brief critical comments regarding the principal distortion of Gramscian theory, the approach of Louis Althusser.

In the second section, and on the basis of the preceding critical discussion, I will attempt to indicate in summary form some of the theoretical characteristics of the capitalist state as it relates to an investigation of the formulation of public policy in education. The final section will provide some questions for establishing an agenda of research on the state and educational policy in Latin America.

A final observation must be made. For distinct epistemological and theoretical reasons, which I hope will emerge in the text, I will try to utilize as an immediate referent of the analysis the conflictual demand for education that the popular sectors have increasingly been making in Latin American societies. Nevertheless, the manifestations, modalities, and determinants of this demand, the role of education in the strategies of survival of the popular sectors, and the repercussions at the level of civil and political society will not be analyzed here.

THE CAPITALIST STATE, HEGEMONY, AND EDUCATION

The contribution of Gramsci to the study of the relations between the state and education can be synthesized in four major hypotheses. First, the relations of hegemony in a capitalist state may be understood as educational relations, even if they arise from mechanisms of coercion and consensus established in relation to a given material basis. Second, although hegemony is exercised by the dominant class, it is organized in capitalist societies by a particular social category: the intellectuals. Third, education is fundamentally a process of the formation of a "social conformism." Fourth, the state, as an "ethical state," or as educator, assumes the function of constructing a new civilizational type or level. The state thus constitutes an instrument of rationalization (Gramsci, 1975: Q 1-XVI, Q 4-XIII, Q 12-XXIX, Q 22-V).

Gramsci's notion of hegemony in civil society is a central theme in his analysis of the social functioning of a capitalist socioeconomic formation. On the one hand, it refers to the relations between groups, especially social classes, where one fraction of the dominant class is considered as exercising hegemonic direction over other (allied) fractions of the bloc in power. This hegemonic direction is based on a moral and intellectual leadership deriving from the economic supremacy the dominant fraction. On the other hand, "hegemony" refers to the relations between the dominant and subordinate classes. Basically, this hegemonic direction signifies the ideological predominance of (bourgeois) norms and values over those of the subordinate social classes. Nevertheless, in the Gramscian formulation, hegemonic direction is established by means of moral and intellectual persuasion, and is only secondarily based on the power of organized violence, the army, political action, or the coercive power of the law. Gramsci states: "The form of power which creates stability is conducted through moral and intellectual hegemony, basing itself in an ample margin of consensus and tacit observance. Each relation of hegemony is necessarily a pedagogical relation" (1975: Vol. II, p. 1321).

The Gramscian notes on hegemony begin by establishing a crucial analytical distinction. Whereas the state (as political society) appears to constitute itself through organized coercion, civil society constitutes itself through spontaneous consensus in the general direction imposed by the dominant classes on social life;[1] yet very often this direction implies the saturation of the political consciousness of the citizenry. The role of intellectuals in this process is to serve as "experts in legitimation" (Karabel, 1976: 146–56), serving as intermediaries between the masses and the hegemonic leadership in the organization of the hegemony of the dominant class. Along with the action of intellectuals, the presence of a matrix of structural (economic) and structuring (the labor force and capital in the social division of labor) relations contributes to the fact that the world view systematized and diffused by intellectuals— which corresponds to that of the dominant sectors—becomes internalized by the dominated classes.

Giuseppe Fiore, the leading biographer of Gramsci, wrote:

> Gramsci's originality as a Marxist lay partly in his conception of the nature of bourgeois rule (and indeed of any previously established social order), in his argument that the system's real strength does not lie in the violence of the ruling class

or the coercive power of its state apparatus, but in the acceptance by the ruled of a "conception of the world" which belongs to the rulers. The philosophy of the ruling class passes through a whole tissue of complex vulgarizations to emerge as "common sense": that is, the philosophy of the masses, who accept the morality, the customs, the institutionalized behavior of the society they live in. The problem for Gramsci then is to understand *how* the ruling class has managed to win the consent of the subordinate classes in this way; and then, to see how the latter will manage to overthrow the old order and bring about a new one of universal freedom. (in Carnoy, 1984: 68–69).

Gramsci argues that the educational system and education in general appear as a privileged instrument for the socialization of a hegemonic culture. He notes:

The hegemony of a directive centre over the intellectuals asserts itself by two principal routes: 1. a general conception of life, a philosophy (Gioberti), which offers to its adherents an intellectual "dignity" providing a principle of differentiation from the old ideologies which dominated by coercion, and an element of struggle against them; 2. a scholastic programme, an educative principle and original pedagogy which interests that fraction of the intellectuals which is the most homogeneous and the most numerous (the teachers, from the primary teachers to the university professors), and gives them an activity of their own in the technical field. (Gramsci, 1980: 103–04).

Gramsci emphasizes that the school and the church are the largest cultural organizations in every country: in the number of people they employ, in the ideological material they manipulate, and above all, in their filling the vacuum between the popular masses and the intellectuals of the dominant classes.[2] This is because "the State, as such, does not have a unitary, coherent and homogeneous conception, with the result that intellectual groups are scattered between one stratum and the next, or even within a single stratum" (Gramsci, 1980: 342). Hence schoolteachers and priests, acting as a labor force, hegemonically link one stratum with the other, incorporating each social stratum with the dominant hegemonic culture. In this sense, the control of consciousness represents as much an area of struggle as the control of productive forces.

It is in this context that the characterization of the capitalist state is important in Gramsci. The state includes a large complex of institutions (including the "private" institutions, such as the church), which are thus apparatuses of the state contributing to the refinement, diffusion, and reinforcement of its hegemony (political ideology). Gramsci notes: "If every State tends to create and maintain a certain type of civilization and of citizen (and hence of collective life and of individual relations), and to eliminate certain customs and attitudes and to disseminate others, the Law will be its instrument for this purpose (together with the school system and other institutions and activities)" (Gramsci, 1980: 246).

In reality, Gramsci concludes, the state must be considered as an educator, inasmuch as it has to create a certain type or level of civilization. Often this is conceptualized by Gramsci as a "passive revolution." "Americanism" and "Fordism," as central pieces of an industrial system of goods production— emerging from the accelerated process of industrialization in the United States, and which so impressed Gramsci while he was writing his reflections in prison— constitute an expression of this "passive revolution." Consequently, for Gramsci it is necessary to consider the state not only as a "superstructural" factor that develops spontaneously and harmoniously, conforming to the development of the productive forces and the social relations of production, but also as a manip- ulator of such economic forces, reorganizing and developing the structure of economic production as well as creating new structures. "The State, in this field, too, is an instrument of 'rationalisation,' of acceleration and of Taylorisation" (1980: 247).

In sum, in Gramsci's thought these relations among state, civil society, and hegemony, even when they often appear to be antinomic and cryptic, are crucial for understanding the process of exploitation and political domination in society. The state contributes in a decisive manner to the process of reproducing the capitalist relations of production, acting as a guard system while participating in the struggle for control over the formation of the citizenry. It is in this sense that the state assumes a complex task: the creation of a "social conformism" through intellectuals and through the school system in particular:

> [E]very State is ethical in as much as one of its most important functions is to raise the great mass of the population to a particular cultural and moral level, a level (or type) which corresponds to the needs of the productive forces for devel- opment, and hence to the interests of the ruling classes. The School as a positive educative function, and the courts as repressive and negative educative function, are the most important State activities in this sense: but, in reality, a multitude of other so-called private initiatives and activities tend to the same end—initiatives and activities which form the apparatus of the political and cultural hegemony of the ruling classes. (Gramsci, 1980: 258)

However rich and captivating in its analysis of myriad complex interactions in political life, Gramscian thought has without doubt been subjected—perhaps because of its seminal yet contradictory and fragmentary character—to a great number of distortions. The most important with respect to the study of rela- tions among state, education, and society has been the approach of Louis Althusser. Althusser has suggested that the primary role of the state is the re- production of a system of class relations, directly through political repression or indirectly by means of the social institutions that function ideologically (such as the school or the means of communication). For Althusser, social reproduction signifies basically the reproduction of the division of labor, but it also includes the reproduction of the habits, abilities, and skills of the labor force. For Althusser, the question of ideology is converted into a central theme for the re- production of the relations of production (and the mode of production in general). The school therefore fulfills the central role for realizing this objective (Althusser, 1971: 132) to the extent that in mature capitalism the dominant ideological apparatus of the state is found in the educational system (1971: 152).[3]

Althusser concludes by suggesting the existence of a duality of state apparatuses: those with a dominantly repressive function and those with a primarily ideological function associated with the church, political parties, trade unions, schools, communications media, and, from a certain point of view, the family.

The criticisms of Althusser's position are well known. First, the limits of the state are not an object of indifference in Marxist political theory; on the contrary, it is essential to be able to classify them adequately. To confound them prevents us from understanding the role and the specific efficacy of superstructures distant from the state in bourgeois democracy, especially when predominantly ideological institutions conserve a high degree of relative autonomy, thus being more capable of masking the character of the state's function, such as the specific contradictions of its functioning (Anderson, 1978; Miliband, 1977: 292). Through inference, it is possible conceptually to distinguish the modes, means, and methods of state action, such as the rules of production of public policy in education. These distinctions allow investigation of modes, means, and alternative modalities in the production of public policy in states that, although of capitalist character, may differ profoundly with respect to their political regime. Here, therefore, distinctions regarding the form of the state and the form of the regime become essential for understanding different formulations in educational policy.

Second, a clear distinction between ideological apparatuses (public and private) and repressive apparatuses (primarily public) in the reproduction of the social relations of production does not appear to correspond completely to objective reality—even in strictly analytical terms. On the one hand, neither of the two types of state apparatuses could function coherently without its functional counterpart: Ideology does not function without a certain dose of coercion, and the mechanisms of coercion become inoperable without a strong dose of ideology to sustain them. On the other hand, the possibility of conflicts, contradictions, and noncorrespondence between diverse state apparatuses—even within a specific apparatus—fades before the supposed solidity of such apparatuses.

Finally, the theme of reproduction can be studied from diverse angles if the reproduction of the technical division of labor and of the social division of labor are considered.[4] Without attempting here to introduce a discussion that has become increasingly intense in Europe (Offe and Wiesenthal, 1980; Przeworski, 1981: 21–45), the question of reproduction also can be considered from the perspective of the logic of class organization and its organizational forms. That is to say, the problem of reproduction abstracted from political struggle (and also ideology, not as an emanation of a mode of production but as a result of the level and character of the daily conflict of classes) and separated from the structuring limits of the activity of the state and civil society, may quickly drift toward the "new" reductionism so justly criticized by José Nun (1982). Just as the technical reproduction of labor cannot be separated from the social reproduction of labor, so education as a mechanism of socialization in a hegemonic culture depends on the structural parameters of the functioning of capitalism. These parameters simultaneously frame and structure the action of formulating state public policy. Here is a tentative list of such parameters. First, the production and distribution of goods and serves are primarily private. Second, the actors in the state apparatus (and particularly in the institutions linked to the ideological apparatuses) depend for their survival, as well as for the success of any global political objective, on the continuous flow of economic resources, which are usually obtained in a form derived from the process of the private accumulation of capital. Third, the state must promote and protect this process of accumulation of capital, which necessitates emergent economic resources and the political legitimacy resulting from economic success, whether this be called the "Brazilian miracle" or the Mexican "stabilizing development." Fourth, the personnel of the state do not possess a base of power *stricto sensu* in the apparatus of the state. That is to say, they need a certain mandate for action, a mandate resulting from some other source of power. In other words, the state depends on the capitalist class not so much for what it decides to do politically as for what it could refuse to do economically (Offe, 1975b).

Finally, imagine that each subject linked to the technical reproduction of the labor force (e.g., a teacher) would always act, whether consciously or unconsciously, as a transmitter of ideology; and then imagine (second presupposition) that this ideology—as a settled complex of rules—is adapted in its formulation and application exactly to the dynamics of the transformation of the industrial sector and the work force—a very simplistic and mechanistic approach to understanding educational dynamics. Consider, for instance, the situation in technical education, in which a curriculum content that tends to be homogeneous is confronted with the demands or the industrial sector, which are persistently heterogeneous.

This elaboration of Gramscian theory has permitted introducing the problematic of the capitalist state. It is now appropriate to synthesize some of the characteristic features of the state, especially its role in the processes of political domination, accumulation of capital, and reproduction.

THE STATE AND EDUCATIONAL POLICY IN LATIN AMERICA

Stanley Moore notes that the social bases of the capitalist state have been constituted by those groups, classes, and sectors which benefit from the system of production, as well as its preservation and rationalization. In general terms, the state can be defined as an institution for the preservation and rationalization of a given socioeconomic order, particularly the system of production and the class relations this implies (Moore, 1957: 17–19; Hamilton, 1982: 6–23). In this sense, F. H. Cardoso has defined the state as a pact of social domination: the basic pact of domination that exists between the classes and fractions of the dominant class, and the norms that guarantee the domination of the latter over the socially subordinated sectors (1974; 1979: 38). But this definition is incomplete if we do not incorporate its character as a system of self-regulated administration held together by the institutional apparatuses, bureaucratic organizations, and norms and codes, formal and informal, that constitute and represent the spheres denominated "public" and "private" in social life (Offe, 1974: 37). These two dimensions reflect the dual character of the capitalist state.

In capitalist societies, the state operates to guarantee the condition of capitalist production. It is thus characterized by private ownership of the means of production, the appropriation of the basic surplus of the salaried work force, and, above all, the management of the contradictions that arise principally in capitalist production but also are created in the state arena. The establishment and maintenance of the conditions of capitalist production include the protection of private property and the provision of inputs (land, labor, capital), either directly (e.g., through training the labor force) or indirectly (guaranteeing the general order of society).

The management of contradictions at the political level involves the management of class conflict as well as myriad conflicts of various types whose origin is found in a form distinct from the class one, for instance, phenomena specific to particular nations (ethnic and minority conflicts, regional and religious problems, patriarchal domination, etc.). In general, the management of conflict presupposes (a) the institutionalization of conflict through labor legislation, state arbitration of labor disputes, and the direct or indirect incorporation of the organizations and parties of the working class within the existing political arena; (b) the design of co-optive reforms for those more radical movements which, per se, cannot be accommodated within the preestablished matrix of political alliances; (c) different forms of socialization of the citizen, with the objective of establishing the legitimacy of the ruling system and social control, which would vary from the elaboration and diffusion of the communications media to the coercion and direct physical repression of opposition sectors. The legitimacy of the state is reinforced by its success in institutionalizing conflict through its reformist efforts, as well as by its successful economic performance with high and persisting levels of economic development; failure in these areas can contribute to a crisis of state legitimation.

It is indispensable to note, as part of a theoretical transition, that some of the Gramscian inheritance consists in emphasizing that the capitalist state possesses a relative autonomy. This relative autonomy constitutes a central theoretical question for understanding changes in the elites exercising political domination and controlling capital accumulation (Skocpol, 1982; Boron, 1982; Hamilton, 1982: 5–39).

For Poulantzas, such autonomy is constitutive of the capitalist state. This relative autonomy refers to the materiality of the state as a complex of apparatuses relatively separated from the relations of production. Relative autonomy also refers to the specificity of classes and to the class struggle in capitalism, the latter being implicitly found in this separation (Poulantzas, 1969: 127). Skocpol, on the other hand, notes that relative autonomy is not a structural characteristic of the state, fixed in some form or system of government. This would suggest that the formulation of state objectives and the capacity of the state to implement its policies are not simple reflexes of the demands or interests of social groups or classes. This relative autonomy does not preclude the state's being conceived as having a certain structural compatibility with certain models of development, ideologies, ways of distributing resources, and mechanisms for formulating collective and national goals or styles of political and administrative management.

It is now convenient to present the problem of the relations between the capitalist state and education confronted with the educational demands of the popular sectors. Michael Apple synthesized what appears to constitute the crux of the Marxist debate on education: (1) Is the principal function of the educational system to reproduce the social division of labor or to constitute an alternative for improving the inequality in the existing distribution of power and knowledge in capitalist societies? (2) Are there strong ideological and cultural determinants external to the academic system, or does it have a significant degree of autonomy? (3) Do theories of economic reproduction offer analytic means for studying the ideological and cultural role that education plays in a capitalist society? (4) What really happens within the school (at the level of the curriculum, social relations, the language and culture considered legitimate)? It would appear that today more and better ethnographic studies at the level of the school could provide answers to this complex of questions (Apple, 1982: 1).

As has been suggested, the capitalist state has a dual character: it is a pact of domination, but at the same time it is constituted as a self-regulated administrative system; it must contribute to the reproduction of the relations of production but at the same time satisfy, within limits, the democratic aspirations of citizens. This dual character of the state constitutes another expression of the contradictory unity and inherent complexity of late capitalism. Education also possesses this dual character. On the one hand, understood as public policy, educational practice, or hidden curriculum, it tends fundamentally to reproduce the division of social labor. In this way it contributes to the process of the accumulation of capital and the exploitation of the labor force by means of assigning roles and positions to the labor force being trained and technically qualified; in the same manner it contributes to the imperatives of the production and socialization of knowledge (as a productive force), and the socialization of citizens in the norms and values of a hegemonic culture. On the other hand, educational expansion, with the growing incorporation of the popular sectors into the educational apparatus, generates advances in the democratic processes in society, thus constituting itself for its part in the expression of the demands of civil society on the state, including criticism of the state and dominant political project. In this way the functions of the mechanisms of mediation and legitimation are altered while processes of popular struggle are introduced into the state arena. Hence education appears linked to the growth of the critical consciousness of individuals, along with growing expectations for occupying better positions in the labor market or succeeding in advancing the substantive democratization of the political and economic areas of our societies.

CONCLUSION: QUESTIONS FOR COMPARATIVE RESEARCH

An important topic for comparative research is the study of the historical crystallization of this dual character of education and its expression at the level of educational policy. Here are some of the questions that appear to be important for such a program: (1) How are class, ideologies, the general objectives of the state, and the concrete formulation of educational policy linked? (2) What are the principal institutional, educational, organizational, and administrative means utilized by educational bureaucracies for molding educational practices to the prescriptions emanating from the ethical state, despite the centrifugal tendencies daily verified in educational practices? (3) Is it certain that education constitutes a mechanism for the elaboration of a collective consensus with respect to the dominant hegemonic culture? If so, how do children and youth react to the working and campesino classes? (4) How profoundly can an ideology sink into the consciousness of citizens submitted to the systematic exercise of educational socialization? Even more important, how are the modes of reception of this ideology established in the student-teacher relationship, the formation and distribution of gender roles, and behavioral expectations in the classroom? (5) If there exists a dynamic of ideological confrontation, and thus every ideological phenomenon does not consist simply in passive reception by agents but is an active process of acceptance and rejection, how is the dominant ideology resisted, rejected, and even redefined within schools by educational actors: administrators, teachers, students, family heads?

Once again it appears that the response to all of these questions can arise only from the concrete analysis of concrete situations. It appears opportune to continue rethinking theoretically and investigating empirically the principles of power and organization that underlie the capitalist states in Latin America, and to investigate above all how these principles are reformulated in the production of educational policy and what are the mechanisms of reception of such policies by the popular sectors.

NOTES

1. The characterization of the state in Gramsci has been the object of many polemics and contradictory opinions (Cerroni, 1973: 151–58; Portantiero, 1981: 221–28; Anderson, 1978: 45–47, 59ff.). According to Anderson, Gramsci oscillates between two major definitions of the state. In the first, an opposition is established between the state

and civil society, and hegemony (direction) pertains to civil society, while coercion (domination) remains the province of the state. The second Gramscian option is very different. Here the state includes civil society in such a way that consensus and coercion appear as coextensive with the state, and hegemony becomes inseparable from the apparatuses of the state. In my analysis, only this second usage will be considered and applied.

2. As a general comment the case of Mexico is worth mentioning: in the early 1980s, 24 million children and youths were tied to the educational apparatus (approximately 33.4% of the total population) and around 800,000 people worked completely or partly in education, as administrators or teachers (Pescador, 1983: 37–54). The Mexican government published and distributed approximately 71.7 million free books between 1985 and 1986 for primary education.

3. The task of this section is not to provide a detailed exegesis, presentation, and critique of the Althusserian position. This has been done elsewhere (see, e.g., Campusano, 1981; Ramirez Cantañeda, 1981; Carnoy, 1984). Nevertheless, I introduce this theme to call attention to two aspects: (1) historically, the Althusserian reading of Gramsci has been the predominant influence in the Marxist analysis of education in Latin America (see, e.g., Vasconi, 1977, 1981) and (2) a complex of theoretical and practical problems, introduced by Gramsci and many of his commentators, is essential for studying the relations between the state and education in Latin America, and must be brought together.

4. I will not devote a long discussion to this topic, which has been treated by Lagrange et al. (1974).

3

THE POLITICAL ECONOMY OF ADULT EDUCATION IN LATIN AMERICA

Why has adult education in Latin America had a marginal role in public policy formation, in terms of financial expenditure and enrollment? I suggest that adult education lacks correspondence with the model of capital accumulation and has little utility for the model of political domination. Additionally, adult education's clientele is socially fragmented, politically disorganized and weak, and economically insignificant in Latin American societies.

Following these analytical premises, I discuss the ideology underlying adult education policies and the main economic determinants of adult education programs, and provide some examples of adult education reform in the region. Finally, I conclude with some theoretical remarks on adult education and public policy in the context of the relative autonomy of capitalist state.

SOCIAL STRUCTURE AND EDUCATIONAL EXPANSION

The Latin American educational expansion during the earlier phase of industrialization in the 1960s accounts for the highest rate of educational growth in the world (UNESCO, 1974b: 167, 227). Between 1960 and 1970, the indices of growth for higher education and secondary education were 247.9% and 258.3% respectively; however, the enrollment in primary basic education grew only 167.5%, while the illiteracy rate remained more or less constant in most countries of the area (UNESCO, 1971). One study of the late 1970s shows a fundamental continuity in this pattern of educational development (UNESCO/CEPAL/PNUD, 1981).

This chapter will seek to explain why adult education[1] policy formation did not follow the same pattern of development as the schooling system, as well as why adult education policy has had a secondary or even a marginal role in public policy formation, in terms of financial expenditures and enrollment.

I claim that the main reasons for this are that adult education lacks correspondence to the specific demands derived from the model of capital accumulation and, with the few exceptions enumerated below, it has little utility in the model of political domination. A major determinant of this low level of development in adult education services and programs in the 1960s and perhaps in the 1970s was the political weakness of the clientele for adult education.

This clientele is composed of peasant and indigenous people; urban marginals; self-employed people in lower-rank positions (e.g., street vendors); urban lower-wage workers, usually located in competitive industries and in the service sector (as opposed to those located in monopolized industries and the higher levels of government bureaucracy); people working in personal services in urban and sometimes rural areas (e.g., household jobs, house cleaning, housekeeping); and the lowest levels of the urban industrial petite bourgeoisie, particularly in those countries with the lowest level of industrial development (C. Torres, 1982a, 1982c). These people could be expected to demand adult education from the state, but they failed to do so because their structural position within the subordinate classes and their lack of political organization and power meant they did not participate in the class alliance that gave rise to the political regimes that increased import-substitution industrialization (i.e., the developmentalist regimes).[2]

Unfortunately, in the political economy of education, there are very few studies that address the origins, constraints, and determinants of educational development in Latin America. These studies have focused mainly on political projects and programs for national development, the interaction between social forces, and the subsequent impact of these interactions on the formulation of educational policy. The focus of analysis has been sharply concentrated on the formal system of schooling rather than on nonformal types of education such as adult education. The analysis has usually been formulated several years after a particular event, thus hampering any attempt to use such an analysis to propose alternative strategies of educational development. Finally, while the critical literature has emphasized a perceived correspondence between the social relations of production and the social relations of education (Vasconi, 1977; Labarca, 1979a, 1979b), by and large it has ignored the political implications and the contradictions between these contrasting types of social relations.

Within this framework, the classic problem of education's contribution to the direct reproduction of the capitalist system has been slightly modified and even amplified. Yet, while these works talk of the relative autonomy of the capitalist educational system (Carnoy and Levin, 1985; Lenhardt, 1981; Hargreaves, 1982), the possibility that the educational system can be a site of contradictory exchanges and a starting point for resistance and societal transformation has not yet received sufficient recognition and analysis (Rodriguez Brandão, 1979;

Giroux, 1981; Freire, 1979a, 1979b; Apple, 1982). Also, those reformist policies which the capitalist state does institute have rarely been thoroughly analyzed. They are simply misinterpreted or dismissed.

There are several lines of reasoning that strengthen the foregoing argument. I shall confine myself to emphasizing three main dimensions of the argument: (1) the ideology underlying the economic and educational development in Latin America in the 1960s; (2) economic determinants of adult education policy formation; and (3) some examples of concrete changes in adult education policy that would constitute departures from these general trends.

IDEOLOGY, EDUCATION, AND POLICY PLANNING

I claim that of the several factors that play a part in the formulation of education policies,[3] the first determinants are (a) the socioeconomic and political characteristics of the educational clientele; (b) the ideology of policy planning held by the policy planners and policymakers; (c) the characteristics of the state bureaucracy and the type of bureaucratic interdependence—including any interbureaucratic linkages and clashes; and (d) the concrete configuration of the political alliance that underlies the political regime[4] in each country. In this chapter, only the first two dimensions will be analyzed.

Regarding adult education clientele, there has been a process of "decommodification"[5] of the labor force, particularly of the labor force that is thought of as having been qualified through adult education. Furthermore, in the aggregate demand for labor skills, the profile of qualifications (basic education) offered by adult education training seems not to have been a decisive requirement of the Latin American industrial structure between the 1950s and the 1970s. In terms of the political society, this "decommodification" of the labor force brings about a relative loss of strength for those social forces involved. Within the general process of political bargaining in the civil society, these social forces lose power, potential or actual, to obtain a higher proportion of available social spending.

Regarding policy-planning ideology, the agenda of modernization theory offers only a very modest place to adult education (La Belle, 1986; Bock and Papagiannis, 1983). This modernization theory was dominant in educational environments during the early 1960s and most of the 1970s—although, with the emergence of military dictatorships in Latin America, policy-planning ideologies sometimes went back to the old conservative theories to support their regressive political economy of education. However, the main assumptions of modernization theory (in spite of the ever-increasing amount of empirical evidence that undermines the theory's conclusions) still survive as a principal policy making view within Latin American ministries of education. Let us start by discussing this superstructural dimension, and then discuss the economic determinant.

Modernization theory has been transferred to Latin America under the label of the "developmentalist" ideology, espoused by developmentalist regimes and underlying the process of industrialization in the 1960s. This ideology attributes very concrete roles to education in the process of economic development. While the literature on the role education plays in economic development is quite extensive, a highly representative example came out of the Conference on Education and Economic-Social Development in Latin America (CEDES) at Santiago de Chile in 1962.

The final document of this conference emphasizes that the role of education is primarily the development of human resources and the training of professionals and technicians deemed necessary for economic development. It stresses the influence education can have in the promotion of technological change through the production and diffusion of innovations. In addition, the importance of education is said to be the generation within social classes of new patterns of consumption, new patterns of entrepreneurial activity, a strong propensity for saving money, the adaptation to economic change, and the promotion of the active participation of all the social sectors in the developmental task (CEDES, 1963).

In this modernization theory, the educational system promotes societal progress by training people and thereby raising productivity; but this objective has been assigned mainly to the formal system of schooling (C. Torres, 1982b). With the exception of a rather elliptic and declamatory argument about the importance of adult education in the promotion of social participation by citizens and the convenience of having more literate than illiterate people, adult education in this document was treated as a marginal instrument for achieving the proposed goals (ECLA, 1963; CEDES, 1963).

By 1965 only seven countries in Latin America had national plans for adult training and only eight had a national program or an ongoing national campaign. In that year, the total expenditure in Latin America on extraschool education, which includes not only adult education but other forms of formal and informal education, was less than 3% of the total educational expenditure (Ochoa and García-Huidobro, 1982: 446).

The educational theory that underlay policy planning and policymaking at that time was a classic human capital theory. In this theory, education is treated as an investment while resources are limited. Therefore, it is necessary to invest in those levels and educational modalities which have a higher private and social rate of return. Expectations are concentrated on the expansion and improvement of the efficiency of the formal system of schooling rather than on nonformal types of education.

Solari, in discussing policy-planning theories and educational financing, made a forceful point: "It is known that there is a great difficulty in resisting the rationality of a theory when it is backed by an instrument as rational as money" (Solari, 1977: 67; our translation).

As Solari argued, there have been important differences among the educational finance agencies in the way they have viewed and supported the educational development of the region. On the one hand, until very recently the World Bank had financed secondary education, which was conceived of as the key to development. According to Samuel Bowles, between 1963 and 1974, the World Bank allocated four times as much funding to middle and higher education as to primary education (Bowles, 1980: 222). On the other hand, the Inter-American Development Bank supported a different policy. It claimed that the major problem in the region was the lack of specialized personnel, and therefore it oriented its educational investments and loans toward the widening and enriching of university resources and toward the training of more highly educated, qualified human resources. Meanwhile, the financing of adult education, as well as primary education, was supported only by national governmental budgets and UNESCO. Since UNESCO has some important financial limitations, its support is very much constrained. Because it is an educational agency created to expand all educational segments, its support of a single level such as adult education cannot be exclusive, as is the case with the other agencies; similarly, since it is not a bank, its funds are limited and are subject to more complex political bargaining with the governments of the region (Solari, 1977: 61–64).

Finally, in addressing the process of educational planning and resource assignment in Latin America, empirical evidence shows that educational policy planners and policymakers have considered adult education more as a consumption expenditure than as educational investment. A good example of the lack of financial support for adult nonformal education is in the data presented by Ochoa and García-Huidobro. In their work they surveyed 1,000 published documents on the research carried out in the region during 1972–1978 (Ochoa and García-Huidobro, 1982: 428–44). The research done on adult education was only 9.7% of the total but, as the authors pointed out, the items grouped under the label of adult education included such diverse types of education as "adult education by all forms," "literacy campaigns," "manpower training," and "supplementary education." They stressed that most studies on adult education were done by research units dependent upon international agencies, such as UNESCO, the World Bank, or foundations, rather than on local or national research agencies. This finding shows the limited concern in Latin America with carrying out research on adult education at local levels. Incidentally, as has been widely recognized in Latin America, educational research supported by state resources depends upon and follows what the policymakers have established as priorities for educational investment. Thus, it could be inferred that adult education matters have not been a high priority for educational policymaking.

However, as a study points out, the process of decision making in education is inherently political and conflictual, and is technically nonrational (McGinn and Street, 1982: 179). In this regard, political rationality has proven to be far more important than technical rationality in the promotion of adult education policies in Latin America.

ECONOMIC CONSTRAINTS, POLITICAL RATIONALITY, AND ADULT EDUCATION REFORM IN LATIN AMERICA

Let us assume that a suitable, simple model with which to understand the economy of capitalist Latin America has four sectors: a monopoly sector, a competitive sector, a public sector, and a residual labor force sector. In fact, however, the picture is far more complex due to the interplay of capitalist forms of production with precapitalist forms of production within a single social formation.

A central assumption of this study is that the state's political economy is organized to support the development of a commodity-production social formation. State economic interventionism should be oriented toward performing those functions which capital is unable to accomplish because it is made up of many fragmented and mutually antagonistic capitals (Offe, 1975a; Altvater, 1979: 42). But state interventionism must also be oriented toward strengthening the legitimacy of the current ruling alliance as a prerequisite to sustaining a given pattern of capital accumulation.

Thus far I have argued that one of the main sources of the political weakness of adult education's clientele results from its structural location as subordinate classes within the Latin American economies. I shall go one step further and argue that this clientele is empirically located in segmented labor markets. These segmented labor markets are composed mainly of the labor force employed in the capitalist competitive sector (i.e., the lower salaried and occupational levels) and of the residual labor force sector (i.e., the reserve army of labor and the economically marginal sectors).

In fairly tentative terms, I shall argue that a process of "decommodification" of the labor force has increasingly been taking place in Latin America (Nun, 1969; Quijano and Weffort, 1973). This process generates a structural discrepancy between abstract, surplus-value-related functions and the concrete, use-value-related forms of labor. It will have important consequences on public policymaking (Offe, 1973: 74; Carnoy et al., 1979: 10–22).

Two processes underlie the "decommodification" of the labor force. On the one hand, despite the claim of modernization theorists, those residuals of precapitalist forms of social life have not been incorporated over time into the market control that provides a capitalist system with its legitimacy. This is so in spite of the fact that those precapitalist forms of production and consumption do contribute to the circulation and realization of capital in some sectors. On the other hand, there is a quantitative growth of forms of labor that are separated from the process of capitalist accumulation; therefore, its exchange value as labor would not be easily exchanged as use value in labor markets.

The political short-term effects are, essentially, that those economic sectors subject to the "decommodification" process, although they are not beyond the impact of the material reproduction of society, have lost their ability to bargain effectively for higher levels of welfare services from the public sector. Of course, this bargaining process should be located within the general frame of political representation of the political regime: in parliaments, political parties, corporations, or the public sector. A corollary of this is that any state effort to build mass loyalty and legitimacy from those social sectors (and social relations of production) becomes very limited. This occurs because the financial ability of the state to tax these sectors is almost nil; therefore, the public funds to support such cooperative "welfare" policies will decline sharply. In addition, this economic determination brings about a significant reduction of the visible importance that these segments of the labor force have for the political alliance holding power. They become at the most another social threat to be either controlled or removed.

In other words, for a class state, it will become crucial to sustain political control over those sectors of labor without its being necessary to gain their consent. Thus, for economic reasons, in terms of fiscal revenues and fiscal expenditure, those sectors in process of "decommodification" will become less important for state policymakers; for political and legitimating purposes, they are negligible. Therefore, state welfare policies will reflect these sets of assumptions in the design and implementation of adult education policies.

Let us consider the formulation of reforms in adult education that might contradict this analysis. Latin American history is rich in valuable experiments in adult education that do not follow the above-stated premises. Examples are the Cuban literacy campaign of 1959–1965; the Freirean "pedagogy of the oppressed" in Brazil between 1960 and 1964; the very different experience, on political and theoretical grounds, of the Movimento Brasileiro de Alfabetização between 1971 and 1983; the Chilean experiences, during the Christian Democrat administration of Frei (1964–1970) and during the period of the Unidad Popular (1970–1973); the Peruvian educational reform (1968–1975) and its rich proposals for adult education; and, most recently, the Nicaraguan literacy campaign in 1980 and the ensuing organization of the Vice-ministry of Adult Education, and the National Program for Literacy Training developed by the National Institute of Adult Education in Mexico since 1981. The questions that can be raised are the following: Why did these developments occur at specific historical moments? Why has a capitalist state, as in some of the above-mentioned cases, launched these new trends of adult education reform?

Usually these experiences have been associated with a change in the political regime and the process of legitimation that the new regime demands. The cases of Cuba, Brazil, and Chile are good examples.

Cuba

In the Cuban case,[6] the process of armed struggle (1957–1959) and the transition to socialism after 1959 have implied the transformation of the political culture of the masses and their resocialization in new values. The literacy campaign was one of the most successful in the world, reducing the rate of illiteracy in only one year from 30% to slightly less than 5%.[7] As a typical example of revolutionary change in the patterns of capital accumulation, which implies a change in the form of the state, socialist Cuba, operating with a model of full employment, has established a new educational demand. It is based not on the free interplay of a supply-demand process in the market, but on centralized social planning.

To this extent, it can be hypothesized that in Cuba, adult education has had two, and probably will have three, decisive phases. At the beginning of the revolution, as some authors have noted, adult education was decisive for the transformation of the political culture of the masses (Fagen, 1969; Dominguez, 1980); from the mid–1960s to early 1970s, there was a phase in which adult education was complementary to the schooling system and to new demands created by the development of the productive forces (Carnoy and Werthein, 1979). Currently, because it is essentially a nonschooling model, the adult education experience might lead, as a methodological and theoretical alternative, to the development of a new systematic outlook for public education that is not necessarily linked to the schooling system (Pescador, 1982).

Brazil

In Brazil, in contrast, between 1960 and 1964, when Paulo Freire's "pedagogy of the oppressed" was developed, there was a high correlation between the populist regime of João Goulart, which needed political legitimation, and the desire for literacy programs. Since until 1983 only the literate could vote in Brazil, the desire for literacy programs should be understood as a mechanism for increasing the number of voters, which would politically sustain the regime in power. To this extent, the figures are impressive: in the early 1960s, northeastern Brazil had 15 million illiterates out of a total population of 25 million; in 1964, the year of the coup d'état, in the state of Sergipe alone, literacy training added 80,000 new voters to the 90,000 already existing. In Pernambuco, the total of voters went from 800,000 to 1 million (Sanders, 1968; Morales-Gómez, 1979).

After the coup d'état, there were profound changes in the pattern of capital accumulation in Brazil and, obviously, in the pattern of political domination. In the early 1970s, the state and the bourgeoisie in Brazil encountered the strong presence of progressive sectors in the Catholic church in Brazilian civil society as a real obstacle to the process of political legitimation and the search for hegemony. Therefore, a reasonable hypothesis with which to understand the political rationality for the creation of the Brazilian Movement for Literacy Training—the most important mass experiment in adult education in the region in the decade (Bhola, 1984; La Belle, 1986; Fletcher, 1982)—is that as a proposed network of educational institutions, it could contribute to building social and political support and consensus for a bureaucratic-authoritarian regime.[8]

Chile

Finally, in the case of Chile, the development of adult education during the Christian Democratic government (1964–1970) might be explained by a complex set of variables, the most relevant of which are the following: on the one hand, Chile was the monitor country of the Alliance for Progress's programs, which were encouraged and supported by the U.S. government as centralist and democratic alternatives to the radical trends emerging from the Cuban revolution. Thus, there was a great flow of financing toward developing key projects such as the agrarian reform, which had an extensive educational network in the form of rural and community development (Freire, 1968a, 1968b).

On the other hand, there were important tensions and contradictions within the Christian Democratic Party. A sector within the Christian Democratic Youth had been working closely, both politically and professionally, with adult education and rural development projects (Chonchol, 1973). Thus, within the government alliance this sector had been a mentor and defender of these adult education projects. In fact, some members of the Christian Democratic Youth later became members of new and smaller parties within the Unidad Popular, such as Izquierda Cristiana (the Christian Left) and MAPU.

During the period of "peaceful transition to socialism" led by the Unidad Popular, adult education and schooling in general were conceived as an instrument of ideological struggle and political organization (Farrell, 1986; C. Torres, 1988b). As one scholar has pointed out, its goal "was to raise the level of class consciousness of the peasants and to contribute to mobilization, each time more conscious and organized for the predominance of its interest" (Gajardo, 1974: 54).

In this regard, two governmental programs were particularly relevant: the National Program of Education for Workers and the National Program of Peasant Unions.[9]

CONCLUSION: ADULT EDUCATION AND PUBLIC POLICY

Any political alliance in power, in order to maintain its political domination, has to consider which clienteles will more forcefully demand and claim which kinds of welfare policies. In so doing, the capitalist state assesses the degree of strength that each social sector has to struggle for social services or welfare spending. These social services include not only education but also housing, health services, and social security.

A second concern for a capitalist state is the probability that each social force has to achieve significant gains or suffer losses in the bargaining process. Finally, the state will take into account the dynamics and configuration of the social relations of production, especially which forms of labor contribute to commodity production and which do not.

In short, a theoretical outcome of this reflection is the need to consider the dialectical relationship between economy and politics in analyzing determinants of educational reforms. But, on the top of that, there is the need to consider which form of state, and particularly which kind of political regime, supports which kind of education, for whom, and for what state purposes. In this regard, the subject of who controls, who sponsors, and who benefits from adult education policies is crucial for a political sociology of adult education (La Belle, 1986).

Therefore, a last theoretical remark on this issue notes the relative autonomy of the state, for if the state "still maintains its character as a national state, this is due among other things to the fact that the State is not a mere tool or instrument of the dominant classes, to be manipulated at will; the task of the State is to maintain the unity and cohesion of a social formation divided into classes" (Poulantzas, 1980: 78).

This relative autonomy allows the participation within the political regime of political programs that are alternatives to the hegemonical ones; this in turn contributes to the explanation of any other reforms, including adult education ones. I have argued elsewhere that the class alliance that benefits from the given pattern of capitalist accumulation through import-substitution in Latin America has supported an educational development that excludes adult education (C. Torres, 1983). Thus, adult education's "vegetative" growth and low-profile status within educational policy formation should be attributed particularly to the socioeconomic characteristics and structural location of its potential clientele, and that clientele's lack of power.

Adult education reforms in the 1980s do not look very different from those of the recent past. In his phrase "an associate-dependent development," Fernando H. Cardoso has expressed the major characteristics of monopoly capitalism in Latin America. That is, it is an economic system built upon an alliance among the state bureaucracy and state managers, the multinational corporations, and the highest strata of the national bourgeoisie (Cardoso, 1974; 1981: 28–29). Its political economy strengthens a more concentrated economic system that is therefore less redistributive. The political system seems increasingly to be excluding the subordinate classes. Thus, the trends already pointed out in the 1960s, 1970s, and 1980s for adult education are likely to continue and, in some countries, even to strengthen in the 1990s.

However, I have also attempted to show, using the Cuban, the Brazilian, and the Chilean cases, that when there is a change in the patterns of capital accumulation, in the form of the political regime, or in the state's needs for increasing political legitimation, adult education plays a relevant role as part of the new educational program and reforms. What are the main reasons for this? As has been pointed out above, the adult education system's practices and policies are in general an expression of a compensatory type of education for the powerless classes. Thus, adult education policies are closely related to the relative autonomy of the educational system as a state apparatus. This is so because education, as a welfare policy, constitutes a particular expression of the "national" component of the class-based capitalist state.

This relative autonomy simultaneously expresses the correspondence of education with the social reproduction and legitimation of the capitalist state and the capitalist economic system, as well as the gains and losses of the subordinate classes in the class struggle and political bargaining (Cole, 1988). The state becomes an object and a product of this struggle for transformation. But, as is always the case, when this newly established dialectic between economy and politics does not lead to a change in the form of the state and in the goals of the national development model, any substantial reform in adult education policies can easily be reversed when there is a change in the political regime.

In the core of many reformist policies, adult education policies may play a significant role. However, it seems that two main restrictions apply to these reformist programs. First, these programs of basic education for adults should not be expensive. That is, they should not draw away fiscal means of the state that might be used to finance other programs—especially those programs oriented toward satisfying immediate demands (and avoiding potential social threats) of specific communities and social sectors (e.g., food-production programs, running-water projects, etc.); those oriented toward improving the employability of the labor force already unemployed or under-employed in the competitive sector of the economy; and those oriented toward satisfying principal demands of specific social sectors (e.g., the demands coming from the lower and middle levels of the petite bourgeoisie that might be greatly affected by the economic deterioration of Latin American economies). In this particular respect, if adult education growth were to undermine the growth of higher education, for instance, any substantial reform in adult education would be challenged and postponed, or dismissed.

Second, from the perspective of the state, adult education policies and programs should never promote the political participation of its clientele in the civic culture and government affairs. When this happens, experience has shown that these processes of increasing citizen's participation are very difficult to control and to co-opt. Thus, a participative adult education program[10] will become a pitfall rather than a meaningful method of political legitimation for the state. That is why participative research or participative planning has not usually had a place in the common stock of adult education policies advanced by the capitalist states in Latin America. However, not all reforms are willingly initiated by the state; some of them result from class struggle and political bargaining. Thus, even within a capitalist public sector, it may be possible to promote new forms of participative adult education. Even if these programs of participative adult education contradict the general views of development of a capitalist state, they are not entirely ruled out (Morales Jeldes, 1986; Latapí, 1988). Moreover, at certain turning points the likelihood that participative adult education will take place is great. If there is a bias of hope, any bridgehead of a political, popular movement within the state will contribute to the betterment of the lower classes, at least as a factor for political mobilization and consciousness raising. This is also possible through adult education programs.

In conclusion, it is doubtful that in the present conditions of Latin American capitalism, adult education can significantly contribute to the "commodification" or "recommodification" of the labor force. It may, however, contribute to the survival, and therefore the reproduction, of the labor force. But any meaningful reform in adult education will be better understood as part of a major project of political change of a political regime and its needs of legitimation, rather than as labor force "commodification" and economic betterment of the adult education clientele.

NOTES

1. From the outset, it is important to define the limits and main assumptions of this analysis. I understand adult education as those programs destined for the population 15 years of age and older who in their earlier years did not have access to or dropped out of the school system. In general, these programs include literacy training and general basic education for adults. The notion of general basic education refers to the minimum limit of education that each citizen in a Latin American country should achieve according to constitutional precepts. In general, it includes six to nine years of compulsory schooling, comprising complete primary and secondary education. Therefore, rural extension, on-the-job training, and professional upgrading programs are not considered in this chapter.

2. A developmentalist regime has several features. First, it claims to rely upon the democratic institutions of a liberal society rather than on the charismatic leadership of an individual or the practices and traditions of a society. Second, this type of regime develops an ideology of "efficiency" as a means to achieve "order" and "progress" in society, to externalize its power, and to institutionalize its authority (Portes and Walton, 1981). A crucial feature is the role of the urban middle class as a chief electoral constituency. In economic terms, this type of regime would expect an interrupted flow of foreign investment to support its programs of economic development and, in general, a partnership with the United States is considered a precondition for the economic development and political stability of the country. Finally, it could be said that the vigorous educational takeoff in Latin America in the 1960s was initiated or strengthened under such developmentalist regimes as those of Frondizi in Argentina, of Frei in Chile, and of Caldera in Venezuela.

3. For a detailed model to analyze public policy formation, see C. Torres (1984a) and Chapters 6 and 7 of this book.

4. A political regime is characterized mainly through the predominant modality of recruitment or access to the higher positions and roles within the state and the current mechanisms of political representation. See O'Donnell (1978, 1982) and Oszlak (1980, 1981).

5. "Decommodified" labor refers to those social groups excluded from the social life form of wage labor yet subject to relations of capitalist domination. The neologism "decommodification" refers to the thesis that "decommodified" forms of social organization of labor power and of the value produced by society are growing quantitatively. These "decommodified" life forms tend increasingly to become a problem of social stability to be dealt with by political means, and represent a potential for rebellion of a special kind (see Offe, 1973; Altvater, 1973: 98).

6. A more detailed analysis of educational development in Cuba is in Chapter 5 of this book.

7. However, as Carnoy and Werthein (1980) have shown, the controversy surrounding these figures is great. Perhaps it is important to remember that a principal goal of the literacy campaign was to provide education to everybody, achieving the level of the first grade of primary schooling. This modest goal was achieved, and the Cuban literacy campaign was considered, even by international organizations such as UNESCO, as a model of a successful literacy campaign in dependent societies. See UNESCO (1965) and Chapter 5 in this book.

8. O'Donnell has defined a bureaucratic-authoritarian state as a system of political exclusion of a previously activated popular sector, based on a military dictatorship, in which the superior positions in the government are occupied by people who have had successful careers in complex, bureaucratic organizations (such as the armed forces, large enterprises, and the state itself). This state promotes a system of economic exclusion that is highly skewed toward benefiting the large oligopolistic units and private capital, and its policies are set through technocratic planning having strong authoritarian overtones (O'Donnell, 1982).

9. The importance of educational policies in the fall of Allende's "peaceful transition to socialism" is insightfully analyzed by Joseph P. Farrell (1986). Farrell's book on the national unified school (ENU)—which was a project combining productive labor, mental education, bodily exercise, and polytechnic training, following the standard Marxist pedagogical principles—attempts to show that "for a minority coalition government (itself internally divided) to attempt to implement revolutionary change in a highly polarized parliamentary democracy is to invite disaster" (p. 239) and that "the debate over the ENU proposal was a critical factor in tipping the balance among these middle sectors away from support for the constitutional order and toward acceptance of a coup" (p. 242). The final explanation, in Farrell's view, lies in the ways this proposal "keyed into the value structure of Chileans" (p. 243) and how its end result was highly alienating for the middle classes. The proposal was perceived to be addressed toward transforming not only education but also the basic family socialization and religious practices of Chileans.

10. A very thoughtful discussion on participatory research and adult education is in Marcela Gajardo (1982).

4

NATIONAL POLICIES OF ADULT EDUCATION IN MEXICO, 1976–1988

INTRODUCTION

Critical perspectives in education, especially those elaborated in the context of advanced industrial capitalism, study the role that the educational apparatus plays in the reproduction of the labor force stratified in terms of race, gender, and social classes. This implies an investigation of the role that education plays in the formation of classes; in the conflicts and contradictions between classes, sectors of classes, and bureaucratic actors; in the accumulation of capital; in political domination; and in the legitimation of the privileges established by the dominant groups in the social formation (Apple, 1982: 3; Giroux, 1983b: 43–56; Cole, 1988).

In Latin America, theoretical refinement has begun to replace first intuitions and initial convictions; at the same time, the most recent analyses have begun to incorporate in an organic fashion some of the principal results of the educational research of the 1980s (even if much of it is not exempt from theoretical perplexities). There is, to put it clearly and simply, a means for criticizing the fundamentals of the theoretical analysis reigning in the established paradigms. But it is a critique that can be realized in light of the main tendencies of educational development as expressed in a significant body of empirical research (Myers, 1980: 19–53).

In this context, it is appropriate to note that the dominant tendency in educational research in Latin America has been to study the social functions of the school and, in a general form, education. The critical agenda of educational research has attempted to respond to the question regarding the reproductive (or not) character of the school with respect to the social relations of production.

In this sense, adult education has been much less studied than, for example, the problematics of basic education or higher education. And, paradoxically, a significant proportion of such research on adult education has delved deeply into the study of contested or contradictory (i.e., nonreproductive) experiences regarding the dominant forms of production, power, or cultural socialization (Giroux, 1983b: 57–87; C. Torres, 1983a; Freire, 1977; Fernández, 1978; De Santa Ana et al., 1970; Martin, 1971; Weffort, 1968).

Even more, adult education, instead of studying institutions from critical perspectives, has primarily studied practices; and instead of taking general social stratification as a fundamental empirical reference, it has focused on the analysis of popular sectors or socially subordinated sectors.

It is appropriate to note as well that given the strongly practical character of the political-pedagogical content of its activity, and a certain backwardness in the theory of adult education, research in adult education is perhaps very scarce and little systematized in the educational context. This is closely related to the low level of budgetary allocations, whether for the development of projects or for research in adult education in the region. Nevertheless, where it exists, this research is among the least conventional and perhaps most stimulating type of educational research.

It is not surprising—given the previous considerations—that the field of adult education has been the most propitious area for the development of the most significant experiments in participative and action research (Gajardo, 1982; Rigal, 1978).

Consequently, it is not typical to find many high-quality studies on national systems of adult education. In addition, often there is a lack of information on the foundations, structures, and modes of organization and administration of programs; human, financial, and material resources; profiles of students and teachers; methodologies of teaching apprenticeships; mechanisms of promotion and examination; didactic materials; terminal efficiency of the system; or educational results and/or social, political, or economic impacts of such programs.

Fortunately, this situation began to change with the appearance of detailed studies of experiments such as the Movimento Brasileiro de Alfabetização (MOBRAL) (Fletcher, 1982); on the Sistema Nacional de Educación de Adultos (SNEA), and the Programa Nacional de Alfabetización (PRONALF) in Mexico (Sirvent and Vergara, 1983; C. Torres, 1984a; De Lella, 1982; CNTE-PRONALF, 1982); and adult education in Argentina (Hernández and Facciolo, 1983)—to cite only studies on the most industrialized countries in the region.

This chapter will attempt to systematize and analyze information and secondary data produced in Mexico during the five-year period 1976–1981: specifically, the National System of Education (SNEA)—the immediate predecessor of the National Program of Illiteracy (PRONALF, later MONALF) and the National Institute of Adult Education (INEA).[1]

Following this introduction, some of the sociological aspects of adult education as a disciplinary field are noted. Then adult education and literacy training in Mexico between 1976 and 1988 are analyzed, distinguishing the characteristics of those being educated and the efficiency of the system. Finally, an agenda of research is proposed.[2]

SOCIOLOGICAL OUTLINES OF ADULT EDUCATION

I have already stated that adult basic education in Latin America is concerned with the needs of the most impoverished social groups that completely lack power and are localized in the lowest level of social stratification in Latin America. Despite the difficulties in measuring this population, let us consider some of the estimates accepted by specialists.

On the one hand, it is suggested that there are approximately 45 million absolute illiterates in Latin America (12% of the total population of the region). Mexico, with approximately 6.5 million absolute illiterates in 1980, represented a seventh of the total in the region. On the other hand, the regional disparities in this regard are very great. For example, in 1970[3] the Federal District (Mexico City) has a rate of illiteracy of 9.1%, which was three times less than the national average. Other states, in contrast, were close to the national average: in Guanajuato 35.5% of the population were absolute illiterates; in Hidalgo and Querétero, 37.9%; in Oaxaca, 42%. The states with the bulk of the Indian population—Chiapas, with 43.3%, and Guerrero, with 44.6% absolute illiterates—represented the extreme cases.

By 1980 the situation had not changed much with respect to the regional distribution. For example, Chiapas then counted 38% of its population illiterate and Guerrero 35.6%; both were triple the national average. Obviously, if consideration were given to functional illiteracy and illiteracy by disuse in these statistics, the population counted in these categories would be much greater. At that time, some estimates have defined approximately 22 million persons as below the minimal limit of basic adult education (Pescador, 1981: 11).

In general, the educational clientele for programs of literacy training are made up of a population of rural origin or urban migrants with a very recent campesino past. This clientele is localized in the major suburban areas of the largest cities or the relatively least developed areas of a country. Many of them belong to ethnic groups and are monolingual, and the rates of illiteracy are higher for groups over 25 years old. The illiteracy of women is proportionally higher than that of men (CNTE-UNESCO, 1982: 17–19; Schmelkes, 1979; Solari, 1982).

The goals assigned to basic adult education vary from offering positive attitudes toward cooperation, work, family, community, and national development or a better individual apprenticeship, to functional literacy training and the teaching of basic arithmetic operations; from promoting a scientific approach in health, agriculture, and related areas, to the learning of knowledge and functional skills for work; from facilitating entry into labor markets or strengthening occupational opportunities for individuals, to facilitating functional knowledge and the skills necessary for civic or political participation (Bee, 1981; Bhola,

1981; Blaug, 1966; Levine, 1982; Lowe, 1975; Mbilinyi, 1977; Schmelkes, 1982; C. Torres, 1980a, 1984a).

The magnitude of the problem of illiteracy and basic adult education, and the importance of the objectives assigned to them, have in recent decades inspired important efforts by international organizations like UNESCO, as well as by governments in the region. These efforts undertake to resolve the problem, or at least reduce the incidence of illiteracy in absolute terms in the total adult population. This intention of designing effective strategies in basic adult education has one of its most important expressions in the Experimental World Program in Literacy developed by UNESCO, which initiated and coordinated this program between 1965 and 1975 in China, Tanzania, India, Vietnam, Iran, Mali, Brazil, Ecuador, and Somalia (Bhola, 1984; Arnove and Graff, 1987). The first systematic evaluations of its results did not suggest promising results but, with the exception of the Tanzanian experience, quite a substantial failure in meeting the stated goals for literacy training (Pescador, 1981; Bhola, 1984; Arnove and Graff, 1987).

In Mexico, the most systematic and significant effort developed in recent decades for confronting the problem of illiteracy and basic adult education resulted in the creation of PRONALF[4] in April of 1981, and the creation of INEA in September of the same year.

In Latin America the evaluation of massive literacy campaigns and basic adult education has presented uneven results. Beyond the complexities of the theme are the difficulties of establishing exactly the contributions of these programs and educational policies to the productivity of labor, increases in employment (and the employability of the work force), and/or modifications in the income or the rising occupational mobility of the beneficiaries of such programs. That is to say, the outcome is that it is difficult to establish the real relationships between basic adult education and economic and social development (La Belle, 1980; La Belle and Verhine, 1978).

ADULT EDUCATION AND SOCIAL RESEARCH

Much of the research in Latin America on these issues introduces the following questions: Is the contribution of adult education decisive for increasing the productivity of workers and campesinos? Is this increase in productivity directly reflected in a better occupation or salary? Is it possible to attribute the increase in the GNP, which cannot be mediated by the productivity of capital, to the improvement in the quality of the human resources of the country? If this is the case, is there a specific contribution of adult education to this process? Is overcoming illiteracy—as an introduction to the initial levels of formal education—and inevitable necessity and precondition for a country to develop? Is learning how to read, write, and calculate at an elementary level reflected in an improvement, in the short run, of incomes and quality of life? Does the skill of the literate person presuppose an automatic increase in productivity? What is the real utility of literacy in rural areas? What are the contributions of adult education to the opportunities of self-employment for graduates? In other words, what is the concrete contribution of massive programs of adult education to employment, incomes, occupational and social mobility, and the cultural capital of the newly literate?

Some of the most conventional responses with respect to the contribution of adult education to development suggest, on the one hand, that literacy and basic adult education contribute to economic development by means of the increase in the productivity of the newly literate, and at the same time enhance the levels of productivity of those who work with the newly literate (the so-called spillover effect). This contribution is verified by reduced costs of transmitting useful information on health or nutrition to a population that knows how to read and write. Finally, it is argued that adult basic education serves as an instrument of selection for potentially more talented subjects, enhancing their possibilities of social mobility and, at the same time, facilitating the rest of society a more elastic response to a modification in economic incentives.

In sum, basic adult education (including literacy training) would be very useful for that part of the labor force with low levels of qualification and a strong tendency to migrate, making them more employable as well as reducing unemployment, underemployment, and interregional and international migration (Blaug, 1966: 393–94; La Belle and Verhine, 1978; Phillips, 1970; Waiser, 1980: 4).

Nevertheless, despite these theories regarding the relations between adult education and the labor market, there is not adequate knowledge, based on empirical research, on the character of such relations in the experiments developed in Latin America and Mexico. Understanding the connections between adult education and labor markets, and understanding in greater detail the impact of massive literacy programs, are indispensable prerequisites for continuing the process of educational planning and decision making in the area on a firmer basis. Especially when it is a question of economically expensive programs, which are presently developing, under the pressure of austerity and administrative rationalization in the Mexican public sector.

LITERACY, IDEOLOGY, AND SOCIAL REPRODUCTION: AN ALTERNATIVE DISCOURSE

The previous considerations do not exempt us from noting that, following Giroux, adult education and, especially, literacy training are themes that, in the context of the present debate on the role and objectives of education, seem to have escaped the ideologies that inform the debate. Especially in the case of literacy training, this is usually reduced to the dominance of fundamental skills, completely subjected to the logic and imperatives of capital and its value as a means for the expansion of the labor process. Giroux concluded that "literacy, in this case, represents a new path for admitting the oppressed in their effort at penetrating an economic sphere which considers them second class citizens" (Giroux, 1983b: 58).

It would require more systematic research in Latin America in order to understand the behavior and real determinants of state programs of adult education and literacy training. Nevertheless, an evident result would be that literacy training is not a politically and epistemologically neutral activity. It is a territory of conflicts and political negotiation between struggling segments, social classes, and groups. Yet it is also an epistemologically differentiated arena where different (and opposing) methodologies, philosophies, ideologies, pedagogical techniques—in short, practically all of the possible dimensions and distinctions in educational practice—coexist (Latapí, 1984: 17–53).

Second, with rare exceptions there has been no demystification of the supposed political innocence of literacy training. Or when it has occurred, as in the case of Freire's theory, over time and with the spread of many of his propositions, the approach has in turn been used as a theoretical justification for very diverse programs. It is clear that this approach has been used by ignoring the critical and radical nucleus, negating the gnoseological and epistemological foundations, and drawing upon only its formal methodological (especially terminological) aspects. This "appropriating" of Freirean thinking, even where partial and in a theoretical and political context that contradicts the principles of a problematizing approach, serves postulates, objectives, and practices that negate the spirit and letter of the initial conception.

Thus it is more and more common in literacy training to encounter concepts, such as the term "conscientização,"[5] that end up becoming vacuous slogans, continuing this process of appropriation—deconstruction and reconstruction of critical theories by the official discourse in capitalism. Obviously such terms could be replaced in official discourses by older concepts in educational planning that undoubtedly would be less expressive of the grammar of the discourse itself (e.g., modernization, increases of productivity, or augmenting civic participation).

At the same time it should not be forgotten that the introduction of a determined problematic in a very distinct theoretical context is not always an epistemological, theoretical, and methodological operation free of complications. Perhaps the most obvious risk arises from analyzing the congruence and coherence of an approach that brings together so many different theoretical aspects. Thus the inclusion of some Freirean terms in public projects, so far in practice from the original approach, produces inconsistencies and tensions that alter the development of the literacy project.

When terminological synonyms are resorted to, for example, in order to evoke a method of the "generative word," like the one adopted by PRONALF in Mexico in 1981, rather than providing a theoretical justification for its (restricted) use, it creates inconsistencies in a method that has a distinct content and pedagogical tone—without the critical character of the original version. Thus a new method results that will be criticized for what it involves or advocates or does not do (i.e., its distance between theory and practice), and for what appears to be the nucleus of its approach, elaborated without sufficient precision and with low operational efficacy.

In the third place, literacy training is commonly discussed from two positions that are at first glance irreconcilable: that of government planning and that of the critique of official educational policy. There is, to be sure, a third voice that rarely is heard: that of the subject of literacy training.

While the planner demands a closer coordination of adult education with the requirements of labor markets, the critic stresses how the conditions that link dominant social and cultural groups to the state, the labor process, and domestic family life are also revealed in the objectives, the curriculum, the planning, and the organization of government literacy programs. While the planner easily justifies such an approach to promote literacy (in an economic and efficient manner) as a contribution to improving the quality of life of the beneficiaries, the critic skeptically observes how the dominant culture inserts itself into adult education programs, and how the ideological form and content of the curriculum simply reproduce the hegemonic culture at the expense of the needs and demands of the communities involved. This is not the moment to judge such positions, which obviously respond not to acquired roles but to contradictory visions of power, the economy, and education.

LITERACY AND POPULAR SECTORS

It is necessary to note, however, that the lack of the voice of the subjects of literacy confronts us with a question posed by J. C. Tedesco that constitutes a true challenge: how to construct a valid alternative pedagogy for the popular sectors in Latin America (Tedesco, 1985), one that is closely tied to their mechanisms of survival; that respects their interests, basic needs, and political-pedagogical programs; or that contributes to diversifying and amplifying their capacity for social resistance. It appears that such a question does not have a single response. Further, what strikes one first in this discussion are the obstacles to offering a plausible response.

It is necessary to be clear when speaking about the "popular sectors" or popular movements, which is not an easy task.[6] The popular sectors, socially subordinated, are subject to the processes of social control, manipulation, domination, and exploitation (in whatever version of critical theory is chosen). These processes are not euphemisms of historical reason. For some authors, there is in the popular sectors a critical discourse in a practical state. For others, there are in the popular sectors a hidden curriculum and an explicit curriculum that are very difficult to decode, given the characteristics of the social segments that construct such a curriculum. Finally, there are others who, on the basis of cultural relativism, deny that such sectors have the capacity to construct a curriculum. Resolving such issues would appear to be a precondition of answering our question.

In any case, the central problem continues: how to structure a curriculum that responds to the demands, needs, and interests of communities; how to establish mechanisms of communication and technical translation of such contents, without the interpretation's in any way disfiguring the grammar, the propositions, and the style of the discourse that is to be redeemed, at the point of proposing a parallel discourse next to that of the popular sectors? These are some of the demands that cannot be responded to at this time and for which research on adult education has responsibilities.

Communication between the discourse of the planner and that of the critic is a difficult task. For some, it is impossible. But having the adult education clientele to intervene in the polemic about the popular sectors is something much more complicated, and without doubt would render the possibilities for the mutual intelligibility of official and alternative discourses in adult education even more complex. Let us now describe the system of adult education in Mexico.

ADULT EDUCATION AND LITERACY TRAINING IN MEXICO, 1976–1981

The magnitude of the problem of adult education in Mexico can be shown by reviewing the statistics on the potential demand for basic adult education in 1976–1977: 6 million illiterates, 13 million adults with primary schooling incomplete, and 7 million with secondary incomplete (Solana, 1980). In other words, 74% of the total population over 15 years old were potentially clients for the services of adult education.

The complexity of the problem grows when the levels of adult education are distinguished: literacy training (an introduction to the rudiments of reading, writing, and calculation), basic education (which would embrace primary and secondary), work training (which implies technical qualification and training for the work force, given the necessities of the industrialization process), and agricultural extension (oriented toward training the agricultural work force, even where distant in its origins from the confluence of processes contributing to the integration of the campesinos in the projects of agrarian reform).

In general terms, adult education has been understood as a systematic activity whose viability depends upon nontraditional (i.e., nonformal, extraacademic) channels and a clearly remedial and compensatory orientation, attending to those sectors of the population that for distinct motives—economic, political, social, or psychological—remain on the margin of the school system, thus constituting those who are educationally "left behind."

From 1976 to 1981 attention was paid to adult education in Mexico by distinct channels, modalities, and institutions. Diverse governmental agencies linked to the agricultural problem, for example, carried out literacy activities, campesino training, or both. It would be difficult to draw an exhaustive chart of the governmental institutions that, in one form or another, could or did intervene in adult education, let alone the nongovernmental institutions that did so.

Nevertheless, for purposes of illustration it is useful to review the principal activities developed under the purview of the Secretaria de Educación Pública by the General Administration of Adult Education (Dirección General de Educación para Adultos, DGEA), which, from its creation in 1978 until its disappearance in 1981, concentrated many of the services consolidated through adult education in the Mexican state. Along with supporting diverse basic institutions, it facilitated the operation of specific agreements with other institutions to deal with a number of other particular populations of adults.

Among the most important services are the centers of basic adult education (centros de educación para adultos, CEDA), which develop activities concerned with an introduction to the primary level (literacy training) and intensive primary training. They are located primarily in urban areas and run on the official calendar. In 1980, 983 CEDA served a total population of 99,903 adults. In the academic year 1978–1979, 24,625 pupils graduated.

Another service was the cultural missions (misiones culturales), oriented principally toward adult education in rural communities, which develop training activities and, to a lesser extent, are concerned with general basic education. In 1980 there were 215 missions with 1,700 teachers that served 645 communities and a total population of 202,800 persons.

There also was the secondary television program, which in 1980 operated as a federal program in 10 states and as a state program in 4. There were 647 federal programs and 120 state ones. In that year there were 2,297 federal television classes and 335 state ones. The population served numbered 79,415 pupils, with a total of 2,692 teachers; in the academic year 1979–1980, 20,095 graduated.[7] There also were reading rooms oriented to providing library services and promoting sociocultural activities in rural communities. During the academic year 1978–1979, 73,245 readers in 99 communities were served.

Another important area of focus was the primary night school. By 1980 there were 450 centers in the states, serving 65,621 pupils. Along with this were secondary schools for workers, which, in the academic year 1978–1979, served 47,828 pupils in the first year (seventh grade), 36,162 in the second, and 27,782 in the third.

Another very important aspect of adult education is the open primary, secondary, and preparatory schools; Table 4.1 presents the basic data for them. As can be seen, the level of efficiency of the open system, as measured by the number of exams taken and passed in relation to the total population incorporated, is very low, and in relation to the total population in need, insignificant. These efforts were insufficient for serving the demand.

The variables explaining the efficiency of an adult education system are multiple. Variables may intervene that represent the sociogeographic context in which the person to be educated is found—for example, the level of development of residences—as well as variables representing social, educational, and personal antecedents of the person, such as age, gender, and level of education and occupation of parents. Also to be noted are variables representing the proc-

Table 4.1
Open Primary and Secondary Schools for Adults, 1980 (in thousands)

	Mar. 1980		Jan.-Mar. 1980		Jan.-Mar. 1979		1979 (1)		1980 (1)	
	OPA	OSA	OPA	OSA	OPA	OSA	OPA	OSA	OPA	OSA
Students of first enrollment	2.4	6.6	6.0	20.6	4.5	22.6	65.8	229.2	71.8	248.2
Students taking an examination	4.7	17.1	11.3	46.3	8.2	54.6	43.3	211.4	11.3	453.0
Examinations solicited	15.3	49.2	36.4	136.4	28.4	178.2	143.3	666.2	36.4	136.4
Examinations accredited	5.2	23.7	5.2	23.7	2.1	7.0	61.1	172.5	5.2	23.7
Students receiving a certificate	0.387	0.649	0.611	0.291	0.474	1.256	3.8	6.6	0.3	1.3
Communities served (nationwide)	164	244	269	351	162	336	444	621	269	361

Source: Daniel A. Morales-Gómez and Carlos A. Torres. The State, Corporatist Politics and Educational Policymaking in Mexico (1970-1988). 1989, table 5.2. (Manuscript.)
(1)= Cumulative since 1976, thousands of persons
OPS= Open primary schools for adults. OSA= Open secondary schools for adults

ess of apprenticeship in the strict sense, such as the quality of the didactic material and the intensity of study. In addition, there are variables related to the expectations and aspirations of subjects—the educational level they would like to complete, occupational expectations—and variables deriving from the determinations produced by the national system of adult education, such as characteristics of the evaluators and the types of service.

In the period 1976–1981, some levels of adult education were more affected than others in terms of quality and coverage, as was true of the attention given to literacy. This will be returned to in a moment.

Characteristics of Users

I have defined nonformal education following La Belle, as any organized and systematic educational activity conducted outside the framework of the formal system and having the objective of supplying selected types of apprenticeship for particular subgroups of the population, whether children or adults (Coombs and Ahmed, 1974: 8; La Belle, 1986).

Nonformal educational programs have rarely been conceived as replacing the formal school. On the contrary, they have been designed as a complement and supplement to the latter, or as a programmatic means for reaching a particular population for which the formal school has been inappropriate or ineffective. Consequently, it is extremely important to know the profile of adult users in this particular population.

Unfortunately, and despite the rough indications that can be derived from a vast and varied bibliography,[8] it is not possible—at least in the case of Mexico—to characterize precisely the profile of the potential demand for adult education. One can, however, analyze the profile resulting from the effective demand (adults registered) and make some inferences about the characteristics of the whole population on the basis of this particular one.

Those registered in the adult education system are preponderantly female (two-thirds are women); a high percentage of women are at the introductory levels, with fewer women as the educational level rises (CENIET, 1976: 8). At the primary level, 34% are men and 66% women; at the secondary level the composition is 40% and 60%, respectively (DGAC, 1978a: 24).

The age structure shows users less than 30 years old, with an average age of 26 at the primary level and 23 at the secondary. Both distributions—primary and secondary—differ considerably from the total population older than 15, which distributes more homogeneously toward the higher ages.

It should be noted that in a population like that of Mexico, with a high birth rate and a relative "rejuvenation" of the population pyramid, it is very important to take into account age groups when considering the problem of education. For example, in the case of literacy, if we consider together absolute and functional (a population with only two years of schooling in the definition proposed by COPLAMAR, a government development agency in Mexico), in 1978 there were 13.39 million illiterate Mexicans, 37.2% of the population 15 years and older. Even during the period 1970–1978, the rate of growth of this group of the population would have diminished with respect to that of the 1960–1970 period (COPLAMAR, 1982: 18).

It is surprising to observe that in the CENIET study there were more older users compared with previous studies. Likewise, it was found that the higher the grade of registration, the younger the population (CENIET, 1976: 84). The results may be very biased because many live in the metropolitan zone (Mexico City) or because there is a "rejuvenation" of the educational population. This appears to be confirmed when DGAC notes that "in general, we see that the SNEA attracts adolescents and young adults, those who have stopped studying only a relatively few years ago in the school system where they did not conclude their studies. This phenomenon is accentuated at the secondary level, where 67% of the users were between 15 and 24 years of age (at the primary level it is 59%)" (DGAC, 1978a: 26).

At the national level, the marriage status is primarily single (which reduces, on the one hand, the possibility of a user who is responsible for a number of persons economically; on the other hand, it is a population with more leisure time not taken up by family responsibilities). In Mexico City, in contrast, the numbers are reversed, with the predominance of married individuals—above all, housewives (CENIET, 1976: 86). Occupationally, two thirds indicate that their principal activity is work, and about half are employed in the public sector (DGAC-CEE, 1979: ch. 3.2), concentrated in the categories of worker and employee (75% at the primary level and 84% at the secondary).

The predominant branches of activity are services (44% of those registered at the primary and 36% at the secondary level) and manufacturing. Nevertheless, it should not be assumed that there is a high percentage of unemployed: in the investigation of 1976, (CENIET, 1976) only 24% declared themselves in search of work, and at the secondary level some 33% declared themselves full time-students (DGAC, 1979: 38).

It is very interesting to observe the situation within the federal public sector—one of the most important employers. In 1975 the Census of Human Resources of the Federal Public Sector noted that of a total of 1,394,396 employees, 685,730 (49.2%) had not reached the level of general basic education: 29,083 illiterates, 196,255 with incomplete primary education, and 460,393 with incomplete secondary education.

Among the adult users, the large majority of their fathers have (or had) manual occupations. The analysis of the index of eating habits appears to indicate that the population served corresponded to the lowest social sectors of the urban areas and the highest in the rural zones (DGAC-CEE, 1979: ch. 3.2). That could, however, sustain the hypothesis that the open systems, given the characteristics of the persons registered, had become basically urban (COPLAMAR, 1982: 122).

In the distribution by state, it is evident that there is a decrease in relative terms of those left behind, (drop-outs and those who never attended school) which reflects an improvement of the conditions of schooling of the adult population (COPLAMAR, 1982: table 3.22). Nevertheless, it is also evident that there is an increase in absolute terms of those left behind in all areas and, further, that there is a relatively unequal decrease between areas, maintaining in general the differences between the more highly educated states (with the higher level of development) and those less educated (COPLAMAR, 1982: 25).

That is to say, the supply of education for adults functioned more efficiently in urban communities, and especially in those regions with a relatively higher level of development. It remains to determine the motivations for entering the different educational levels, and the academic and occupational expectations of the subjects, a fundamental issue, according to a state-of-the-art survey (Lind and Johnston, 1986).

The motivations were diverse. Married women, especially those who defined themselves as housewives, indicated their principal interest as participating in systems of adult education in order to help with the schoolwork of their children. In general terms, they did not manifest any interest in accreditation, but they did want to master the content (CENIET, 1976: 86). The increase of the male population at the secondary level reflected, in some investigations, the utility that possession of a secondary certificate had in the work place.

These facts reveal, first, that nonformal education may offer a small change in the status or the salary of the employed labor force that occupies the lowest socioeconomic positions. From this perspective, there may exist, at a specific level (e.g., at the secondary level for adults), distinctly economic motivations for participating in adult education. At the same time, the acquisition of a primary certificate would not have any compensation in this sense—nevertheless, one study indicated the opposite (DGAC-CEE, 1979: ch. 2.31).

Second, there are indications sustaining the hypothesis of La Belle and Verhine that education acquired after taking a job has a large impact on status and salary (1978: 13). Clearly, adult education cannot be very attractive for the unemployed adult, especially if it involves expenditures that increase opportunity costs. Despite the fact that books at the primary level are free, it is necessary to consider other expenses, such as (in 1976–1979) paying for accreditation exams, transportation, minimal supplementary materials, or photographs. Finally, the studies indicate that many of the users have expectations of being able to complete a subprofessional program.

The Efficiency of the System

The evaluations of the efficiency of the system are critical. One study notes:

> The individuals who have taken this decision were not obtaining the benefits that —under conditions of greater efficiency—they would have been able to derive from the advantages this system offers (with respect to the number of hours of

study that are necessary for completing each cycle and with respect to the flexibility of hours) if one compares it with the conventional academic system.
(DGAC-CEE, 1979: ch. 7)

Even more drastically: "As is noted in the diagnosis, presently the educational
services for adults do not constitute a coherent subsystem and are unarti-
culated, are without priority, and function with scarce resources, all of which
translates into low levels of attention and efficiency" (COPLAMAR, 1982: 119).

It is convenient to introduce three relevant aspects that follow from the conclusions of such research. First, why are the adult education services not attractive to the male population? Second, what are the principal problems that must
be resolved with respect to the instructors and tutors of adults? Finally, if the
objective of the system of adult education is attention to and accreditation of
studying, what are the results?

If we review the distribution of the Mexican population over 15 years old by
gender, we find that in 1970, 50.03% were men and 49.97% women. In 1980 a
similar distribution was maintained (SPP-CONAPO-CELADE, n.d.: 8). The fact
that two-thirds of the users of adult education services in 1976–1981 were
women does not correspond to the population distribution. Why are these services not attractive to the male population? Here is a first problem to resolve.

Some of the factors that, from 1976 to 1981, discouraged male participation
in the system include greater participation in the labor force, less leisure time,
the occupational devaluation of primary schooling certificates, and the extensive
duration of studies (2,450 hours for passing the primary examinations, 3,360
for the secondary ones). Has a service of promotion and motivation been designed that is especially directed to male, adult users, including new educational
forms that permit a greater participation by men in these programs?

What are the principal problems to resolve with respect to the instructors? At
the outset it is appropriate quickly to characterize them. The instructor in adult
education was, from 1976 to 1981, on the average 27 years old, and predominantly female at the primary level and male at the secondary level. They generally did not have training courses, but typically had completed junior high school
or higher. They dedicated approximately an hour a day to the system and had
less than a year of experience in adult education.

As one study put it: "The analysis indicated as well that, in some cases, the
age, level of education, experience, training and level of dedication of the instructors intervenes significantly in the determination of the levels of output of
the system" (DGAC-CEE, 1979: 16).

These aspects contribute to outlining the qualitative problem of the instructors; let us now look at the quantitative one. "To reach 1.29 million adults in
1980 required 57,346 instructors, a number that would rise . . . to 267,290 instructors in 1991, assuming an optimum of one instructor for each 20 pupils in
the open systems and one adult education teacher for each 32 pupils"
(COPLAMAR, 1982: 128). As can be inferred from these figures, the demand

for instructors in Mexico has been, and will probably continue to be, very great. This is a challenge for designing multiple, flexible, and efficient mechanisms of development and training of instructors to meet the demand.

Finally, one of the principal problems that was debated in 1976–1981 was the low productivity of the system. According to the data, the attention to illiteracy had a negative rate of increase (−21.3%) between 1978 and 1980. In contrast, the primary training of adults increased substantially (81.3% annually). The total number participating increased at a rate of 20.8% annually, on the average. Despite this, in absolute terms the growth was not so significant, given the magnitude of uneducated adults in Mexico (COPLAMAR, 1982: 39).

Considering, for example, the proportion of the population reached compared with the total of the population within the minimum in some areas, it can be observed that, of the total number of those registered at the primary level, only 63% effectively pursued their studies and of these only 23.3% were certified. At the secondary level, the relation between registration and attendance improved substantially, but the rate of certification was lower than that at the primary level, with a total of 14% graduating. That is to say, the more academic systems, like those of the CEBA, have a high level of efficiency with respect to attendance and graduation, even if they behave very erractically in relation to registration and attendance.

The CEBAs, the secondary programs for workers, and the open primary program, despite having a higher relation between registration and attendance than the other services, never reached 20% graduating relative to those registered. Beyond the questions arising from evaluations and studies, there is that of revitalizing programs directed specifically to reaching illiteracy and, at the same time, giving a differential impulse to the process, emphasizing more the necessities of the rural as opposed to the urban areas.

ADULT EDUCATION POLICIES IN THE 1980S

By the early 1980s, educational policymakers considered that the SNEA was not fulfilling its mission. There were declining enrollments and increasing dropout rates, and SNEA was mostly serving as a channel for middle-class youngsters to complete secondary education through open systems. A major overhaul of the system was quickly planned and implemented in light of the abundance of fiscal resources resulting from the oil boom. In 1981–1982, the National Program of Literacy Training (PRONALF) began, and the National Institute of Adult Education (INEA) was organized. The main aim of PRONALF was to reduce illiteracy to 10% by the end of 1982—the end of the "sexenio" (the administration of President López Portillo)—obviously a very ambitious educational goal that was reached, according to official statistics, by 1985, during the administration of President De La Madrid (Morales-Gómez and Torres, 1990). A method partially inspired in Freire's work and termed the "method of the generative word," was designed and implemented to achieve these goals.[9]

The INEA, an institute created on the model of the Brazilian MOBRAL, was in charge of coordinating all adult education policies and programs promoted and sponsored by the Secretariat of Education (SEP)—and eventually it would have incorporated the diverse services and programs of adult education offered by other agencies of the Mexican state. The INEA incorporated PRONALF as its main agency of literacy training; coordinated its activities with all state (provincial) organisms, using a decentralized scheme; and incorporated job training programs, elementary and secondary education for adults, public libraries for rural communities, community education programs, and some research activities carried out in SEP.[10]

The operation of INEA boosted adult education policies and programs in Mexico, becoming a central component in the strategy of educational modernization advanced by the technocratic fraction of the Mexican state. In addition, the activities of INEA exposed the texture and dynamics of adult education as part (indeed, a central one) and parcel of a comprehensive package of compensatory legitimation policies advanced by a corporatist state (Morales-Gómez and Torres, 1990; C. Torres, 1989b).

INEA claimed substantial gains in literacy and adult education training, and until approximately 1987, it had access to a fair amount of monetary resources, even in the midst of the most serious fiscal crisis in the recent economic history of Mexico. When the new government took office in 1988, the perverse combination of growing external debt (and more pressing payments of the debt interest), devaluation of the peso, and inflation had further affected the financial resources of the state, and budget cuts across the public sector were undertaken. By then, however, INEA was in a poor position to bargain for more resources. It had claimed that some states had virtually wiped out illiteracy (Tabasco, Baja California Sur, etc.) or that illiteracy rates were at levels lower than 6%, hence making the remaining target population difficult to reach. Priorities were shifted from literacy training to bilingual literacy (i.e., literacy training in both Spanish and one of 13 out of the 52 indigenous languages spoken in the country) and to more advanced forms of adult basic education. Paradoxically however, the Mexican state dropped most of its programs for job training and on-the-job training; not only programs controlled by INEA but also many of the programs conducted by other state agencies. These programs were supposed to be picked up by the private sector and particularly industries, and be tailor-made to their own training needs. This, in light of recent research evidence, did not happen (Schmelkes and Narro, 1988).

These fiscal and policy developments severely curtailed any attempt to move from a policy rationale to support adult education expansion on grounds other than promoting (symbolic) participation in citizenship, individual and family well-being, or reinforcing the self-identity and pride of individuals and specific groups of the population. In short, any attempt to use adult education policies to contribute to labor force commodification or recommodification was severely undermined. Once again, compensatory legitimation policies—which could be expensive in the context of diminishing fiscal resources and policies of rationalization and austerity—cannot compete with modernization policies that try to promote capital accumulation. Coming to grips with the tension between expanding capital accumulation and increasing the legitimation of the political regime seems to be a principal task of the capitalist state (C. Torres, 1989a), and more so in corporatist Mexico. In the context of profound economic and fiscal reforms, reindustrialization, and forced modernization, educational policies promoted through nonformal education and based on cultural or political rationales may not have a bright future.

CONCLUSION: RESEARCH PROGRAM ON ADULT EDUCATION AND LITERACY IN MEXICO

The points noted in this agenda constitute fundamental aspects of research on adult education in Mexico and perhaps all of Latin America. This research could be initiated as part of participative planning in adult education and, if that were the case, would be able to link up with action research or participative research.

Participatory action research has certain epistemological and theoretical-methodological presuppositions that differ, often drastically, from the conventional procedures of social research. Without claiming to note all of the characteristics of participative research, some of them are: (a) an explicit political intention articulated in relation to the dominated classes and social groups and the impoverished in society; (b) an effort to combine in a proper balance educational activities with research processes and with popular participative action; (c) an effort to incorporate within the same process researchers from the population studied; (d) activities of research and education supported by an organized base or social group; (e) in understanding knowledge as a means of social transformation, a radical critique of any separation of theory and practice; (f) a critique of the methods and techniques of social research that inhibit the simultaneous understanding of the object as subject of the educational research process; (g) an effort to develop a systematic process for transmitting the knowledge realized to the population studied; (h) incentives for the participation of the members of popular sectors in the understanding of the political and community locus and in the exercise of recovery actions; in the design of self-management mechanisms or political reorganization (including economic organization) and in the transmission and collective analysis of the information gathered and conclusions reached (Gajardo, 1982; Rigal, 1978; Vio Grossi, 1982: 51–58; Yopo, 1983; Latapí, 1988).

In the context of a participatory action research approach:

1. It would be useful to develop a socioeconomic and cultural profile of those illiterates who participate in adult education and literacy programs, including their social, educational, and family antecedents, employment, income and ex-

penditures, reasons for participating in a given program, and knowledge and opinions with respect to Mexican society.

2. It would be useful to determine the role of basic adult education and literacy in family and individual improvement of the beneficiaries of this program on the basis of the self-perceptions and experiences of the newly literate.

3. Another fundamental aspect is the determination of the specific contributions of reading-writing and the mastery of basic arithmetic operations for enhancing and/or modifying the means of self-employment of the beneficiaries of the program.

4. It is indispensable to develop an analysis of the modifications in the level of income, employment, type of occupation, occupational mobility, and cultural capital of the beneficiaries of these programs once a certain period of time has passed following their departure from the program (e.g., one year after).

Beyond the specific objectives of research projects oriented toward literacy programs, the following should be pursued:

1. Elaboration of an analytical framework for the relations between massive literacy programs; improving the conditions of life of popular urban, suburban, and rural sectors in Mexico; and the continuity of formal apprenticeship in reading, writing, and arithmetic.

2. Elaboration of a follow-up model for graduates of literacy programs that would allow studying the change, in the short and the long run, of specific variables (e.g., working conditions or type of occupation) once the program of studies has been abandoned.

3. Elaboration of a systematic analysis of the possible contributions of literacy and basic adult education programs to the processes of self-employment of graduates on the basis of the experience of a select group.

4. Design of a complex of organizational alternatives and pedagogical activities for postliterates that could be implemented to give continuity to the process of learning–apprenticeship and, at the same time, link the newly literate more closely with work channels, especially the informal marketplace (self-employment).

5. Compiling the complex of experiences of the newly literate, especially in terms of access to and use of information, and in terms of reading and writing new materials. Experiments could be incorporated for the critical analysis and diffusion of a system of training for regional organizers, instructors, and teachers of adult education dedicated to designing and operationalizing alternatives for postliterates in Mexico.

Once such an agenda of research has been satisfactorily carried out, the results would contribute more elements of judgment and analysis to an ever more detailed theoretical and methodological discussion about the effects of educational variables in adult education upon the beneficiaries of such systems. Increasingly, there is a heated polemic regarding whether there are psychological, political, economic, and social returns, and if there are, how to estimate their magnitude or diversity. However, a more comprehensive debate should take place regarding what, if any, alternative strategies and models of adult education can be initiated in dependent-development capitalist countries, given the new economic and social conditions of the 1980s: political redemocratization in the midst of economic recession, growing external debt, and increasing poverty of the masses.

NOTES

An abbreviated version of this chapter was published in mimeographed form as "La educación de adultos en México, 1976–1981" (Facultad Latinoamericana de Ciencias Sociales [FLACSO], December 1984). My analysis of adult education policies in Mexico is further developed in Chapter 5 of Morales-Gómez and Torres (1990). I would like to thank José Angel Pescador and Alberto Arnaut Salgado for useful comments on preliminary versions of this chapter. As usual, the author alone is responsible for the opinions expressed and not the institution that supported the research.

1. In 1975 the Ley Nacional de Educación para Adultos was passed, which gave rise in 1976 to the setting up and initial opeation of SNEA under what was then the Subdirección del Sistema Abierto. From this followed a great number of institutional transformations in the educational agencies of the public sector responsible for non-formal education. In 1977 the Coordinación de los Servicios Educativos para las Zonas Deprimidas y Grupos Marginados was created; under it were, among others, the Dirección General de Alfabetización y Educación de Adultos (DGAEA) and the Coordinación Nacional de Sistemas Abiertos, both of which were under the Secretariat of Public Education (SEP). In 1978 the Coordinación General del Plan para Zonas Deprimidas y Grupos Marginados (COPLAMAR) was created, responsible directly to the president of the republic; it ceased to exist at the end of the 1970s. In February 1978 the Coordinación Nacional de Sistemas Abiertos disappeared from the domain of the SEP and the Dirección General de Educación a Grupos Marginados (DGEGM) was created. In September of that year the majority of the services under the responsibility of the DGAEA and the DGEGM were combined, giving rise to the Dirección General de Educación para Adultos (DGEA), responsible initially to the Subsecretaría de Planeación and, beginning in 1980, to the Subsecretaría de Cultura y Recreación. In April 1981 PRONALF was created, and in September 1981, INEA, which incorporated PRONALF under the Dirección General de Alfabetización, as well as the majority of the services under DGEA (C. Torres, 1984a; Rubio, 1983).

2. For more documentation on SNEA, see Sirvent and Vergara (1983); Cuéllar (1981); and Morales-Gómez and Torres (1990).

3. Population ten years or older. Data from the Dirección de Estadísticas, *IX censo general de población 1970*, abbreviated summary (Mexico, DF, 1972).

4. The total cost of PRONALF was set at 2,676,100 million pesos (approximately $55 million). For 1981, it was planned to make literate one million people. Subsequently, serious difficulties in the implementation and operation of PRONALF forced the selection of new and more moderate goals for the program. It is interesting to note that origi-

nally PRONALF was designed as a program oriented toward illiterates who resided in localities with more than 500 inhabitants and who were not monoligual.

5. Paulo Freire has criticized in diverse contexts the mystifying use of the concept (see Freire, 1980a, 1980b). For complementary references see Darcy de Oliveira and Dominice (1975) and Snook (1981). I have developed a critical analysis of the political content of the concept (C. Torres, 1980b: 101–24).

6. In a very incisive article, Carlos Rodriguez Brandão has stressed that the notion of popular movement includes all those forms of mobilization and organization of persons from the popular classes directly linked to the productive process, in the cities and the countryside (Rodriguez Brandão, 1984: 34, fn. 11).

7. An evaluation of the secondary television program as an educational tool, which includes such diverse aspects as an analysis of the cultural policy of the Mexican state and the development of television, and an evaluation of the educational efficiency and inclusive costs of the system, is in Montoya and Rebeil (1981).

8. See, for example, the bibliography at the end of La Belle and Verhine (1978). For the European case consult Kulich (1982), Titmus (1985), and Titmus et al. (1979).

9. But, as De Lella (1982) has rightly pointed out, the method was used purely as a technique for teaching reading and writing, and not as part of a comprehensive process of consciousness raising or "conscientization," as proposed by Freirean educators. Further, this use of the method not only stripped it of its political and ideological overtones, but also deeply affected its technical component, and hence its effectiveness in literacy training (Morales-Gómez and Torres, 1990).

10. In the established symbolism of a powerful presidentialist system such as the Mexican state, there are not ministers (who may have strong autonomy in decision making at the cabinet level), and hence ministries, but appointed secretaries of the president in charge of specialized functions. For all practical purposes, however, the Secretariat of Education is the Ministry of Education in Mexico.

ADULT EDUCATION AND THE TRANSITION TO SOCIALISM IN CUBA, NICARAGUA, AND GRENADA

This chapter offers an overview of the educational situation of three revolutionary and socialist-oriented nations in Latin America, with special focus on the state and adult education reform. Almost 30 years after the first socialist experience in the area, it is appropriate to review the changes in the adult educational systems in some socialist-inspired transitional projects that have taken place in the region. The analysis will focus especially on Cuba and Nicaragua, although some insights into the Grenadan experience will be offered.

Several questions can be advanced at the outset: (1) How can these experiences be understood in the context of the current discussion about the relationship between socioeconomic and educational changes and the state? (2) What were the major modifications made in the educational system in general, and in adult education, particularly, in the socialist experiences? (3) Why were the literacy campaigns in socialist countries considered so successful in contrast with many of those carried out in other Latin American nations? (4) What factors have undermined the educational reform in socialist-oriented nations? (5) What seem to be the main differences between adult education systems in capitalist and noncapitalist Latin American countries when issues such as democracy, political participation, and social mobilization are taken into account?

The chapter is divided into four main parts and a postscript. The first part briefly describes the main features of the socioeconomic and educational situation in dependent Latin America, in order to provide a context for the discussion. The second part analyzes educational reform processes in Cuba, Grenada, and Nicaragua. For a better understanding of these changes, a comparison between the prerevolutionary and postrevolutionary situations is made using available data. The third part analyzes changes and contradictions in the three nations. The fourth part, focusing both on the achievements and on the problems of adult education in these nations, draws some preliminary lessons for adult education reform in transitional societies. The postscript briefly addresses the relationships between democracy and adult education in Latin America.

LATIN AMERICAN DEPENDENT SOCIETIES

Cardoso and Faletto (1978) have proposed the notion of a structural dependency to understand Latin American history. They have argued simultaneously against vulgar, mechanicitic Marxism and modernity theory, rejecting the notions that (a) the fundamental periods of change at the international level have marked the significant moments of transformation of Latin America and (b) that the history of central capitalism is, at the same time, the history of peripheral capitalism. In short, they do not derive mechanically significant phases of dependent societies only from the "logic of capital accumulation."

Dependency studies have conceived the relationships between external and internal forces as forming a complex whole whose structural links are rooted in coincidences of interest between local dominant classes and international ones; and, on the other side, are challenged by local dominated groups and classes. Peter Evans, drawing upon this "dependency tradition" in his highly commended study of associate dependent development in Brazil, discusses a triple alliance of international capital (embodied in transnational corporations), local capital, and the state. In this alliance, "the centrality of the state to accumulation on the periphery is incontrovertible" (Evans, 1979: 43).

Cardoso and Faletto have identified two basic situations of dependency: (a) a dependency where the productive system is nationally controlled, and therefore accumulation is the result of the appropriation of resources and labor exploitation from national sources, and production is oriented toward the external and internal markets (Argentina, Brazil, postrevolutionary Mexico, Colombia are cases in point); and (b) dependency in enclave situations, where accumulation is promoted by foreign interests and external capital, and the process of accumulation is oriented toward the external market (some republics in Central America and the Caribbean, and Bolivia are good examples of enclave economies).

In enclave economies, Cardoso and Faletto identify two types of situations: in the first, foreign enterprises assume control of enterprises that have been created and expanded by local entrepreneurs (such as copper mining in Chile); in the second, the enterprises were originated by foreign investment without the participation of local entrepreneurs.

This last situation implies the local bourgeoisie's loss of control of fundamental sectors of the economy, exemplified in the production of nitrate in Chile, of guano in Peru, of cash crops in Central America and Panama, and the basic situation of Venezuela before the oil boom. Obviously, the situations of dependency where the local entrepreneurs kept tight control of the means of production in the long run allowed the country to operate with more freedom in its model of development, with national control of the productive system. Industrialization took place in this way in Argentina, Mexico, Brazil, and, to a lesser extent, in Chile and Colombia.

In this process of industrialization several periods can be identified. To put it simply, industrialization was initially oriented toward import substitution in the 1940s and 1950s, oriented toward a growing domestic market from the late 1950s until the early 1970s, and oriented toward exports (particularly in Brazil—appliances, arms, and computers) in the late 1970s and early 1980s. Cardoso and Faletto have rightly noted that peripheral industrialization is based on products from central, mass-consumption economies that typically represent luxury consumption in dependent societies.

The crisis for the model of development in the nationally controlled economies was brought about by a perverse combination of (1) industrialization bottlenecks, a drop in foreign investments in new areas of these economies, and serious difficulties in the balance of trade in some of these countries; (2) the activation of the masses, particularly the working and middle classes; (3) the predominance of technocratic roles in the state and the increasing difficulty of economic and social planning in the face of intense corporative and social negotiation with unions and traditional political parties; and (4) the role of the army, which since the national reorganization of the Southern Cone democracies has been less oriented toward defense against external threats and more toward internal control of unwanted (by the state bureaucracy) reactions to state policy.

This combination of economic, political, and social variables produced the emergence of the early authoritarian experiences in Latin America with coups d'état in Brazil (1964), in Uruguay and in Chile (1973), and in Argentina (1976), and in Bolivia one of the most extreme expressions of political destabilization, a series of changes of governments from civilian to military in the late 1960s and early 1970s. The Argentine political scientist Guillermo O'Donnell (1982) termed the new form of authoritarian state that emerged in Latin America in the 1970s the "bureaucratic-authoritarian state," a description that, although captivating, has been the subject of controversy concerning its analytical value (C. Torres, 1989c). After this brief introduction to the structural and historical dynamics of dependent societies, let us discuss the economic and educational situation of Latin America.

The population of Latin America is nearly 280 million people. Of those, 112 million (40%) live below the poverty line.[1] Among these 112 million, 41 million live in cities and 71 million in the countryside. This means that in Latin America, poverty is fundamentally rural. It is also estimated that 53 million (19% of the total Latin American population) was at or below the destitution line.[2] Almost two-thirds (34 million) of these extremely poor people lived in rural areas, and 19 million lived in urban areas (Avalos, 1987).

In the context of the economic crisis of the 1970s and 1980s, the gap between central and peripheral economies seems to have increased.[3] Since the beginning of the 1980s, the majority of the Latin American and Caribbean countries have shown an abrupt decline in their rhythm of growth, less controlled and high rates of inflation, a large deficit in the balance of payments, a reduction of real income, higher unemployment, a proliferation of poverty, deteriorating terms of trade, inflated interest rates, and huge external debts.[4]

Economic crisis notwithstanding, the political map of Latin America in the early 1980s had substantially changed, showing some progressive trends. At present, Latin America is showing, after many years of military regimes, processes of political redemocratization (particularly in the Southern Cone and Mexico) but also conflictive and violent deadlock scenarios in Central America.

Regardless of the particular differences that can be identified among the Latin American countries, almost all of them are in a situation of economic, political, financial, and technological dependence[5] with respect to the metropolis. This is a historical relationship that, for some scholars, can be traced to the conquest and colonization nearly 500 years ago. In the countries today experiencing attempts at transformation (under revolutionary or liberal-democratic models) the governments usually suffer internal and external pressures that limit their possibilities of success, especially if they search for real sovereignty, more egalitarian distribution of wealth, greater participation of the socially subordinated sectors and classes in the power structures, or the provision of higher standards of living for the majority of the population.

Although a great diversity exists among Latin American countries, many of them share some common economic and social problems. In a fairly oversimplified way, they are the following: First, natural resources, labor, and capital are flowing increasingly toward the markets of the industrialized societies. As in colonial times, raw materials, whose prices started to decline in the first quarter of the twentieth century, are feeding the factories of the advanced industrial countries and return to Latin America in the form of expensive manufactured goods—perhaps with the exception of some items in the export-oriented industrial model of Brazil. Second, the "brain drain" of Latin American professionals and intellectuals continues to constitute an important supply of the scientific and technological research and applied knowledge process of the industrial advanced countries, especially the United States. This results in difficulties for the development of an autonomous scientific and technological system, particularly in the less industrialized countries of the region. Finally, a large portion of the national income from exports in the late 1970s and 1980s was channeled to the payment of the external debt, which constitutes a serious limitation for self-development, and a deterrent for any autonomous strategy of capital accumulation.[6]

Similarly, the concentration of resources in a few industrialized metropolitan areas and the lack of opportunities in the countryside have created profound distortions in the patterns of development. This situation is forcing the rural population to migrate to urban areas, which provide few economic and social benefits, dashing the hopes of millions of peasants. Unemployment and underemployment are widespread among the newcomers to the urban settings, who remain socially and economically marginalized, and unable to practice subsistence agriculture.

The educational system cannot escape this situation. In a context of poverty and inequality, on average 60% of the children who enter elementary school do not complete it. Most of these dropouts belong to the poor social classes, and most of them live in rural areas. Undoubtedly, many of these young school leavers will be added to the 45 million Latin American absolute illiterates, and the even greater number of functional illiterates.

Although an important expansion of the educational system occurred in Latin America, and the number of children enrolled in school has increased, there is also a rapid increase in population that is now pressing for more and better education (Carnoy et al., 1979) in the context of persistent high dropout rates throughout the system. While the policymakers, still mostly using human capital theory assumptions, have expected that educational expansion would contribute to economic growth, to the equalization of educational and social opportunity between classes, and to the development of a more employable labor force, the reality of the last decades has been different:

> The absolute number of illiterates in Latin America has also increased, the poorest fifty percent of the population has remained as poor as before, income distribution has, if anything, become more unequal, and open unemployment has also increased. Poverty has been transferred from rural to urban areas while rural areas continued to remain desperately poor. (Carnoy, et al., 1979:1).

Carnoy concludes by arguing that "education has not been relevant to the development of Latin American societies and for that reason, it has not served to fulfil the distribution and employment needs of those economies" (Carnoy et al., 1979:2). Similarly, Beatrice Avalos synthesizes the main problems of the Latin American educational system as follows: "Three major issues dominated the discussions and in a way have coloured the concerns of the first half of the present decade. These are equality, quality and relevance in respect of educational provision" (Avalos, 1987: 153).

Regarding the problem of equalization of opportunity and democratization of society, the educational system has not been very successful. In the analysis of this failure, it is possible to resort to two types of explanation. The first understands the problem as an internal deficiency of the educational system. In this technical-financial perspective, the resolution of the income distribution, employment, and educational opportunity dilemma depends basically on the incorporation of new educational technology, more skilled teachers, curriculum modifications, and the provision of more material and financial resources. The second type of explanation emphasizes that the problem is inherently involved with the economic and social structure, and is related to the pattern of dependent development followed by the Latin American countries; hence, no incremental change will substantially modify the educational conditions. Similarly, although the dynamics of the process of modernization will not necessarily be wiped away by the present deep crisis, it will definitely affect the process of capital accumulation and the future of the model of development pursued in the region (Morales-Gómez, 1990; Fagerlind and Saha, 1984; Simmons, 1980). The following section will discuss in detail the educational and social developments of Cuba, Nicaragua, and Grenada as transitional and socialist experiences.

EDUCATIONAL REFORM AND SOCIALISM

Cuba

Education before the Revolution

To understand the changes that have occurred in the educational structure of Cuba, it is necessary to examine the state of education prior to the revolution. The prerevolutionary years of Cuban education show a concrete example of a country having the potential for educational development but hindered by a lack of leadership, corruption, and structural obstacles (Valdés, 1971). Let us examine some figures.

In 1899, 56.8% of the population did not know how to read or write. Half a century later, the illiteracy rate in the island had decreased to 23.6% (UNESCO, 1965: 16), although the absolute number of illiterates had increased from 690,565 to 1,032,849 (an increment of 49.6%).

Economic and political inequalities among regions were reflected in the access to reading and writing. Looking at the provinces, we observe that in 1953, the illiteracy rate in the province of Havana was 9.2%, while in the provinces of Oriente, Pinar del Río, and Camagüey it was 35.3%, 30.8%, and 27.3%, respectively. Observing the general differences between urban and rural areas, the gap was still greater: in the urban sectors it was only 11.6%, while in the countryside it reached 41.7%, almost twice the national average.

In 1953, 84% of the children between the ages of 6 and 9 were illiterate. The percentage of illiterates among those 6–14 years of age in urban areas was 44.5% in Havana and 81.2% in Oriente Province. In rural areas, the percentage reached 64.1% in the former and 89.5% in the latter (Valdés, 1971). In the mid–1950s, Cuba was in seventeenth place in primary school enrollment for all of Latin America. By 1958, one year before the revolution, approximately half of the Cuban children of primary school age (6–14 years) had no education, while the Latin American average was 36%. There was an acute deficit of classrooms: in 1958 there were only 17,000 classrooms, whereas approximately 35,000 were required (UNESCO, 1965).

At the time of the revolution, only 24.2% of the total population aged 15 years and over had ever gone to school (Valdés, 1970: 424; Morales, 1981:31). The 1953 census stated, "It is possible that this high percentage of Cuban school age population who do not attend school is the cause of the illiteracy index yielded by the population census" (Republic of Cuba, 1953). In summary, when the new government took power, close to 75% of the Cubans were either illiterate or had failed to complete primary school.

Furthermore, the educational pyramid of Cuba during Batista's regime challenges any hope of considering education as a channel for social mobility. For instance, in 1953, 52% of Cubans had not gone beyond the third grade, 44% had between the fourth and the eleventh grade of education, 3% had between the twelfth grade and three years of college, and only 1% had four years of higher education. Among the latter, less than half acquired a university degree (United Nations, 1963: 314).

What could be inferred from the above statistics is that the conditions of the rural schools were less than satisfactory: in 1953, 385,394 peasant children between the ages of 6 and 14 had no access to schooling. In 1959, there were 732,000 children of school age in the rural areas, but available classrooms could have served only 279,000 students. In a study by the University of Las Villas in 1959, it was reported that 96.2% of all schools in the province had just one classroom, and in that classroom pupils ranging from first to sixth grade met at the same time and were served by only one teacher. On average there were 38 students per classroom, but only 20 desks. Furthermore, 86% of the schools lacked bathrooms, and there was running water in only 3% of the schools. The average number of textbooks per student was one, although approximately 15 different subjects were taught (Feijoó, 1959; University of Las Villas, 1959, cited in Valdés, 1971; Morales, 1981).

The Cuban Revolution took place in the mountains, not in the cities, and an alternative educational policy was developed by the insurgents along with their combat guerrilla tactics and agrarian reform. It is well known that the organization of the revolutionary army in the Sierra Maestra was cumbersome (Guevara, 1967). In December 1956, there were 82 survivors of the boat *Granma* that brought Fidel Castro and his insurgents to the beaches of Cuba. By March 1957, the guerilla group was as few as 18 men; however, by May of that year there were 127, even though some of the insurgents had to be expelled from the group to create greater ideological and combat strength. By July 1957, the 200 members were divided into two battalions and the Sierra area was established as a "liberated area." In his diary, Ernesto Guevara says that there was a lot to learn and teach among the group, since membership was unstable and recruits were unprepared. Instruction included military training, ideological lessons (with topics such as the importance of agrarian reform, collectivization, and principles of social change), and literacy programs. Other mechanisms of nonformal education, such as radio, were used by the rebels to inform the urban population about the goals and values of the revolutionary cause, and the different stages of the military struggle (Guevara, 1967; La Belle, 1986). On January 1, 1959, the new revolutionary army took control of Havana, and sweeping changes were begun.

Educational Reform after the Revolution

When Abel P. Morales, the Cuban Minister of Education, was in Italy, some-
one at an education conference asked him: "'Is the school in Cuba an instrument
of the State?' His answer was 'yes, of course, just as it was before the triumph of
the Revolution, and as it is in the present day in Italy'" (Leiner, in Manitzas and
Barkin, 1973:6). Just four months after the triumph of the revolution, during the
Labor Day celebration (May 1, 1959), Ernesto Guevara synthesized the diagnosis of the situation and the task for the government in the following way:

> There are more illiterates in Cuba today than were twenty-five years ago, be-
> cause the whole Government educational policy has consisted of embezzling and
> of building a few insignificant schools at the more central crossroads of the coun-
> try. Our task is another, comrades: we can rely on the people as a whole. We do
> not have to go beg for votes by building an insignificant school next to a highway.
> We are going to put that school where it is needed, where it fulfils its educational
> function for the people's benefit. . . . And not only schools. We will build centers
> for technical agricultural training, large technical schools where thousands of
> children can go to receive a much more systematic education which will enable
> them in the future to enter Cuban society with a great wealth of knowledge. (Na-
> tional Press of Cuba, 1960)

The emphasis was placed on the role of education in the structural transformations of the Cuban society. This was in the context of the traditional educational system in Latin America (Weinberg, 1984), which would soon be strongly
influenced by modernization and human capital theories as a reaction to the
Cuban Revolution, and by the fact that popular education had not been fully
developed,[7] and the experiences of educational innovation inspired by popular
education were still in need of more systematization and theorizing (Puiggrós et
al., 1987).

The new government viewed education as a key factor in achieving economic
and political transformation of the society. Cuban leaders did not see revolutionary programs as limited by lack of human resources so much as limited by the
difficulty of mobilizing and utilizing the population at large and the resources of
mass organizations (Fagen, 1969).

The principal reforms in postrevolutionary Cuba centered on mobilizing the
entire population into productive activities and transforming the ideological
base through which these productive activities functioned. The most important
reforms after 1959 were, according to Carnoy and Werthein (1980), the radical
change in the purpose and structure of adult education, the expansion of schooling at the primary and secondary levels, the shift of schooling to rural areas, the
improved fit between schooling and work (including the schools as productive
units), and changes in the socialization in the school (changing from individual
motivation to collective work). What follows is a brief examination of some of
these reforms.

In 1961, all private schools were nationalized, and education became free and compulsory, with 11% of the GNP assigned to this area. The enrollment in elementary schools grew from 717,000 in 1959 to 1,666,267 in 1961. In the same period, the number of teachers increased from 17,355 to 33,916. In secondary schools, enrollment increased from 90,192 to 151,091, and the number of teachers grew from 5,120 to 8,620. From 1959 to 1960 enrollment climbed rapidly, doubling the number of children attending classes. An indicator of the emphasis on primary education is that students at this level in 1961 represented 80% of the total number of young people receiving regular education (Carnoy and Werthein, 1980; Valdés, 1971).

Castro summarized the early achievements in the following way:

> The Revolutionary Government in only twenty months has created ten thousand new schools; in such a brief period of time it has duplicated the numbers of rural schools that had been created in fifty years. And Cuba is today the first country in America that has satisfied all the school needs, that has a teacher in every last corner of the mountains. (quoted in Kenner and Petras, 1969:3).

Schoolchildren were not allowed much leisure. The primary school year, which in 1958 consisted of 810 hours, was increased in 1964 to 1,080 hours in the urban areas and 900 hours in the countryside. Technical education was expanded, diversified, and given priority by the revolutionary government.

Polytechnic education[8] was created in 1965, as the method by which children "from the outset in the primary schools learn the scientific principles underlying all subjects and acquaint themselves with the handling of tools and machines so as to acquire the abilities, habits and dexterity, and communist attitude toward work which are important in society today" (UNESCO, 1965). Polytechnic education introduced an important innovation in the Latin American educational system, where teaching had been, and still is, highly verbal, intellectual, and formal, with a disdain for the technical and practical implications of education. Such a curriculum is considered irrelevant not only by students but also by a considerable number of teachers (Avalos, 1987).

The notion of polytechnic education implied that students must do work that is simultaneously educational, productive, and socially useful. They take care of the school and its surroundings; they plant trees, work in garden plots, and raise animals; study different jobs; visit factories and farms; discuss speeches of revolutionary leaders; and learn the fundamentals of literacy and numeracy. In summary, polytechnic education was established to combine education with technological principles, productive work, and research. Higher education was another important target of these revolutionary policies, and was linked with the notion of polytechnic education.

After 1959, the university also became a school of higher technical training, preparing people for specific kinds of jobs in short supply in the economy. The egalitarian aims of the revolution were so predominant in its early years that expenditures on university education, which usually caters to middle-class or elite demands for upward mobility, were curtailed relative to the heavy emphasis on primary and lower secondary education (Carnoy and Werthein, 1980).

The university has been incorporated into the country's development. Since the mid–1960s students have aided in carrying out economic plans. For several months per year they worked in factories and on farms, and assisted in the building of dams, roads, or hill terraces. They were also involved in coffee and citrus plantations, as well as in the analysis of soil. Political science students, for instance, worked in sugar mills, doing research on factors that contribute to greater productivity or ameliorating absenteeism (Valdés, 1971). Fidel Castro commented on these first experiments, saying that they moved universities from their traditional seats, "which convert a mountain-work project into a university classroom and the physical planning room of an administrative office into an architecture classroom." For Castro, "These examples show the process through which the present university will gradually disappear. . . . The old idea of the classic university will wither away" (*Granma*, March 16, 1969).

During the first stages of the Cuban Revolution, Castro and the revolutionary leadership believed that, in the future, practically every factory, farm, and hospital would have the appropriate facilities to do the research and higher studies previously undertaken by the universities. Furthermore, Castro foresaw that revolution in education would lead to the universalization of universities, promising that "in Cuba someday the university will become universal and the entire nation will study at the university level" (quoted in Read, 1970:134). Two decades later, the university had not withered away but, on the contrary, had become the center for graduate training of a new intellectual elite while a parallel system of universities for workers was open to the general population (Pescador, 1982). Perhaps one of the main accomplishments of revolutionary politics, however, was in the field of adult education, including the cuban literacy campaign.

The Literacy Campaign

In September 1960, Prime Minister Castro appeared before the General Assembly of the United Nations, where he gave a four-and-one-half-hour speech. He announced the Cuban literacy campaign in the following terms:

> In the next year, our people plan to wage a great battle against illiteracy with the ambitious goal of teaching every last illiterate person to read and to write. To this end organizations of teachers, students, workers, that is, people as a whole, are preparing themselves for an intense campaign, and Cuba will be the first country in America which, at the end of a few months, will be able to say that it does not have a single illiterate person. (quoted in Kenner and Petras, 1969:3)

In fact, in 1961, designated by the revolutionary government as the "Year of Education," the whole population was mobilized during an eight-month period to eradicate illiteracy on the island. A quarter of a million men and women (one person for each four illiterates) were transported all over the island and supplied with 3 million textbooks. The campaign was undertaken in four clearly defined stages. The first stage was preparatory, from September 1960 to January 1961. This period took advantage of research conducted under the sponsorship of the National Commission for Illiteracy and Fundamental Education (created in March 1959).[9] Several methods of literacy training were explored, including Ana Echegoyen's idea-phonic method, the method of normalized words developed by María L. Soler, and the Laubach method. Research on the vocabulary universe of Cubans was also conducted, by randomly sampling 3,000 adults 16 years of age and older, of whom 360 were found to be illiterate. The conclusion of this first stage was that all the methods, although technically appropriate, failed to correspond to the political and ideological requisites of the Cuban process. Hence, a revolutionary primer was devised. The second stage took place between January and April 1961. In this stage the structure of the campaign and the technical elements of it were conceived. The third stage was developed between April and September 1961. In this period, the political direction of the campaign was conceived through active participation of mass organizations. The final stage, between September and December 22, 1961, the date on which the campaign was officially declared concluded, is properly considered the teaching-learning stage.

The revolutionary primer, entitled *Venceremos*, was based on a compounded analytical-synthetic method, including levels of increasing phonetic, linguistic, and grammatical difficulty. Unlike the majority of the primers at that time in the region, it presented 15 topics related to the tasks and accomplishments of the Cuban Revolution, including subjects as politically sensitive as agrarian reform, the role of the Organization of the American States (which had expelled Cuba from its membership under pressure from the United States), as well as subjects such as poetry and the alphabet. There were 1.5 million primers distributed. According to a UNESCO study, the results of the campaign were astonishing: At the beginning of the year the official illiteracy rate was 21%; by December it was reduced to 3.9%—the lowest rate in Latin America. Overall, as seen in Table 5.1, of the total of illiterates enrolled in the campaign, 72.2% become literate.

The achievement of the campaign notwithstanding, many problems were faced by its organizers. One of the main problems was the difficulty in locating the illiterates, largely because they tended to hide their condition. In addition, in pedagogical terms the level of knowledge achieved in literacy training was considered insufficient for daily needs: only first grade levels of reading and writing were officially claimed for the new literates, and such levels were too low to be of real or immediate use either at work or at home. A third important problem was the limit to avoid the relapse into functional illiteracy: according to the final statistics of the campaign, about 28% of the located illiterates could not or would not be taught to read an write during the year (Carnoy and Werthein, 1980).

Table 5.1
Illiterates and Literacy Workers in the Cuban Literacy Campaign, 1961

Illiterates	Total	Percentage
Enrolled	979,207	100%
Literate	707,212	72.2%
Remained Illiterate	271,995	27.7%
Literacy Training Workers		
Total	268,420	100%
Popular Works	120,632	45%
Workers' Brigade	13,016	4.9%
Students' Brigade	100,000	37.2%
School teachers	34,722	12.9%

Source: UNESCO, Misión de la, 1965: 40.

Despite these difficulties, international experts considered the campaign a success. The UNESCO report (1965), for example, concluded that "the campaign was not a miracle but a difficult conquest achieved by virtue of work, technique and organization." Fagen (1969) argues that although the campaign was not an overwhelming and unquestionable triumph from a scholastic point of view, this is not the principal criterion by which to evaluate it. The campaign—Fagen claims—was intended to mobilize and to change Cuban political culture. Other effects of the campaign were the provision of medical services for the poor (including the free supply of spectacles to illiterates needing them) and the contact between two social groups that had been separated by dependent capitalist development: the illiterate peasants and the educated urban residents. Postliteracy courses were organized thereafter: in 1962, a total of 58,749 classrooms and 55,767 teachers were employed in postliteracy courses, serving a total of 1,470,545 students (UNESCO, 1965:56).

Adult Education System

The overall system of adult education was organized after the conclusion of the campaign, and a program to elevate the educational level of workers and farmers began. Primary and secondary education was offered in farms, factories, offices, and night schools. In the "worker-farmer education," adults could take improvement courses to advance to the third grade, sixth grade, or the secondary level. With that preparation they could continue their education by going to vocational schools or the workers' university. An idea of the dimension of this effort is given by Read when he states that "more than 15 million textbooks, technical pamphlets, workbooks, magazines and newspapers have been printed by the Ministry of Education and distributed without charge to participants in these programs" (Read, 1970:141).

In the worker-farmer education program the rates of enrollment were high: for instance, there were 468,000 students in 1962 and 818,000 students in 1964. With unusual flexibility for a Latin American adult education system, teaching hours were adjusted to fit the work schedules of the students. Three different calendars were created for the rural, mountain, and urban areas, adapting schedules to the harvest. Most of the teachers in worker-farmer education were not professionals. In 1966, for instance, instruction was provided by 21,696 amateur teachers and 8,899 professionals (Huberman and Sweezy, 1969:29).

Internal efficiency of this program can be considered high when compared with similar programs in developing countries. Between 1961 and 1973, 575,573 adults completed the sixth grade, practically one adult for every two children who finished primary school. In 1954, 53% of the labor force were absolute illiterates, 28% were functional illiterates, and only 13% had finished their elementary education. Ten years later, 59.2% of the labor force had completed or surpassed this level. In 1986, the minimum level of education reached by every Cuban was nine years, double the Latin American average.

Adult education also included the Women's Educational Advancement Program, which brought thousands of farm girls and women from isolated regions of the country to boarding schools that prepared them politically and educationally. Adult education programs were exceptionally important during the 1960s, in view of the massive exodus of the educated classes from Cuba after the revolution. An example of this brain drain is that although professionals, semiprofessionals, and the managerial sector constituted only 9.2% of the total population in 1953, they represented 32.8% of the Cuban emigré community from 1959 to 1966 (Fagen, 1969). At the end of the 1960s it was common "to find people with a sixth grade education in charge of state farms, factories, and other important work centers" (Read, 1970:142).

Experience derived from this program and increasing levels of schooling was achieved by adults.[10] In fact, in the 1980s, adult education in Cuba, unlike compensatory programs carried out in the rest of Latin America, is developed mostly at the work place, enhancing technological, scientific, and social knowledge related to the work. It is even possible to argue that the organization of this system of adult education accounts for the impressive gains in the education of the labor force compared with the rest of Latin America. Table 5.2 presents the pertinent data.

Table 5.2
Educational Levels of the Labor Force in Cuba, 1964 and 1974

	1964		1974	
	Workers	%	Workers	%
Illiterates	584,487	53	...	...
Third grade	309,821	28	734,204	40.8[1]
Fourth and fifth grade	60,410	5	...	...
Sixth grade and above	147,435	13	1,065,796	59.2
All levels	1,102,153	99	1,800,000	100
(1) Workers with less than sixth grade of education				

Source: Jorge Dominguez, *Cuba Order and Revolution.* Cambridge, Mass. The Belknap Press of Harvard University Press, 1978, page 170. Reprinted with permission.

That is to say, in 1964, 53% of the labor force was illiterate, 28% was functionally illiterate, and only 13% had finished or gone beyond basic education. A decade later, while the average education of the labor force in Latin America was less than 4 grades of elementary instruction (CEPAL, 1976), 59.2% of the Cuban labor force had completed primary education or gone beyond.

The principal reforms in the quantity and type of postrevolutionary education reflect the mass mobilization and redistribution orientation of the Cuban leadership. The whole educational system was oriented toward the search for the "new man,"[11] defined as a "person with scientific and technical knowledge, a humanist culture and a mentality that identifies personal and community interests as one and the same" (Valdés, 1971) or as one "for whom work is enjoyment and not obligation, and for whom study is a permanent process. A man of culture, science and technology" (Llanusa, 1969).[12]

The emphasis on egalitarianism and centralized planning resulted in a much slower university expansion than that of lower schooling levels for adults or children. The need to replace the large number of technicians and professionals who left Cuba after the revolution (estimated at 15,000 to 25,000) and the necessity to develop an independent technology and technological know-how resulted in an important shift to vocational and technical education in the university. In general terms, the orientation of the Cuban educational system was toward staffing lower and middle technical positions, raising productivity of ordinary workers and peasants, and transforming the values of the masses to the new socialist society (Carnoy and Werthein, 1980).

In the 1980s Cuban society provides a free education—including lunch and materials—for every child of school age, while in the rest of Latin America more than 22 million children have no schools, and some societies are turning to user fees in public education. Cuba has no illiterates, while in the rest of Latin America 45 million people cannot read or write, and many more can be classified as functional illiterates. Cuban workers have access to educational services similar to those achieved by Italian workers with the 150 hours' agreement (Yarnit, 1980a). While the success story of Cuban educational reform has been told by many observers (e.g., Kozol, 1978), what needs to be highlighted is the importance of adult education in the context of the transformation of the educational system and the political culture of revolutionary Cuba.

Nicaragua

Education during the Somoza Period

Twenty years after the Cuban Revolution, the Frente Sandinista de Liberación Nacional (FSLN) in Nicaragua was able to overthrow a cruel, dynastic dictatorship in its struggle for a new society based on justice and equality. In July 1979 the FSLN brought an end to the U.S.-backed authoritarian and corrupt regime identified with one family that controlled much of the Nicaraguan economy.[13] In the words of Anastasio Somoza Debayle himself, under his government Nicaragua was "not a Third World country but a country economically, politically and militarily dependent on the United States" (quoted in Arnove, 1986:5).

The general situation in those times was synthesized by Carnoy and Torres in the following terms:

> Under the Somozas the Nicaraguan capitalist state was oriented primarily to maximizing the economic returns of the Somozas and their friends. Rather than seeking any widespread legitimacy through popular public projects, the Somozas used their monopoly over the repressive apparatus—in the form of the National Guard trained in the U.S.—to terrorize and control the population. (Carnoy and Torres, 1989)

When the Sandinistas came to power on a wave of popularity, they began to redistribute land to the peasants and develop a socially oriented economy.

Nevertheless, the number and dimension of the difficulties facing this project were perhaps larger than they expected.

To begin with, the revolution inherited one of the lowest-income economies in the region, an economy tied closely by primary exports and foreign loans from the United States, and corrupted by 40 years of a single family's repressive control (Carnoy and Torres, 1989). In addition, the housing and production infrastructure was heavily damaged by both an earthquake (1972) and the civil war (1974–1979). As if this were not enough, the deposed president had escaped with most of the reserves of the Central Bank.

Another problem, shared by many revolutions, was the lack of qualified professionals in the various areas of government, as well as in production and services. The Sandinistas had no political experience outside of guerilla warfare, and very few people within or even outside the movement were able to carry out the plans of rebuilding and reform. At the same time, as in Cuba, a significant number of professionals left the country because of the revolution.

A third problem—maybe the most important one—is that, only two years after the end of the civil war and the establishment of the new government, the Sandinistas had to wage a war, this time against remnants of the National Guard who were, and still are, backed publicly by the U.S. administration. As will be examined later, this external aggression creates great obstacles to achieving economic growth and to the expansion of social services such as health and education. Since 1983, almost half of the national budget has been channeled to the defense effort. The indirect costs of the war (material resources, productive young people who must leave the farm or factory, the loss of lives, psychological effects, destruction of work centers, etc.) could raise this percentage still higher. According to an informed observer, "The total value of all the destroyed crops, farms, transport, infrastructure, schools, clinics, etc., over the last six years is more than the total foreign exchange earned by Nicaragua's products on the world market" (Judson 1987:10).

All these problems have produced negative effects in education, which was deficient at the beginning of the revolution. In fact, the Sandinistas, as was the case in Cuba, inherited one of the least developed educational systems in Latin America. In the mid–1970s, about 65% of Nicaraguan children 7–12 years of age attended primary school, and only 18% of those 13–18 years old were in secondary school. In those years, just 39% of the population 6–23 years-old was in school, one of the lowest enrollment rates in the region.

Between 1965–1966 and 1977–1978, primary school enrollment grew at only 3.9% annually, slightly more rapidly than the 3.3% annual increase in population during that period. Likewise, 28% of the teachers in elementary schools and 78% in secondary schools were underqualified (Carnoy and Torres, 1989). Preschooling and special education were almost nonexistent. Enrollment in the former was 9,000 children, and in the latter, 500 children.

Moreover, about 50% of the population over ten years old were absolute illiterates, and in the countryside the illiteracy rate reached 76%. This means that in the rural areas, only one in four Nicaraguans could write or read. In Somoza's time, the United States played an important role in the shaping of the Nicaraguan educational system, especially in curriculum development and implementation, textbook provision, teacher training, and educational planning (Arnove, 1986:5). According to Arnove, the textbooks—which did not always reach rural schools because of the corruption—were extremely biased in content and therefore not suited to the needs of Nicaraguan children. Furthermore, the school system was intended to meet the manpower needs of the economy, determined by Nicaragua's dependency on the United States for markets and capital.

Therefore, the educational apparatus was oriented to train an elite segment of the work force serving foreign interests and the Somoza oligarchy. In fact, the amount spent on university education was greater than the amount spent in any other sector of the educational system. At the same time, a kind of counterhegemonic education was developed in the mountains controlled by the guerrillas and in poor urban areas. This education, inspired by the thinking of Augusto Sandino and Carlos Fonseca Amador, founder of the FSLN, was conceived as an element for consciousness raising, popular mobilization, and military training (Tunnerman, 1983).

Augusto César Sandino, who led his peasant army for seven years against the U.S. Marines, created Nicaragua's first school of liberation at Las Segovias in 1928, explicitly linking pedagogy and politics (Arnove, 1986; La Belle, 1986). He attached great importance to literacy as well as to combat, and established a special department in his army for adult education (CAN, 1982). He advocated an education "based on common problems and aimed at improving living conditions," but he is also remembered for the organization of agricultural cooperatives, an area that was later highly recommended by various international institutions as an important field of adult education programs. Sandino was assassinated in 1934.

Carlos Fonseca Amador, the FSLN founder and main ideologist until his death in combat, exhorted his soldiers not to confine themselves to instructing combatants in the use of weapons but also "to teach literacy and to raise political consciousness." He perceived guerrillas not merely as dogmatic rebels who engage in military combat but, more important, as intellectual workers and writers converted into both generals and "teachers of humanity." Thus, in the mountains of Nicaragua, both in the 1930s and in the 1970s, the roles of guerrilla, educator, and student appeared to be interchangeable (Tunnerman, 1983; Arnove, 1986:17–40).

While the Sandinista guerrillas were operating these instrumental and ideological schools for the peasants in the "liberated territories," in the cities Catholic priests and Protestant ministers adhering to liberation theology and university students were active in promoting popular education. For example, Fernando Cardenal (a Jesuit priest, and the minister of education since 1985) had been instrumental in introducing participative, popular education among the poor during the Somoza period.

Educational Reform after the Revolution

When the Sandinistas took power in July 1979, under the principles of a mixed economy, political pluralism, and social justice, a new cycle of development began in Nicaragua, and the objectives of the educational system were rapidly transformed. They fostered full participation, increasing political awareness, and critical analyses of underdevelopment, and encouraged the integration and understanding between people of different classes and backgrounds (Arnove, 1986).

In the early stages of the revolution, as in Cuba 20 years before, the emphasis was on mobilization through popular education, first in the form of the literacy campaign and later a system of popular basic education. At the same time, the educational system was greatly expanded. In a complicated situation aggravated by external military aggression and economic boycott, these educational reforms faced new challenges. What follows is a review of the most important postrevolutionary educational events.

Expansion of formal education has been quite important in the last few years, as measured by pupil enrollment, teacher recruitment, and the number of schools built or classrooms opened. Compared with 1978, in 1986 there were twice as many students in the Nicaraguan educational system (see Table 5.3).

As was mentioned above, when the revolution took power, only 9,000 children attended preschool and only 500 were enrolled in special education programs. By 1984, these figures had increased to 67,000 and 1,500, respectively, and preschool had been incorporated into the compulsory basic education system.

Before the revolution, the total teaching force was less than 13,000. By 1984 there were 20,000 teachers working in basic education centers, including 2,000 Cuban teachers of the Augusto Sandino Brigade. In the same period, 1,400 new primary schools and 700 new secondary classrooms were built, mostly in rural areas.

As in Cuba, expansion in secondary education was accompanied by shifting from an academic, preparatory orientation for university education to technical training directly applicable to production, and the students were asked to be involved in communal and productive work. Also, a substantial effort was made to improve the quality of education as measured, for instance, by the teacher/student ratio. (see Figure 5.1).

The ratios have been improving over time in all systems, and the student/teacher ratio in adult education is significantly lower, compared with the other levels. Impressive gains have also been made at the junior and senior high school levels, from a ratio at the beginning of the revolution of 45.4 students per teacher, to 29.9 students per teacher by 1986. In adult education ratios are very low, and perhaps due to the contribution of paraprofessional teachers and volunteers who form the bulkwark of the system.

Table 5.3
Initial Student Enrollment, Educational Centers, and Teachers in Nicaragua, 1979/80–1986

Year	Adult Education			Pre-School			Elementary			Secondary		
	Stud.	Ctrs.	Teach.	Stud.	Ctrs.	Teach.	Stud.	Ctrs.	Teach.	Stud.	Ctrs.	Teach.
1979/80	...	...	...	18,292	n.d.	n.d.	411,315	3,601	11,741	95,682	243	2,107
1980/81	143,816	15,187	18,449	30,524	463	924	472,167	4,577	14,113	120,522	258	2,581
1982	148,369	15,397	21,607	38,534	646	1,212	500,924	5,107	14,711	114,868	294	2,865
1983	166,208	63,467	62,999	50,163	953	1,420	536,656	4,061	15,639	125,357	293	3,609
1984	129,290	17,428	20,312	60,557	1,057	1,686	534,317	4,783	16,486	117,315	324	4,104
1985	104,165	13,614	15,976	62,784	686	1,983	517,811	4,008	16,872	99,984	290	3,212
1986	120,851	13,197	12,792	72,569	841	2,254	563,928	3,659	17,199	119,055	220	3,982

Source: Oficina de Estadística e Información, División General de Planificación, Ministerio de Educación, unpublished information

Figure 5.1
Student/Teacher Ratios, 1979–1986

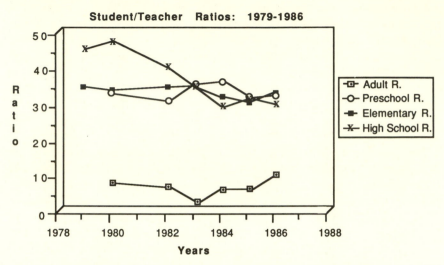

This improvement in the light of continuing increases in enrollment implies a substantial financial contribution. The relationship between educational expenditure and total government expenditure is as follows: in 1979 it was 14.2%, by 1983 it reached its lowest level of 8.5% (perhaps as a result of the intensification of the war in the north and the pouring of increasing resources into defense), and by 1986 it had climbed back to 12.8%. The relationship between educational expenditure and GNP has been improving since the revolution: in 1979 it was 2.9%, in 1983 it reached 5%, and by 1986 it achieved its all-time high of 6.2% of GNP. This means that the Nicaraguan revolutionary government has kept its educational commitments in spite of the shrinking war economy of the mid–1980s.[14]

At the tertiary level, as also happened in Cuba, a polytechnic university and several technical institutes have been set up. Enrollment in economic sciences, humanities, and law, so popular during the previous regime, has dropped considerably, with a shift toward the professions needed for the development of a new technically and mass-social, service-oriented economy. By 1984, for example, enrollment in humanities and law had dropped from 18% to 5%, while enrollment in technology, medicine, and agricultural, natural, and physical sciences and mathematics rose from 41% to 53% (Carnoy and Torres, 1989).

Differences exist between Nicaragua's and Cuba's higher education policies. In the first place, unlike Cuba during the first stages of the revolution, university enrollment in Nicaragua was expanded. Second, higher education, with less than 4% of the total school enrollment, received 25% of total public spending on education; and the public spending per student on higher education in the five years immediately after the triumph increased twice as rapidly as spending on primary and secondary education. This suggests the existence of different rationales in the determination of priorities, and it is probably due to distinct conceptions of the economic and political roles of the educational system—and, in consequence, to distinct strategies of educational and social development. According to Carnoy and Torres (1989:318), "Unlike Cuba, which de-emphasized university education while building up its primary and secondary system, Nicaragua is placing much more of its effort into developing highly-schooled cadres, cadres with specific skills relevant to the revolutionary project."

The Literacy Campaign

The literacy campaign—also known as "Literacy Crusade"—was one of the first educational policies advanced by the new government. It was planned just three months after the triumph and carried out before the first anniversary of the revolution, improving all previous records in this respect. As in the case of Cuba in 1961, when the Sandinistas announced that the campaign was about to be launched, skepticism arose not only among the international experts but also among several prominent members of the government. The suggestion, in both cases, was to wait until material, human, and technical resources were available. Nevertheless, in both cases it was demonstrated that in the struggle against illiteracy, it is more important to have political will and the capacity to mobilize human resources than to have a large budget or highly technical qualifications (R. Torres, 1985; Lind and Johnston, 1986).

The Nicaraguan Literacy Crusade was inspired by those carried out in Cuba (1961) and Tanzania (1970), as well as by the philosophy and methods of Paulo Freire, who consulted with the teams of educators designing the campaign and is reported "to have announced his enthusiastic support for both its content and pedagogy" (Arnove, 1986: 41). However, the method of the "generative word" was expanded from one word to a sentence (Cardenal and Miller, 1982), to facilitate the transition from a complex discussion to the reading of a concrete syllable. This innovation did not have the expected success, and it was reformulated (R. Torres, 1985: 169; Cardenal and Miller, 1982).[15]

The literacy campaign was organized as a "second mass insurrection," not against Somoza but against ignorance. It involved more than 80,000 *brigadistas* (literacy workers)—50,000 youth brigade members and 30,000 literacy teachers—and more than 400,000 adults (Carnoy and Torres, 1989). This implied that, in a total population of 3 million people, approximately one in six Nicaraguans participated in the campaign either as a teacher or as a student. Taking into account all of the ways of participation, one in three Nicaraguans were involved in the movement (R. Torres, 1985: 18). Although Spanish was the official language of the crusade, it also included literacy training in indigenous languages, with material specifically designed for the ethnic minorities of the Atlantic Coast (Miskitos, Sumas, Ramas, etc.).

The achievements of the campaign were astonishing. In only five months, according to official estimates, illiteracy was reduced from 50.35% to 12.9%. Arnove points out that a more correct figure is 23%, because the 12.9% is based on "the government decision to subtract from the target population of illiterate adults approximately 130,000 individuals who were considered unteachable or learning impaired" (1986: 27). Even accepting this correction, to decrease the illiteracy rate of the country by half in such a short time and without resources is a significant event in the history of Latin American education.

However, although the fundamental goal of the campaign was to teach as many people as possible to read and write, at the same time it attempted to enable teachers, students, and workers who participated in the movement to obtain a better understanding of the revolution, its causes, its purposes, and its ideals. In the words of the government, Nicaragua understood the literacy campaign as "a political act with pedagogical implications" (MED, 1980). In this respect, the Literacy Crusade was perceived as an instrument of resocialization and national integration in a very polarized society. On the one hand, the high school students from the urban middle class, through living for several months in the rural villages, were able to discover unknown realities of their own country. This was part of the Sandinista strategy, in a context of a mixed economy, to incorporate the middle class into the revolution and to sensitize them to the problems and rights of the poor. On the other hand, the peasants were also resocialized, not only because they were led through the first steps of literacy but also because they learned to accept their compatriots from the urban areas. Under the previous regime the rural areas had been the least incorporated and most oppressed, economically as well as politically and militarily. This last aspect was clearly expressed by a peasant interviewed during the campaign: "Previously all we knew of people in the cities was that they [the National Guard] came and killed people. Now we know that city people and country people can live together" (CAN, 1982: 39). In fact, the peasants accepted the *brigadistas* as members of their families, and the *brigadistas* constantly spoke in terms of "my campesino mother" or "my campesino family" (CAN, 1982; R. Torres, 1985).

Another important achievement of the campaign was the reestablishment of dignity in a people "whose dignity had been withheld over more than two generations" (Carnoy and Torres, 1989). The feeling of dignity and pride, as well as confidence in one's ability and experience, reaffirm the necessary self-esteem to think of oneself as capable of participating actively in the new process. As another peasant said, when he finished the course, "For the first time in my life I feel able to walk with my head up" (CAN, 1982: 33).

The campaign also produced some other significant results. To some extent, it reduced the high degree of inequality between countryside and city, male and female, and the Atlantic and Pacific coasts. It mobilized previously marginal populations into new roles related to national reconstruction. It strengthened mass organizations, especially the Sandinista Youth, the Teachers' Organization, and the Nicaraguan Women's Association. It was the first national task where women had equal participation, with resulting implications in other fields of society. It created a national publishing industry and initiated the process of the administrative decentralization of the country (Arnove, 1986; Carnoy and Torres, 1989).

These achievements have won the acclaim of the international community. In August 1980, UNESCO granted Nicaragua the Nadezhda Krupskaya Literacy Achievement Award, in recognition of "that exultant experience, whose goals transcend the educational area and aim for a profound modification of the relations between the different sectors of the country," as the director general of UNESCO, Amadou-Mathar M'Bow, expressed it.

Shortcomings in adult education policies and programs can be indicated, however. Literacy statistics may not be accurate, due to the exclusion of the "unteachable" or "learning impaired," and the poor measurement criteria and means to assess literacy levels. La Belle considers the Nicaraguan definition of literates—individuals able to write their names, read a short text aloud, answer three questions based on the reading, write a sentence dictated to them, and write a short composition—as too modest (La Belle, 1986: 241).

Second, the process of conscientization through literacy may have been undermined by the fact that the *brigadistas* were quite young, inexperienced, and perhaps insufficiently trained. They may have lacked the required methodology to conduct an effective process of consciousness raising through literacy, and this may have prompted some of them to relapse into the kind of teaching that Paulo Freire called "banking education." Often the dialogue, as an instance of communication, reflection, and debate may have been reduced to a kind of oral questionnaire where the educator made questions (and decided the validity of the answers) and the adults answered them (R. Torres, 1985: 119). In practice, despite the planners' intentions, in some regions and areas the pedagogy used may have resembled a traditional teacher-directed one with an almost mechanical approach to literacy instruction (Arnove, 1986: 25). Furthermore, consciousness raising requires time and patience on the part of the educator, and these conditions may not be easily achieved under time pressure. The relatively short period in which the campaign was carried out (six months) perhaps was insufficient to guarantee an adequate development of this educational process.

Whatever the shortcomings, the achievements in adult education have been numerous, and the exercise has served to maintain and even to boost a momentum that generated the enthusiasm and sense of participation necessary for the collective construction of a different society.

Adult Education Programs

Popular basic education (PBE) is a system of nonformal education created to enable newly literate adults to attain the standard of primary school graduates. When this program began in 1981, after the Literacy Crusade, it had four educational levels (grades). In 1983 it was extended to six levels, and in 1984 to nine (R. Torres, 1985; Carnoy and Torres, 1989; Arnove, 1986).

The curriculum for the first four levels focuses on language arts and mathematics, and it includes an introductory level to render permanent the literacy acquired in the Crusade. In the fifth and sixth levels, importance is attached to the social and natural sciences, and in the final three levels, emphasis is placed on vocational skills with a view to preparing these learners for the work force.

In PBE, on average 15 adults in the cities and 5 in the rural areas meet in a private house, in a school after hours, or in a church, under the leadership of a coordinator (adult education teacher). The themes of study are organized around problems of interest to the students, such as agricultural production or health care. Periods of study take into account work schedules. Although PBE is directed to adults, during the first four years about 20% of the students were under 15 years old (Carnoy and Torres, 1989).

Approximately 400,000 adults completed the literacy campaign in 1980. In March 1981, 143,816 of them had enrolled in the PBE program. Although this figure could seem low, it is relatively high, considering (a) the high number of adults involved in the Literacy Crusade who conceived of it as a terminal stage in their own education, and (b) the conditions of life of the popular sectors—giving up two or more hours of leisure or rest after the day's work to continue their education is a major sacrifice. Regardless, the enrollment and the number of popular education collectives increased in the following semester from 143,816 to 167,852 and from 15,187 to 20,561, respectively. The proportion of the educational budget assigned to PBE increased from 4% in 1980 to 12% in 1984.

As in the Literacy Crusade, the PBE programs were carried out by nonprofessional but enthusiastic young people. More than half of the popular educators are younger than 19 years old, and only 30% are older than 25. Moreover, only 2% have any university education, 19% are housewives, 39% are farmers, and 43% have no relationship to any mass organization. Furthermore, 52% of them have not completed primary school. These volunteers, by teaching in their own neighborhoods, represent for some scholars an antibureaucratic force in education showing that creative, committed, nonauthoritarian teaching can be developed by using volunteers (R. Torres, 1985). Nevertheless, although these teachers are highly motivated, there are significant problems in the quality of the teaching-learning process: most popular educators do not have adequate knowledge to teach beyond the course's introductory levels. The pedagogy to be used—based on notions of dialogue and active, inquiring learners—requires teaching skills that are well beyond the preparation of these nonprofessionals, and is rarely implemented (Carnoy and Torres, 1989; Arnove, 1986; Shor and Freire, 1987). Popular educators are beginning to address some of these concerns through training workshops on the weekends, but PBE programs still face other obstacles. Let us mention some of them.

Classroom activities (also called "collectives") are characterized by frequent absences and dropouts, due fundamentally to work commitments of the adults. The lack of a formal contract means a higher turnover among the volunteers than among the professional teachers. In border regions, Contra attacks have concentrated on these centers of mass public education, hence reducing attendance: by May 1984, 158 teachers had either died in combat against the Contras or had been assassinated while fulfilling their teaching chores; 135 of these victims were adult educators.

Similarly, there is no equivalence between the levels of PBE and those of the formal system, so PBE students do not obtain a regular primary school diploma, and have some difficulties shifting to conventional schools if they want to continue their education. This puts pressure on the PBE to expand to higher levels, even beyond its teachers' capacities. Finally, the lack of coordination between vocational training and work opportunities creates a greater pressure for formal secondary education as a continuation of PBE training, instead of offering practical or terminal alternatives to the system (Carnoy and Torres, 1989).

By 1989, due to the boycott and external aggression, material conditions of existence and economic indicators have been worsening in comparison with before the 1979 revolution. Very real difficulties are experienced by Nicaraguans in transportation, health care, education, electric power and water supplies, and food production and distribution, and each problem has a negative, compounded, and exponential cumulative impact on the others: "The accumulation of difficulties was, up to a point, a quantitative matter. Now it has made a qualitative difference. The costs of the war, against the background of an inherited poverty and high degree of under- and misdevelopment, with a lack of experienced administrators and the inevitable mistakes made, have created a situation that is exceedingly difficult" (Judson, 1987: 10).

In this context, it is no surprise that the educational situation has largely deteriorated. The rate of illiteracy has doubled in a few years, and dropout rates have increased. In addition, year by year, more educational centers have closed their doors because of sabotage or threats to teachers and students in areas of intense counterrevolutionary activity.

A prominent member of the government commented: "Unfortunately, at this moment education cannot be our first priority. In this context of war, poverty and hunger, our priorities are defence and production, and education could be considered in third place, with health and other basic services. It is painful for me to say this, but it is so" (quoted in Schugurensky, 1987: 6).

In concluding this section, let us quote Paulo Freire, who, commenting on the Cuban and the Nicaraguan experiences, asserted:

For me the issue is that in the process of revolution, people take history into their own hands. The other issue is to know whether the revolution, in losing itself, takes history out of the people's hands. When people get their history into their hands, it's very easy to get letters into their hands. This is why the campaign in Cuba many years ago was successful, as was the recent campaign in Nicaragua, which in my opinion went beyond what the Cubans did. (Freire, in Bruss and Macedo, 1985: 15)

Grenada

Education in the Gairy's Period

Education before Grenada's independence in 1974 reflected British colonial policy, and therefore reinforced the colony's dependent status training only limited manpower and playing a fundamentally symbolic role in the Caribbean society (Bacchus and Brock, 1987; Bacchus, Pannu, and Torres, 1988). During the first half of the century, education was elitist and oriented to satisfy the needs of the colonial power and the upper-class Grenadan settlers. In the 1930s and 1940s, only 2% of primary students reached the secondary schools. During that period

> Education was not concerned to develop and diversify local production, technical skills and various forms of indigenous technology. The system practiced resulted in the majority of Grenadians being largely unemployed and unemployable. Many emigrated and others undertook forms of subsistence self-employment using the rudimentary skills at their disposal and living on subsistence agriculture or trade. As the colonial system was not based on education for production and employment it was not only generally irrelevant but often wasteful. Education in the early 20th Century taught the Grenadian to adore and even deify the British. (Brizan, 1984: 295).

According to Brizan (1984: 290), in 1939 "an average class consisted of 50–60 children, presenting a formidable task for untrained teachers, and leading to the destruction of any inclination to learn for the majority of students." Bishop emphasized: "The history of our country, as with the history of Latin America and all Third World countries generally, has been a history that has said that education is for the elite" (quoted in Searle, 1984: 52).

Nonetheless, the students who were in secondary school performed well on the external exams administered by the universities of London and Cambridge. After World War II, the Colonial Development and Welfare Organization, based in England, did make some improvements in Grenadian education. Nevertheless, Premier Gairy's misappropriation of public funds in the 1960s[16] and the stagnation of the economy in the 1970s substantially reduced the flow of funds to the schools, and they deteriorated considerably until the revolution (Jensen, 1987).

From 1967 to 1979, Grenada was under twelve years of a cruel dictatorship whose atrocities and lack of scruples can be compared with the Nicaraguan and Cuban dictatorships of Somoza and Batista. Both Gairy's personality[17] and his repressive and elite-oriented policy constituted the ferment of the revolution.

Unemployment, idle cultivable land, and repression were normal under Gairy's regime. At the beginning of the 1970s, nearly 50% of the population was unemployed, and the bulk of the unemployed were young. By 1972, many of the peasants' holdings were fragmented due to archaic inheritance laws. By contrast, since many larger farms (located in the most fertile areas) were owned by absentee landlords who had emigrated, much cultivable land lay idle (Payne et al., 1984).

In comparison with Cuba and Nicaragua, the educational system inherited by the revolution in Grenada was not underdeveloped by Caribbean standards. In 1979, Grenada had 61 primary schools with 761 teachers and 22,861 students. The secondary schools numbered 21, employed 295 teachers, and had 6,381 students (Jensen, 1987: 110). Only 11% of the school-age population, however, attended secondary school.

School buildings were in poor condition, especially preschools and secondary schools. A painted wall often replaced a chalkboard, sanitation was deplorable, and toilet facilities—if they were available—usually functioned very poorly (Marcus and Taber, 1983: 45; Jensen, 1987: 115).

The quality of the teaching-learning process can be assessed by considering the level of teachers' qualifications and the teacher-student ratio. In regard to the qualifications of teachers, before the revolution only 30% of the primary teachers and 7% of the secondary teachers received any form of professional training. Preprimary teachers were, as a rule, not trained at all (Marcus and Taber, 1983: 45). The teacher-student ratio under Gairy's regime was the same as 40 years before, 1:50 (Bishop, 1984: 182).

Unlike Cuba and Nicaragua, the illiteracy rate in Grenada before the revolution was only 15% (R. Torres, 1984). Nevertheless, according to Maurice Bishop, functional illiteracy reached 40%, measured by the inability fully to appreciate what is presented in the newspapers or fully to comprehend a commentary on the radio.

The major problems of the prerevolutionary period were not quantitative but qualitative. In this regard, Bishop described the educational legacy as "perhaps the worst crime that colonialism left our country," because the system was used "to teach our people an attitude of self-hate, to get us to abandon our history, our culture, our values . . . to get us to accept the principles of white solidarity, to destroy our confidence, to stifle our creativity, to perpetuate in our society class privilege and class difference" (quoted in Marcus and Taber, 1983: 42).

At the same time, the civil society developed different forms of adult, counterhegemonical education. When in 1970 Maurice Bishop returned to Grenada from Britain, he helped to found FORUM, a discussion group of young radical professionals. This was succeeded by the Movement for the Advancement of Community Effort (MACE), which stressed political research and education among the urban population (Payne et al., 1984). Four years later, MACE and the Committee of Concerned Citizens joined to create MAP (Movement for the Assemblies of People). MAP and JEWEL (Joint Endeavour for the Welfare, Education and Liberation of the People) later started the New Jewel Movement (NJM). Unlike other political movements, the NJM leadership was well represented by teachers (e.g., Unison Whiteman, Jacqueline Creft, George Louison, and Bernard Coard). Since the NJM political bureau had only 16 members, obviously the influence of these educators was considerable (Jensen, 1987; Thorndike, 1985). From 1974 to 1976, the party's paper *The New Jewel*, expanded its circulation to over 10,000 copies, becoming the most widely read newspaper in the island (Latin American Bureau, 1984: 26). Another kind of alternative education was the public meeting. These meetings, held in almost every village, were sometimes interrupted by Gairy's forces. At these meetings the NJM militants first presented the effects of Gairy's dictatorship, and immediately advocated a "non-capitalist alternative that would provide the material needs of the society (food, housing, clothing, education, health facilities and jobs) while restoring the dignity of the people" (Jacobs and Jacobs, 1980: 112).

Educational Reform after the Revolution

Educational reform must be analyzed in the context of other social reforms. To mention some of them, after the revolution unemployment was reduced from 49% in 1979 to 14% in 1983. Repair of school buildings and homes of the poorest population was a task of massive proportions (the latter, for example, benefited 17,240 families). Health care and dentist services doubled. A program of free milk distribution benefited 50,000 Grenadans. Lower income workers were exempted from paying taxes. Several laws benefiting women were established (e.g., "equal work, equal pay" and maternity benefits). However, in spite of these distributional measures, in economic terms Grenada was the only Caribbean country with a steady, positive GNP growth between 1979 and 1983 (R. Torres, 1985).

Regarding educational reforms, at the opening of a national training seminar in 1980, Bishop outlined the four main elements of the revolutionary educational system:

> Firstly, it attempts to teach people a greater understanding of their own reality in order for them best to understand how to change it. Secondly, it attempts to develop the innate abilities of the masses of our people and not just in entrenching the privileges of a few. Thirdly, it should seek to develop the productive capacity of our society since it is only through an expansion of production that the standard of living including the educational system can be improved. And fourthly, it tries to promote the democratization of our society encouraging the people to take an active part in all major decisions that affect our lives. (quoted in Jensen, 1987: 95)

The Literacy Campaign

Although in 1979 Grenada had only 15% absolute illiteracy, a literacy campaign was launched from April 18, 1981, to March 1, 1982. This becomes a keystone of the new policy for adult education. Enrollment figures vary, depending on the source. Rosa M. Torres (1984), for example, estimated 2,738 students, while Jensen (1987: 177) estimated between 3,500 and 4,000 students. The primer materials were influenced by Freire's ideas, and a massive volunteer effort took place.

While in Nicaragua the ratio of literacy workers to adults was 1:3 and in Cuba was 1:2, in Grenada practically each volunteer worked with only one literacy student. Among the main principles of the literacy campaign were the following: (a) the revolution should be the central theme; (b) it would be essential to utilize the vocabulary used by the Grenadian people; (c) step-by-step introduction of new vocabulary was suggested; and (d) repetition was considered a key factor for the acquisition of the new linguistic skills (R. Torres, 1984).

As a result of the campaign, 881 illiterates and 287 semiliterates became literate, with a substantial proportion of youth: 40.6% of these 1,168 people were between 14 and 25 years of age (Cornwall, 1981). Nevertheless, the success of the campaign cannot be judged by the absolute number of individuals who became literate. It was the ability to mobilize Grenadans in a mass campaign that was considered an important success. Cultural components of the campaign were important to this mobilization strategy. As in Cuba and Nicaragua, Grenadans were encouraged to write poems, plays, or songs about adult education:

> Educational achievements of the campaign have naturally been over-shadowed by the organizational achievements and the social and cultural impact of the programme. These are achievements which cannot be measured by numbers, but by the popularity of the program in our communities, the resulting organizational ability to our villages and the extent of people's participation. (Cornwall, 1981: 14)

Following Bishop's murder in 1984, and the U.S. Marines' invasion of the island, the Grenadian Revolution was brought to an end. Many of its educational measures were inconclusive or the real impact on the population could not be evaluated.

CHANGES AND CONTRADICTIONS IN THE THREE EXPERIENCES

In the three revolutionary experiences analyzed, it is possible to observe important reforms in the educational systems. The changes were both quantitative and qualitative, and some problems did arise. A critical review of those changes and problems follows.

Regarding the quantitative changes, it has been observed that the educational budget was in all three cases significantly increased (in the case of Grenada, the budget represented 21% of government expenditure; in Nicaragua, educational expenditure was 6.2% of Gross Domestic Product in 1986, from a low 2.9% in 1979). There were similar rates of increase in public expenditure for other important welfare services, such as health and housing.

The expansion of the educational system in all three countries was enormous. Within a few months, the number of schools created was more than were built in the previous decades. Enrollment at all levels increased rapidly. There was a special emphasis on the levels of the system and the educational clientele previously neglected, including preschooling, elementary schooling, and adult education.[18] The number of teachers also increased dramatically, and a massive and efficient system of teacher training was quickly organized. The elaboration and free supply of new learning materials (specially written materials) had massive influence at all levels of the educational system.

Regarding the political will to offer equality of opportunity, both the rate of attendance and the terminal efficiency increased. In other words, students were able to perform successfully and to graduate.[19] Similarly, historically high illiteracy rates were greatly reduced in a short period of time. In addition, in the three countries the literacy campaigns were followed up with the development of important postliteracy efforts. Finally, in an attempt to increase the quality of education, the ratio of teachers to students was substantially reduced.

Several qualitative changes took place in all three nations. Under the rationale of a centrally planned economy,[20] a close relationship between social needs and the educational system was sought. A first outcome of this statement was a new distribution of careers at the tertiary level, promoting technical and professional training related to programs of national development. In general terms, the educational system was tailor-made for the perceived social demands, and not oriented toward the satisfaction and reproduction of a given elite. A second implication was an important change in the content of the curriculum, from a verbal, encyclopedic, and formal one to a more scientific, technical, and practical one. The development of polytechnic education was an attempt to reduce the gap between manual and mental work, and to promote a productive and socially useful education. Some outcomes of this process, such as the teaching of foreign languages in Cuba, have shown results that are surprising for a Third World country.

Overall, a new rationale for the allocation of resources was provided by the revolutionary governments. Educational reform was related to concerns with social justice, in terms of access and permanence in the system for those who were excluded in the past. Therefore, special attention was given to disadvantaged groups, such as peasants, ethnic minorities, and women. Overall, some of the main distortions between educational systems and the labor market were ameliorated through the principles of the centralized planned economy. Some of the features associated with credentialism in dependent capitalist societies (unemployment of university graduates, brain drain, etc.) seem to have diminished, especially in Cuba (Dore, 1976).

The educational system reveals a new ideology oriented toward the principles of social solidarity and radical egalitarism. National mobilization and interaction of people of different social classes during literacy campaigns, and the role of university students researching issues intimately connected with the new model of economic development, constitute examples of this new political philosophy.

In startling contrast with principles proclaimed in liberal-pluralist democracies, education was conceived explicitly as a political act. Hence, the most meaningful educational problems (i.e., financing, quality of the teaching-learning process, distribution of enrollment, content, etc.) could not be addressed only from a technocratic perspective but also needed a consistent set of political answers. The basic assumption held by policymakers in these transitional societies was that political or social problems could not be solved exclusively through technical means. This new approach to cultural action and education explains the relevance attached to adult education in all three transitional nations. Literacy campaigns not only achieved instrumental goals (reading, writing, and arithmetic) but also contributed to social solidarity, critical thinking, and ideological support for the revolution.[21] Curiously, in the three countries analyzed, literacy campaigns were conceived in a Freirean way, as "a political act with pedagogical implications, rather than a pedagogical act with political implications" (Freire, 1985). To be sure, according to Arnove and Graff (1987: 202), "both historically and comparatively, literacy campaigns have played a role in larger transformations in societies."

The content and the teaching-learning process in literacy campaigns have changed radically. Reinforcement of people's dignity and pride has also been an intended goal of these campaigns. In contemporary experiences, Freirean-inspired methodologies have become a central feature. In Nicaragua and Grenada, Freire's advice was sought and his presence was celebrated as an indicator that the campaigns were going in the right direction. Furthermore, a mass, national system of adult education was created in a relatively short period of time. Unlike many adult education services in Latin American countries, which are conceived as a "second chance" service, and in some cases use children's didactic materials, in the socialist experiences these programs have teachers trained in adult education issues; a curriculum and textbooks specially designed for adults; and real possibilities to advance to further educational levels. The themes of study are organized around problems relevant to the students, and periods of study take into account work schedules. At the beginning, in the three nations analyzed, adult education programs (or popular education) were seen as a means to equalize the society and to legitimate the revolution. Afterward, as the Cuban case shows, with the expansion of schooling, adult education plays a role in the specialization of workers and becomes a more formalized system.

These changes notwithstanding, the transitional nations are not exempt from problems. A centrally planned economy will usually place the interests of society well above the interests of the individuals. Thus, individual freedom may be, and in fact is, severely constrained at the level of choices, preferences, and so on. With the passing of the years, the initial mysticism and emotional commitment to the revolution decrease. In that case, moral incentives seem to be insufficient, and material incentives become more prominent. As a result, in some cases intrinsic motivation for learning is overridden by extrinsic interests—with Pavlovian overtones of reward and punishment.

Teachers tend to retain their old values, beliefs, and professional behavior, in spite of the structural, short-term transformation that may have occurred. It is perhaps fair to say that, as agents of the ideology of the former regime, they continue to perform (at least for a while) according to their old behavior, practices, and knowledge at the classroom level. The explicit curriculum may be changed more easily and more quickly than the hidden curriculum. This is because every dependent society usually faces shortages of resources (technical manpower, financial resources, etc.). The mounting pressure from the world capitalist system tends to isolate the countries in social transformation, worsening the resource crisis. Indeed, as has been shown in the case of Nicaragua, the situation brought about by the war and the commercial boycott has thwarted some of the advances of the revolution in social welfare, and has exhausted the government's fiscal resources.

There is also the tension between centralized planning in education and decentralized interests of the local communities: "certain populations will resist nationally directed programs" (Arnove and Graff, 1987: 203).[22] This is part of a standing problem of all revolutions: the contradictions between the unifying, ideological, and political leadership (which is thought of as a precondition for building a new state and government in the face of external aggression or civil war) and the libertarian, autonomy-oriented trends (and the diversity of critical-radical thinking) sponsored by, and arising from, these processes of radical transformation.

A successful adult education programs always faces the need to develop a sustained postliteracy system (Bhola, 1984), which was achieved in the nations analyzed. However, in the short term, the problem of the integration of nonformal and formal systems remains, including how to link accreditation, evaluation, and curriculum design to policy planning and work certification. In addition, any substantial expansion of education does not necessarily imply a similar improvement in the quality of the educational system.

Policy planning is always a matter for political bargaining. In some cases, internal conflicts arising from opposing conceptions about the revolutionary process—which are intelligently exploited by foreign agencies—generate severe consequences. These contradictions can undermine, and even abort, not only the educational reforms but also the revolution itself (e.g., discrepancies between Bishop's and Coard's supporters in Grenada or, to a lesser extent, the separation of Omar Pastora from the FSLN in Nicaragua).

Methodologies are always subject to change and refinement in literacy training. In the Nicaraguan Literacy Crusade, the attempt to change the "generative word" of Paulo Freire's method to a "generative sentence" did not come up to expectations. A second problem was to conciliate the tension between time pressure and the expected quality of the consciousness-raising process. Furthermore, limitations in the follow-up of the new literates generated functional illiterates in a short time, increasing the illiteracy rate from 12.5% to 25% in five years.

CONCLUSION: LESSONS FROM THESE EXPERIENCES

There is a degree of correspondence between changes in the socioeconomic system and educational reform. If education is always and everywhere an "instrument of the state" (as suggested by the Cuban minister of education), relevant modifications of the educational system can be possible as a result of structural changes in society.[23]

Although educational institutions are dependent in the socioeconomic context, they have a relative autonomy (Morrow and Torres, 1987; Fritzell, 1987) and, under certain circumstances, can play a counterhegemonic role. This autonomy is mostly enjoyed in nonformal education, and it is more evident in prerevolutionary processes. Examples of this assertion can be found in the educational work carried out by the revolutionary guerrilla movements in Cuba and in Nicaragua, by the Jesuits of the Universidad Centroamericana in Nicaragua, or by the repatriated intellectuals of MACE and *The New Jewel* newspaper in Grenada (Guevara, 1967; La Belle, 1986; Arnove, 1986; Payne et al., 1984; Latin America Bureau, 1984).

It is evident, from the analysis presented above, that socialist-oriented experiences tend (1) to expand the system in the areas previously neglected—usually associated with services to the poorer sectors of the population; (2) to reduce illiteracy drastically; (3) to develop notions of polytechnic education, attempting to remove the distinction between manual and mental labor—and attempting to narrow the gap between education, the work place, and social needs.

Almost by definition, successful literacy campaigns were conceived and carried out in the three transitional nations. Even though technical qualification and financial resources are important, these successes could be attributed mostly to an effective political will, the capacity for mobilization by the mass organizations, and the political momentum of the revolution. This combination of will, capacities, and momentum gives the educational symbols a natural place in the new development model, as pointed out by Bhola (1984) and Arnove and Graff (1987).

Undoubtedly, a set of fundamental problems besieged these revolutions: they included the tensions between material and moral incentives; the belated development of the forms of conscience vis-à-vis the structural changes in economy and power; pressures from the world capitalist system (Arnove 1986: 11); the issue of democratic centralism (i.e., directiveness versus autonomy); tensions between mass expansion and quality of education; and the interplay of power and bureaucratic struggles.

Adult education teachers' training always faces a fundamental dilemma in dependent societies: the choice between highly motivated but poorly trained para-professional teachers and professionally trained, although sometimes bureau-cratized, corporatively oriented, and more expensive teachers. In most cases, both volunteers and professional teachers behave according to the old frame-work. Teachers' practices have the same degree of authoritarianism as in the past while they seek to establish the same pattern of relationships with adults that they had with children. Paraprofessional helpers rely upon their own schooling experience, instilling verticalism, and eventually authoritarianism, in class discussions. In short, the transformation of teachers' values, behavior, and world views is a Herculean task.

In Latin American dependent-development capitalism, adult education is basi-cally compensatory; it represents a "second chance" type of education. In spite of the complexity and variety of institutions dealing with adult education, policy rationales usually highlight the economic and political payoffs of adult education. It may be argued that adult education plays several major roles, among them (a) to act as a mechanism of social control (by creating mass expectations for up-ward social mobility while claiming to improve the equality of educational oppor-tunity, access, and permanency); (b) to contribute to a carefully controlled and manipulated political mobilization (e.g., to improve voting patterns in rural areas); and (c) to act as a means of economic investment directed toward the marginalized segments of the population (e.g., increasing the trainability and discipline of the labor force or enhancing the propensity to consume).

In socialist societies adult education seems to fulfill similar roles. The main differ-ence is that the fit between adult education and the labor market is much tighter. Similarly, adult education is not considered a neutral, apolitical activity of possessive individualism. Adult education takes an explicit political-ideological orientation to-ward strengthening the legitimacy of the political regime. In those societies where the paradigm of popular education prevails, a process-oriented rather than a prescriptive-oriented approach predominates (La Belle, 1986). In a revolutionary situation, political mobilization—although endorsed by government apparatuses—always has a degree of spontaneity and/or is stimulated and sponsored by genuine mass organizations that are rarely found in more status-quo-oriented societies. In spite of some inevitable dogmatic situations, the experiences outlined above have shown that critical thinking and participatory planning can be part and parcel of the educational process in adult education, particularly when this form of education is related to economic democracy and the state.

When discussing dependency and the fragility of the state institutions in Latin America, and hence political turmoil, the following are most often emphasized: (a) the role of external forces in the region, especially the United States and the multinational corporations; (b) the conspiratorial role (and/or political failure) of the national bourgeoisie in holding back democracy in favor of accelerated capi-talist development, and/or its inability to promote a full capitalist development; (c) the presence of elements of a feudal past that does not allow for moderniza-tion and democratization of the social structures; and (d) the role of the army as a central political institution that regulates conflicts and disagreements within the ruling classes, and blocks any anticapitalist initiative or the presence of the masses on the streets demanding their rights.

In short, dependency, underdevelopment, and political instability or crisis are seen either as a problem of incomplete capitalism and capital accumulation or as a persistent conflict over the distribution and allocation of resources (including political resources) in highly activated civil societies. These features are reflected in the consolidation and articulation of the educational system, particularly in adult education.

The incomplete capital accumulation and the political history of Latin America (including the political culture and the failure of a labor or workers' alternative) has, as one of its main dimensions and products, a weak state. This type of state has been termed by Martin Carnoy a "conditioned capitalist state" (Carnoy and Samoff, 1990), a state that falls short of fulfilling its mission in capital accumulation and political legitimation. In Cuba, Nicaragua, and Grenada, this state was extremely particularistic, with Batista, the Somoza family, and Gairy (respectively) taking over the country and ruling it as a profit-making enterprise.

Carnoy (in Carnoy and Samoff, 1990) argues, following Nicos Poulantzas, that the political practice of the capitalist state is said (a) to individualize, socialize, fragment, and reintegrate disciplined individuals into the labor force by separating workers from their means of production; (b) to elaborate, promote, and enforce the law; (c) to consolidate the nation and the internal market; and (d) to create an ideology that separates knowledge from power.

The conditioned states have not been able to carry out these functions properly because, in the case of individualization (a) the fragility of the local economies made local dominant groups unwilling to allow the pluralist participation of the masses in the selection of state bureaucracy, and (b) the state historically has been identified by the popular sectors more as a pact of domination on behalf of the dominant classes, or as a surrogate state, than as a nation-state.

In the case of law, the vast social gap between the dominated and the dominant classes, both in material and in cultural terms, inhibited the state from performing its function as a lawmaker ruling on behalf of the entire citizenry. Since the state is not subjected continuously to the laws of the political market, where everybody agrees or disagrees by conventional institutional means (i.e., regular voting) on the performance of the state's personnel, the state ends up overruling the law by increasing the degree of repression of the civil society instead of improving its own legitimation through consensus. It is the sociology of fear that rules, not the law, and property rights always predominate over personal rights (Bowles and Gintis, 1986).

As for the nation-market, since the boundaries of the market are externally defined by the presence of U.S. hegemonic powers and multinational corporations in the region, the nation is continually and historically redefined by a complex matrix of exogenous-endogenous processes. More often than not, the conditioned state has little control over its own dynamics.

Finally, regarding knowledge and power, the position of a state at the periphery of the creation of technology and the use of science and technology for improving capital accumulation, makes this state impotent to link the capitalist division of labor with science and technology. The brain drain of the nation's intellectuals is a typical example.

The nature of political conflict in Latin America is related to the nature of the state, the more so in revolutionary societies. Questions and areas for further research on adult education include the following: To what extent has the revolutionary state eliminated the feudal elements that prevail in lower-income economies, and their expression in educational policymaking? Have the previous loyalties between bureaucratic groups in the educational arena disappeared as a result of the revolution? Have the "institutional feudalism" and corrupt tendencies in public education disappeared with the revolutionary triumph? If the answer to this last question is "no," because of the short time that has elapsed, what forms are they taking in the educational system of the revolution? Is the revolutionary leadership aware of and coping with these traits? If so, how is it doing this?

How has the process of individualization, socialization, fragmentation, and reintegration of disciplined individuals as labor force been redefined in the new education? Besides the empowering of illiterate people through the Literacy Crusade and the ensuing adult education systems, how are the relationships between knowledge and power being redefined in Sandinista education and in the Cuban system? In short, how are the adult educational programs in Cuba and Nicaragua attempting to overcome the historical traits of a "conditioned state"?

Finally, what are the modes and methods of operation in educational policy formation? What are the extent and type of bureaucratic organization? What are the educational bureaucracy's ideologies, and how are they contained in policy planning? What are the material and nonmaterial outcomes of a given educational policy? What are the role of educational policy within the overall state public policy and the relative role of a given sectoral policy, say adult education, in the overall educational policy (C. Torres, 1989a)?

When these questions can be answered systematically, the role and function of adult education in socialist transition will be perceived more clearly, and the relationships between state, democracy, and adult education will become central in understanding past changes and new directions for the future.

POSTSCRIPT: NONFORMAL EDUCATION
AND DEMOCRACY

It is fundamental to understand the relationships between democracy and education in transitional societies. It will be convenient to distinguish at the outset, as the Italian political scientist Humberto Cerroni does (1976), between democracy as content and democracy as method. Democracy appears to be primarily a method of political representation that includes regular voting procedures, free elections, parliamentary and judicial systems free from the control of the executive (including the notion of checks and balances in the system), the predominance of individual rights over collective rights, and freedom of speech.

The notion of democracy as a content is related to the notion of democracy as a system of political participation by the people in public affairs. It is related to the power of the people (over any other regulatory institution, such as the kingship), the idea of equal rights for all citizens, and, particularly in the U.S. Constitution, a political philosophy of egalitarianism.

The question, then, is to explain how the notion of democracy became associated with the notion of capitalism. Bowles and Gintis (1985) offer a very persuasive argument. They argue that the dynamics of democracy relies on two logics of expansion of the capitalist system: personal rights and property rights, which often are opposed. The dynamics of the conflicts between these two logics (represented perhaps in the clash between business ideologies and social movements in industrial advanced capitalism) is over the use and appropriation of societal resources, as well as ethical standards of social behavior. However, capitalism as an economic and social system of accumulation, production, reproduction, and distribution of commodities is intrinsically conflictual and marked by internal contradictions. In late capitalist societies, social power is essentially heterogeneous and diffused, and the same dynamics of democracy has created over the last two centuries several social movements that strive to change the direction or the nature of the democratic system. These movements have concerned issues of class and labor, race, gender, the environment, nuclear disarmament, and global peace. Finally, the most recent social movements in the United States and Western Europe (from right and left) are not distributional in nature but express moral and cultural aspirations.

If capitalism is a conflictual system, and democracy has two different logics of development, then the question is why democracy and capitalism become intermingled, and why this working relationship of politics and economics does not fall apart. Bowles and Gintis claim that the connection between democracy and capitalism has been made through four historical accommodations of the system: (a) in Europe, the Lockean proposal that accommodates the system by limiting the political participation of the propertied; (b) in the United States, the Jeffersonian proposal that distributing property widely among the citizenry (of Anglo-Saxon origin) reaccommodates the system in the face of increasing political strains; (c) the political proposal of Madison to foster a sufficient heterogeneity of interests among citizens to prevent the emergence of a common political program of the nonpropertied; (d) the Keynesian model, in which economic growth and distribution of income generate a commonality of interests between the dispossessed and the wealthy.

Now, what are the notions of democracy that we find in Latin America, and to what extent have the four accommodations mentioned above worked as efficiently as in the advanced industrial societies? First and above all, it is possible to find the notion of liberal democracy in the origins of the postcolonial, independent Latin American countries. This was, at best, a concept for describing a system that worked (and still does in many countries) with extremely powerful executives (e.g., Mexican presidentialism) without sufficient checks and balances, with limited exercise of citizens rights, and centralized and centralist public bureaucracies. With the army and landowning aristocracies that effectively controlled the economic system of production, and/or the external influence of British interest until the 1930's and the overwhelming presence of the United States after War World II, particularly in enclave societies, this notion of democracy becomes paradoxical.

Second, there is also the notion of a nationalist democracy, associated with populist governments at the outset of industrialization in Latin America. This promotes a strong capitalist state that, it is hoped, will be able to implement the political and economic independence of these countries while searching for a balance of power between the propertied and the nonpropertied classes through the creation of social wage policies and the implementation of Keynesian policies.

There is the notion of a popular democracy, based on the defense of popular sovereignty and national sovereignty, the idea of public property as a common good, and the predominance of the right of collectivities over the right of individuals. Thus, the notion of democracy as content rather than as a method of political representation was prevalent in many of the Latin American revolutions and uprisings, including the Mexican Revolution of 1911–1921, the Bolivian revolution of 1952, the so-called peaceful transition to socialism in Chile during 1970–1973, and perhaps the Nicaraguan experience since 1979. Finally, there is the notion of a socialist democracy in Cuba, which alters most of the political reaccommodations between democracy and capitalism outlined above.

It has been argued in this chapter that in Latin America, there is a dependent, incomplete, and peripheral capitalist development (with different national situations): a system of production where power is concentrated, encompassing the rule of capital (class domination), the power of state elites (bureaucratic domination), and the power of men over women (male chauvinist domination). The dynamics of bureaucracy are tied to the dynamics of capitalism, where property rights are much more important than personal rights.

In liberal democracies, adult education usually plays a subsidiary and marginal role in achieving the premises of possessive individualism (Kozol, 1985). In transitional societies, with the predominance of radical forms of popular democracy, including the fundamental role of mass organizations, popular education may become a key element in breaking the ties between liberal institutions of formal representation and the political socialization of the citizenry, and in downplaying the role of the market in closing the gap between education and work—which will upset any attempt to pursue a neo-Keynesian reaccommodation of capitalism. This key role of nonformal education policies is in part due to the flexibility of the systems of nonformal education compared with the highly stratified, hierarchical, and bureaucratized schooling systems (C. Torres, 1989a). In part because of the new revolutionary ideology, a new set of assumptions regarding power and individual rights may be implemented in these new adult education programs, and a strong emphasis is placed on the notion of democracy as content as opposed to the notion of democracy as a method of political representation—which is the basis for establishing the relationships between education and democracy in Western societies.

NOTES

1. The poverty line is defined as the minimum threshold necessary to satisfy the basic needs of nourishment, health, clothing, housing, and education (Latapí, 1987).

2. A family is on or below the destitution line when its income is not sufficient to satisfy the minimum nutritional requirements of its members, even if the entire family income were to be spent on this purpose (Latapí, 1987).

3. The notion of crisis poses particular problems to any serious analysis in the social sciences. To put it simply, there are many types of crisis from a theoretical perspective. Without attempting a taxonomy of the different types, let us note that there are social crises (e.g., the complete disorganization of the dynamics of reproduction of the social structures in El Salvador today); there are fiscal crises of the state, which are clearly perceived as a gap between revenues and expenditure in the context of increasing mass demands and pressure for social services (typical of most of the industrial advanced societies today and definitely a feature of the most industrialized societies in Latin America); there are crises of representation between the masses and their natural institutions of political representation (e.g., the political parties, the church, etc.), and between the dominant classes and the political alliances that control the public sector apparatus; there are crises of legitimation and crises of hegemony, which are related to an overall crisis in the social formation, a crisis between the vertical and social controls established in any society, with a particular emphasis on the perceived role of the state as guaranteeing and safeguarding the reproduction of the social system while simultaneously appearing as the representative of the general will. This discussion on crises has, obviously, practical implications and connotations. For instance, speaking about the debt crisis, Beatrice Avalos quoted the magazine *South*:

A recent World Bank Study of the impact of depression on Latin America noted a reduction in primary school enrollment rates in Chile, a rise in infant mortality rates in Brazil and evidence of falling consumption of cooking oil, meat and milk in Mexico's poorest households. Argentina has had to introduce a food programme covering 5.5 million of its 30 million people. It takes a long time for cutbacks in medical and educational services to affect health and literacy indicators, but there is increasing concern that the large reductions in government spending since the debt crisis broke will undo years of slow progress in these areas. (Avalos, 1987: 152)

4. At the end of 1986, the long-term debt of developing countries amounted to $1 trillion, more than double their total export of goods and services. The total payment of interest amounted to $65 billion; and in Latin America only, by the end of 1985 the total

service of the external debt cost the countries $105 billion in interest payments and some of the principal.

5. In cultural terms, however, Octavio Paz is right when he observes, "The concept of 'underdevelopment,' for instance, may be applied to economics and technology, but not to art, literature, moral values or politics" (Paz, 1982:5).

6. The dilemma of the external debt was clearly expressed by Latin American leaders at the negotiation table with the creditors: "to pay or to grow." At a summit of presidents in Acapulco the following points were made: "Each of us has the right in the name of our people to not pay more than what its economy can pay if its social situation doesn't permit it" (Alan Garcia, Peru); "Today it is vital to adjust debt service to the ability to pay and the need for growth in Latin America" (Miguel de la Madrid, Mexico); "The current economic conditions impede our development and condemn us to decline" (Raul Alfonsin, Argentina); "The political will to bring Latin America out of its tragic decline does not exist in the industrialized nations; we will have to fight with our own efforts" (José Sarney, Brazil) (*Toronto Globe & Mail*, November 28, 1987: B14).

7. This is consistent with the African experience, as reported in Kruss (1988).

8. It was conceived as the contribution of truly Marxist pedagogy to educational reform (Price, 1977).

9. On March 17, 1959, the Law of Agrarian Reform was passed, and the Institute for Agrarian Reform later constituted a fundamental institution in facilitating the literacy campaign in the rural areas.

10. The ratio of students to teachers has improved in Cuban adult education over time: in 1961 there were 161 students per teacher; by 1965 this ratio was 18; and by 1973 it was 11 (Carnoy and Werthein, 1980: 62).

11. This was the term used by the revolutionaries, particularly in the writings of Ernesto Guevara. The patriarchal implications of the term deserve to be criticized in light of feminist scholarship.

12. This is somewhat idealistic. The insufficiency of moral stimulus and the switch to material rewards suggest that such self-motivated revolutionary persons have yet to form the majority.

13. Roxborough argues:

> Prior to the 1950's Somoza did not rule simply on the basis of terror and repression, as was the case in the later stages of the regime. Indeed, in this early populist stage of the Somoza dynasty, Anastasio Somoza was engaged in a bitter political struggle to free himself from the tutelage of the traditional "oligarchical" parties, and turned to the labour movement for political support. . . . By promulgating a labour code and giving support for union organizing Somoza could operate a sort of balancing act between the oligarchy and the nascent, but combative, working class. . . . By late 1947, the growing strength and independence of the labour movement posed a threat to Somoza and he moved rapidly to repress it and to remove its Communist leadership. This also fitted with the emerging anti-Communist Crusade by the USA in Latin America as a whole. With labour defeated, Somoza could then establish a pact with the oligarchy and set the basis for the rapid expansion of agrarian capitalism which was the distinguishing characteristic of Nicaraguan development in the post-War. (*London School of Economics Newsletter* no. 1, 1987: 4)

14. Data from unpublished documents of the Ministry of Education, Office of Educational Financing Planning, Managua, January 12, 1987.

15. *El amanecer del pueblo* (People's dawn), the literacy primer, was organized through photographs and sentences. The sentences were elaborated under thematic considerations rather than didactic ones. The assumption was that a sentence allows an easier transition from a complex discussion to the concrete study of the syllables. In this meaning, it would constitute an expansion of the Freirean approach of only one word. The result of this was unsatisfactory: the adults could not read; therefore, they were limited to a passive and frustrating role. In the second version of the primer, these problems were solved.

16. E. M. Gairy, then minister of finance and later prime minister, was the leading player in this scandalous affair, called "Squandermania" by the population. The report of the Commission of Enquiry into Public Expenditure in Grenada led to the dissolution of the Grenadian United Labour Party government in 1962.

17. Jacobs and Jacobs stated: "At the United Nations, Gairy enhanced his reputation as an international buffoon by repeatedly calling upon that august body to set up an agency for "psychic research into Unidentified Flying Objects, what he called 'Ufology', the Bermuda Triangle, and other psychic phenomena" (1980: 109).

18. In Nicaragua, preschool enrollment increased from 9,000 to 67,000 in only five years; in a few years elementary school enrollment doubled in Cuba and in Nicaragua; adult education, practically nonexistent before the revolution, enrolled 818,000 students in Cuba, 167,852 in Nicaragua, and 20,000 in Grenada.

19. In Cuba all citizens have at least nine years of schooling, while in the rest of Latin America dropout rates in basic education are above 50% and the average level of schooling is 4.5 years.

20. In a centralized planned economy (CPE) "regulation of the market" means that employment is not left entirely to individuals' attributes or ascriptive characteristics (social class, race, gender, etc.); resource allocation and the flow of the labor force are tied more closely to the forecast of social needs. Hence, CPE helps to reduce the uncertainty of the market. Second, CPE smooths out the trends of supply and demand of labor (regulating the ups and downs of labor supply). This is so because (a) it reduces the hierarchical articulation of a segmented labor market; (b) it reduces the size of the underground (nontaxable) economy; and (c) it reduces the distance between the dominant mode of production and precapitalist ones. Third, it reduces the income inequality in society through (a) the provision of free services (real wages) and (b) the egalitarian structure of nominal wages. Finally, it regulates access to consumption and protects social wages from inflation.

21. A hypothesis could be advanced in this regard. The success of revolutionary campaigns hinges upon the momentum in which they are conceived and carried out. High participation and mobilization facilitated by mass organizations, revolutionary rhetoric and morale, and the new national project based upon social solidarity usually are features of revolutionary transitions. In short, these elements, taken altogether, could explain the different outcomes of revolutionary experiences and the more carefully planned, resource-rich campaigns implemented in capitalist Latin America, with their litanies of failures (cf. La Belle, 1980; 1986). The latter, even when they could be more systematic, "may lack both urgency and passionate fervour" (Bhola, 1984: 211). How-

ever, there have not been that many revolutionary experiences in Latin America to test out this hypothesis.

22. The Miskitos question on the Atlantic Coast of Nicaragua is an example of this situation.

23. Particularly after many years of dictatorship, extreme concentration of income in a few hands and cruel repression of any opposition (as was shown in these three cases), both structural and educational changes occur very quickly.

6

TOWARD A POLITICAL SOCIOLOGY OF ADULT EDUCATION: AN AGENDA FOR RESEARCH ON ADULT EDUCATION POLICYMAKING

This chapter is organized in two main parts. The first presents a brief discussion and overview of the literature on adult education, emphasizing the main short-comings and weaknesses of the major arguments and underlying conceptualizations. The second presents an alternative theoretical view of adult education and the research problems that arise from it. The thrust of the argument in the second part is that a theory of the state is needed to understand current adult education practices and policies in dependent capitalist societies.

CURRENT CONCEPTIONS AND GOALS OF ADULT EDUCATION PROGRAMS

By definition, adult education and literacy training programs have a broad range of goals and use several methods and strategies. In general, adult education is conceived of as a means of providing a vast range of skills, abilities, intellectual patterns, and social and political values for a growing sector of a nation's population. Sometimes overlapping with the notion of "basic education" as defined by the World Bank (World Bank, 1974), adult education is assumed to be different from universal primary education insofar as it is concerned with the minimum learning needs of a specially identified group, particularly in Third World countries. It tends to transcend the hierarchy of the educational system and is provided in different forms in different countries, through both nonformal and formal means.

Nonetheless, the range of aims and goals of adult education activities varies from developing positive attitudes toward cooperation, work, community, and national development, and further learning to the teaching of functional literacy and numeracy; from providing a scientific outlook on health, agriculture, and the like to incorporating functional knowledge and skills; from preparing individuals to enter the labor market or strengthening their current occupational position to making available functional knowledge and skills necessary for civic participation (Coombs, et al., 1973).

From a different and more radical point of view, literacy training and adult education have enormous advantages as a field for the development of innovative educational and political practices. Paulo Freire and the other educators for liberation originally developed their educational/political strategies in this field through their work in Latin America and Africa (Freire et al., 1980; C. Torres, 1982b).

Advantages of Adult Education
(Popular Education) Programs

From this more radical political perspective, there are several significant factors that underscore the advantages of adult education over formal education, as part of a political strategy. First, so far as community needs and problems are used as a basis for designing the content and vocabulary of adult literacy programs, the political implications of adult education vastly exceed those of formal schooling. Second, adult education programs are usually better linked to community needs and are more responsive to community pressures than the formal schooling system. Thus, in certain circumstances, this popular education can be understood as a form of education developed *by* the oppressed rather than *for* the oppressed. Third, this education has the curricular and organizational flexibility that formal schooling lacks. Fourth, the results of adult education are more immediate than the results achieved through formal schooling. It is not necessary to wait for 10 to 15 years, as with formal training, for the graduate to be incorporated into the labor market or into political activities. Fifth, those who are likely to demand adult education in peripheral capitalist societies tend, according to this educational perspective, to be the dispossessed. This is due to their lack of power. Furthermore, it shows that illiteracy, far from being a "social illness," as is often claimed, is an outcome of a hierarchical class struggle or of violent historical processes such as colonization. Finally, adult education and literacy programs have demonstrated their importance as instruments for developing political and critical consciousness in some processes of transition to socialism in such countries as Cuba and Nicaragua (Fagen, 1969; C. Torres, 1982a; Arnove, 1986).

Popular education becomes a central feature of educational systems in transitional nations. The concept of popular education is not a conventional term for an English-speaking audience. In Latin America, however, the term has had widespread importance and is now the subject of an intense debate, as was pointed out in Chapter 1. For instance, in Nicaragua, the "Sandinista education" has been defined as "popular education." First, this notion means that education is a right for all Nicaraguan people, particularly the lower classes, which were excluded from the benefits of the educational system in the past. Second, "popular education" means that this education cannot be constructed without the active and conscious political participation and support of mass organizations. Third, popular education is considered a powerful ideological weapon in the process of ideological class struggle during the process of transition to socialism. Fourth, it means that the revolution is, in and of itself, an immense and continuous "political workshop" where revolutionary politics becomes a sort of pedagogy for the masses and the leadership. Finally, "popular education" means, following Sandino's pedagogical principles, that a learning process can be carried out only through praxis and fighting, thus combining manual with intellectual labor, theory with praxis, productive skills with political consciousness raising (Tunnerman, 1983: 15; Carnoy and Torres, 1989). Thus, this somewhat extreme example of a political perspective of popular education differs from conventional views of nonschooling education, and popular education as a versatile educational perspective cannot be restricted to nonformal approaches to education, nor can it be understood outside the context of a dialectical theory of pedagogy and its relationships with social and political mass movements in Latin America (Bruno-Jofre, 1984; La Belle, 1986).

Ambiguous Terminology or Confused Theory?

This wide range of aims and goals attributed to adult education nonformal education, and literacy training policies creates a feeling of elusiveness about this field of study. On the one hand, there is conflict over terminology, and some terms that might be considered similar to, synonymous with, or related to adult education include a wide range of programs, such as nonformal education, distance education, open education, continuing education, lifelong education, extraschool education, and popular education. Any attempt at clarification by undertaking a terminological screening usually results in position papers on the subject (see, e.g., Titmus et al., 1979) with empty, highly abstract, categorical and taxonomic definitions, all of which would be very different in their practical application. In addition, they are all different from the concrete rationality that underlies adult education and literacy training policy formation.

So far, the most detailed attempt to define in international terms what adult education signifies has been undertaken by UNESCO, which refers to it thus:

> [Adult education] denotes the entire body of educational processes, whatever the content, level and method, whether formal or otherwise, whether they prolong or replace initial education in schools, colleges and universities as well as in apprenticeship, whereby persons, regarded as adult by the society to which they belong, develop their abilities, enrich their knowledge, improve their technical or professional qualifications or turn them in a new direction and bring about changes in their attitudes or behavior in the twofold perspective of full personal development

and participation in balanced and independent social, economic and cultural development. (UNESCO, 1976)

This definition, although acceptable, is incomplete because it lacks a precise identification of the different factors involved in the organization and structure of adult education and literacy training programs. Also, explanations of the motivation for adult education learning or adult education policy formation are missing. In fact, the definition does not address the main problems of scale, types of providers of adult education and clienteles, changes in and scope of legislation, forms of learning experiences, or the mechanisms of evaluation and certification of these programs.

With the complexity of contemporary social formations, particularly the vast array of intersections between precapitalist and advanced capitalist modes of production in capitalist-dependent societies, the growing interdependence-dependence linkages between advanced industrial and Third World societies, and the economic and fiscal crisis of the 1980s in those societies, there have been substantial changes not only in the pace of growth in the provision of adult, nonformal education but also in the quality of educational opportunities for adults. Hence, it would be very difficult to provide an "international" definition of adult education institutions, policies, practices, and pedagogies; that is, it would be difficult to provide a comprehensive definition that would account for and coherently summarize what actually has been going on in this field internationally in the 1980s.

In addition, as John Lowe has emphasized, the traditional confusion and ambiguity about the purposes, functions, and means of adult education are "compounded by the fact that the term is regularly used with three separate connotations: first, to designate the education of adults, second, to describe collectively all the persons and agencies in a country or globally which provide for education of adults, third, to specify an area of academic scholarship" (Lowe, 1975: 20).

There is an ongoing debate in which some authors argue that adult education practices differ totally from those of the formal schooling system, while others claim that adult education programs reflect bureaucratic procedures, cognitive knowledge, and values and assumptions that are identical to those which inform any standard schooling system. In this chapter it will be argued that the institutional configuration of adult education and literacy training practices and policies differs sharply from that within the schooling system. However, concerning the hidden and the explicit curriculum or the hegemonic political culture in adult education, one sees that governmental programs hardly differ from the dominant agenda in the formal schooling system. Thus, any alteration in the formal prescriptions and organization of the services could indeed make a difference in the quality of the curriculum and the overall service, a difference that should be analyzed.

Adult Education for Whom?

The main differences between adult education and school-based education lie in the age and experience of the students, the overall character of the adult education network of programs and its close connections with the processes of legitimation of the state, the modality of organization and (sometimes) administration of the system, and above all in the socioeconomic and political characteristics of the clientele that these programs are supposed to serve (C. Torres, 1982a, 1984b).

The ages at which one can become incorporated into basic education services are marked by a minimum age beyond which a person could be considered an adult and able to use these services. Overtly, this age limit is usually 15 years in Latin America, which corresponds to a conventional decision in educational jurisprudence regarding the estimated age for completion of compulsory basic education. In almost all Latin American countries, compulsory education is six to nine years of completed schooling—the number of years it takes to complete primary and secondary education programs, respectively. This conventional age limit coincides with the estimated age for entrance into the labor force as part of the active economic population. In some cases, this threshold is estimated to be 15 years; in other cases, it is 12 years (UNESCO, 1974a; Altimir, 1975; Torrado, 1978; CEPAL, 1977).[1]

In spite of the contrasting goals attributed to adult education, most of its expected social functions are thought to be similar across diverse social formations. Nonetheless, the clienteles to whom adult education policies are usually addressed differ sharply across these diverse social formations. For example, a survey of adult education, recurrent training, and lifelong learning programs in advanced industrial societies indicated that adult education policies are usually devised for people who are above the age of compulsory school attendance, estimated to be 15 or 16 years.[2]

These programs have defined the different sectors of the population that are targeted by adult education programs in the following manner: (1) workers, both white-collar and blue-collar, a category that is virtually synonymous with those employed (except that the study is also concerned with training of adults seeking employment); (2) older persons, broadly defined to include people from midlife through relatively advanced age; (3) women entering the labor force, defined as adult women seeking to enter or reenter the labor force after having been away from education or work; (4) parents, including men and women with children up to age 18 in the home, who want parent education programs; (5) "undereducated" adults, a category that, although understood as a country-specific definition, includes, in general, those who fail to complete the normal sequence of compulsory education (Peterson et al., 1982).

The amorphous nature of the field, as John Minnis so nicely puts it, calls for programs as diverse as the education of migrants, community-oriented programs and/or programs for the aged, on-the-job-training programs, second

chance education, nontraditional programs in postsecondary and higher education (e.g., the open university in Great Britain or the Universidad Simón
Rodriguez in Venezuela), functional literacy, mass literacy campaigns, continuing professional education programs, business-oriented programs, applied behavioral science programs, coping with changing job needs, parenting,
self-assertiveness programs, life planning, or even certain outdoors and field
programs (Minnis, 1984; Coombs et al., 1973; Hayden, 1982; La Belle, 1986).

But is it theoretically useful to describe those who would potentially demand
adult education along the lines suggested above? To define the clientele of adult
education in those terms does not tell us exactly what is the sociological profile
of the adult education clientele in different societies. This lack of a specific analysis of social classes, and the particular social segments that would demand adult
education, perhaps rests on an underlying assumption that capitalist societies
tend, in the long run, to achieve a certain degree of social integration and har-
mony, and that adult educators have "attempted to forge a middle ground between those who want to impose a definite curriculum and those who want
education to bring about radical social change" (Minnis, 1984: 127). Therefore,
for some authors, the class composition of the adult education clientele does not
really matter, since, sooner or later, everybody will be included in the "melting
pot" of capitalist societies. But the classification used above does not tell us if
this educational clientele may be found in occupational institutions, specific organizations, or particular corporate settings. Neither are the above-mentioned
categories mutually exclusive.

Adult Education Clientele in Latin America

In the Latin American dependent states, adult education policies, even
though formally similar in terms of the goals set forth to complete mass compulsory education, usually have striking differences from the policies and experiences of advanced industrial capitalist social formations.

Since the early formulation of dependency theory, there has been a challenge
to the notion that international dependency relies on a set of countries that constitutes a central core (advanced industrial capitalist social formations) and a set
of countries that constitutes a periphery (the Third World). New phenomena in
the capitalist periphery have caused theoreticians to identify certain countries
that have increased involvement in the international arena. These countries,
known as newly industrialized countries (NIC), have assumed new functions in
the overall world division of labor by constituting industrial platforms of development because of their labor-cost advantages. They have shown—until the dis-
closure of the financial crisis brought about by the mounting external debt—a
sustained pace of growth in the midst of a world recession. Other features of
NICs include having abundant strategic mineral resources and, usually, presenting a particular modification in the form of the state (i.e., its autonomy) identifia-
ble in the process of political bargaining with the transnational corporations and

the imperial country. This may be the case with Mexico, Brazil, India, Singapore, Korea, Hong Kong, and Pakistan since the 1970s.[3] As in the previous chapter, I wish to call the reader's attention to the notion of dependency and the dependent state because, to clarify the social settings where adult education takes place, it is essential to develop a political sociology of adult education on theoretical grounds. To understand the peculiarities of adult education in peripheral or semiperipheral societies, we must understand the development of public education and the rules of policy formation in the dependent state (Carnoy, 1984). In these dependent states, adult education tends to have a clear-cut class orientation, in its target clientele and in its policy formulation, as well as in its links and relationships to economic, social, and political development.

As has been pointed out elsewhere (C. Torres, 1984a), despite the argument that there is no solid information available about the characteristics of illiterate adult learners (Burke and Chiappetta, 1978: 6), there is ample evidence that the adult education clientele in Latin American societies is composed mainly of peasants and indigenous peoples, urban marginals, self-employed people in lower-rank positions, lower-wage urban workers (usually located in competitive industries and in service sectors, as opposed to those located in monopoly industries and the intermediate and upper levels of government bureaucracy), and the lowest levels of the urban industrial petite bourgeoisie, particularly in those countries with the lowest levels of industrial development (Gajardo, 1982: 2–54; C. Torres, 1982a; Muñoz Izquierdo, 1982a).

Some research findings in Mexico, reported in Chapter 4 of this book, also seem to confirm this description. The characteristics of students enrolled in a program of adult education during 1979–1980 were as follows: Two-thirds of all the students declared paid work as their principal activity—roughly half of them were employed in routine, low-paid occupations in the public sector. The vast majority (75%) of the students in programs for elementary education for adults were classified as workers and employees. The service sector was the more important type of economic activity in which they were engaged. In general, two out of five students did not work, one out of four worked in the service sector, and one out of nine worked in manufacturing industries.

In Latin America, the population in need of adult education and literacy training is therefore highly specific: it is comprised mainly of a rural population or of very recent migrants to the cities. These people are found in very large numbers in the more underdeveloped countries in the region or in the most backward areas of the less underdeveloped; some of them belong to ethnic minorities, are monolingual, and have higher rates of illiteracy, especially among the groups above 25 years of age and among women.

According to conventional theories of education and development, these sectoral characteristics of the groups demanding adult education and literacy programs and policies could be considered highly relevant for economic and political purposes. However, in general, I have argued in Chapter 3 that the principal social characteristics of these adults in dependent societies are not taken into account when government programs are designed.

The Contribution of Nonformal Education to Development

One could next raise the question of the contribution of nonformal education to socioeconomic development. What are the social and economic returns of adult education? Several studies summarize the most important research done on this subject (Waiser, 1980: 4ff.; IDRC, 1978). Waiser shows that some authors believe adult basic education contributes to economic development in the following ways: (1) by raising the productivity of the new literates; (2) by raising the productivity of individuals working with literates—the so-called spillover benefits of literacy; (3) by expanding the flow of general knowledge to individuals (e.g., instruction in health care and nutrition), thus reducing the cost of transmitting useful information; (4) by acting as a device for selecting the more able individuals and thereby enhancing their occupation mobility; and (5) by strengthening economic incentives, that is, the tendency for people to respond positively to a rise in the rate of reward for their efforts (Waiser, 1980; Phillips, 1970; La Belle and Verhine, 1978; Fuller, 1984). Particularly in farming activities, better allocative decisions that could be made as a result of adult education, could increase the economic return from primary activities. It has been argued that shifting from production of subsistence crops to the production of grain or fruit for the market could in the long run increase farmers' productivity and welfare, and adult education programs could play a role in such processes of change (Muñoz Izquierdo, 1982a).

The contribution of (adult) education to growth is smaller than the early human capital theorists and development economists thought. The correlation between earnings and education includes many other influences on earnings that are also correlated with schooling but should not be attributed to it (Carnoy, 1982; C. Torres, 1988a). Hence, much of the research has cast some doubts on the validity of the above-stated premises. First, available evidence tends to suggest that the wage structure depends upon variables exogenous to individual productivity. These variables include gender, race, the nature of a firm's market, maintenance of class structure in the face of meritocratic rules, degree of monopoly power in the market, and/or social class background (Carnoy et al., 1979; Carnoy, 1977: 39). Thus, differential rates of return to education are not the result of inequality in the distribution of schooling, but refer instead to the basically unequal structures of commodity production societies (Carnoy, 1975: 5–6; Levin, 1980; Bowles, 1980: 207; Bowles, 1975: 47; Bacchus, Pannu, and Torres, 1988).

In addition, the role of the state in education and income policy is a crucial variable in determining income distribution. In this sense, taxation, wage fixing, price control, and inflation and employment policies are the means by which the state exercises this power—policies that are out of reach of adult education programs.

A decisive standpoint from which to study the relationships among education, income distribution, and capital accumulation is the theory of labor market segmentation. In the light of this theory, labor market conditions can be understood as outcomes of four segmentation processes: (1) segmentation into primary and secondary markets, (2) segmentation within the primary sector, (3) segmentation by race, and (4) segmentation by gender. The primary and secondary segments are differentiated as follows:

> Primary jobs require and develop stable working habits; skills are often acquired on the job; wages are relatively high; and job ladders exist. Secondary jobs do not require and often discourage stable working habits; wages are low; turnover is high; and job ladders are few. Secondary jobs are mainly (though not exclusively) filled by minority workers, women and youth (Reich et al., 1975: 71).

Although the theory of segmented labor markets has particular relevance to advanced industrial societies, it does help us to understand that adult education in dependent capitalist societies prepares people for improving their chances to enter the secondary labor market. The notion of segmented labor markets is assumed in the context of monopoly capitalism, and therefore implies a high degree of homogeneity for a given social formation. In Latin America, the segmentation processes could be considered simultaneously as a horizontal and a vertical process. In the vertical process, the segmentation is due to the combination of modes of production (precapitalist and capitalist), which implies different labor markets for different workers. In the horizontal process, however, the process of segmentation of labor markets, particularly in the most advanced modes of production, is similar to that of the advanced industrial societies vis-à-vis historical specificities of the dependent societies.

The notion of labor market segmentation cautions us not to assume that education and training lead automatically to better income distribution through increasing per capita productivity, which leads, in turn, to higher earnings. And perhaps, through adequate theorizing, it would be possible to link a theory of labor market segmentation with the theory of the combination of modes of production, and therefore to explain in a more precise fashion how adult education intersects with precapitalist and capitalist forms of production in a given dependent society.

In analyzing craft training programs in Guyana, K. Bacchus argues that the labor market for craftsmen was not homogeneous, and that it was segmented into a "high wage" market and a "low wage" market in terms of demand for and supply of skilled labor. This heterogeneity is further reflected within the "modern," high-paid sector. However, focusing on the low-wage sector, Bacchus forcefully argues that while the effect of upgrading skills through training undoubtedly resulted in a higher rate of private investment in their training by these artisans, "the effect of this [improved training] was that they were pricing themselves out of the 'low wage' sector of the economy and, since the demands in the 'high wage' sector were not increasing fast enough to absorb them, a high percentage of them remained unemployed" (Bacchus, 1976: 120). So, looking at the linkages between the precapitalist and capitalist forms of production in peripheral capitalism, it is important to note that despite the hopes of policy planners and politicians, adult education training cannot easily cope with the economic needs of the poor and ever-increasing marginalized social sectors. This is particularly true when the situation is one of economic stagnation, and chronic and increasing unemployment, and when the economy cannot grow as fast as the labor force to provide enough jobs in the primary markets of the economy while the same combination of modes of production is undermining the traditional basis of subsistence of farmers, artisans, and other groups. It is obvious that adult education programs could not solve the gap between traditional and advanced modes of production, nor could they contribute significantly to the short-term needs of the poor. Thus, it is not surprising that adult education and training programs are less and less appealing to men and women seeking jobs: the private investment is high but the economic return insignificant in the low-wage sector of the economy.

Modernization theorists have overwhelmingly assumed that adult basic education is useful for improving skills among low-technical levels of workers and peasants, particularly those with a tendency to migrate, thus making them more employable and reducing unemployment, underemployment, and migration of the labor force—which, in turn, has demographic consequences. Other authors have identified types of outcomes produced by literacy training, distinguishing purely cognitive effects, social effects, and instrumental effects (Bhola 1981: 9–11). However, other authors are skeptical of the profitability, productivity, and expected "per se goodness" of adult education programs and policies (Giroux, 1983b; Mackie, 1981; Levine 1982).

ADULT EDUCATION POLICIES AND THE ROLE OF THE STATE

What is missing from the conventional framework outlined above? First of all, it does not offer a—or any—theory of adult education reform, or of the underlying political rationality of reformist efforts in this area of research and policymaking. This is due, in part, to the lack of an explicit theory of the state that could come to terms with the process of public policymaking in dependent capitalist states. Even the radical approach in adult education is faulty in this particular regard. For instance, Freire and Macedo have distinguished four approaches to reading: the academic approach, the utilitarian approach, the cognitive development approach, and the romantic approach, all of them criticized on grounds that "they . . . ignore the role of language as a major force in the construction of human subjectivities" (Freire and Macedo, 1987: 147). Arguing that literacy training is a form of cultural politics, Freire and Macedo view literacy as a set of practices that either empower or disempower people (1987: 141). They argue that when literacy is seen as a form of cultural production and not as another form of cultural reproduction (i.e., as a function of the cultural interest of the dominant groups in society), it is "an integral part of the way in which people produce, transform, and reproduce meaning" (1987: 142). When literacy training goes beyond helping people to develop skills to master the dominant standard language, literacy becomes an emancipatory practice.

However, although emphasizing the political nature of literacy training while arguing for a theory of culture and radical pedagogy, Freire and Macedo tend to neglect the nature of literacy as a state practice. The overall analysis places little emphasis, if any, on the political, analytical, and practical categories—the political mediations, in Hegelian terms—that are needed to understand adult education as public policy or as part and parcel of "resistance practices" in civil society (Giroux, 1983a). Since radical analysis will emphasize the concepts of reflectivity, structure, agency, and human learning (Jarvis, 1985: 111), this approach will contrast sharply with the mainstream views regarding the contribution of adult education to development. However, it still needs a more refined theory of the state and politics, as well as a systematic assessment of the institutional, organizational, and economic constraints on human learning and agency.

Second, adult education programs are not seen (as perhaps they should be) as part of a series of factual responses to the legitimation crisis of capitalist societies (to borrow a term from Habermas), and therefore related to the needs for political legitimation of the capitalist state (Morrow, 1983). Paradoxically, this is due to the overemphasis placed by researchers and policy planners on the economic determinants of educational policies, either from a functionalist perspective (always looking for a functional policy to improve the performance of the economy and the productivity of the labor force) or from an orthodox Marxist perspective, which addresses reality only through the lens of the role of education in the extraction of surplus values, and in so doing has failed to capture the significance of superstructural activities for social reproduction.

I will argue, instead, that since any capitalist state has a class content reflected in its policymaking, adult education policies constitute an example of class-determined policies oriented to confront the political and social demands of the powerless and impoverished sectors of that capitalist society. The issue is, then, why and how the capitalist state addresses the needs of the masses by means of adult education programs, instead of simply leaving them alone. Indeed, the political economy of the state is organized to support the development of a social formation directed toward commodity production. State economic interventionism is therefore oriented toward performing those functions with capital is unable to perform because it is made up of many fractionalized and mutually antagonistic parties. However, state interventionism tends to be oriented toward strengthening the legitimacy of the current ruling alliance as a prerequisite to sustaining a given pattern of capital accumulation. Therefore, any mode of state intervention and most of the state's policies are linked to a changing pattern of potential or actual threats to the political system, or to structural problems that emerge from the process of capital accumulation. Thus, the modes of state activity can be seen as responses to these social threats and problems (Wright, 1978; O'Donnell, 1978a, 1978b; Offe and Ronge, 1975: 137–47).

In this regard, it is important to note that adult education policies, like any educational policies, are subject to an intense bureaucratic struggle in central-ized educational systems, and therefore, many of the policy outcomes reflect these bureaucratic clashes. In fact, the process of educational decisionmaking in dependent societies seems to be inherently political, conflictual, and techni-cally nonrational (McGinn and Street, 1982: 179). What does this mean for adult education?

The issue is how adult education policies relate to the process of capital accu-mulation and political domination in capitalist dependent societies. Has political rationality proven to be far more important than technical rationality in the pro-motion of adult education reforms in these societies? In this respect, what has been the role of distinct and factional bureaucratic ideologies in adult education policy formation?

The questions posed above are much more fruitful for concrete research on adult education policies than the conventional view of adult education programs as a tool for development or as an agent of change. This is particularly so be-cause the available empirical evidence shows hardly any contribution of adult ed-ucation policies and programs toward those ends.

Grasping the inner rationality of adult education programs will help us to un-derstand under which social and political conditions and for what purposes a cap-italist state will undertake a new substantial reform in adult education programs and policies. To what degree can new policies in this field, as a minor part of the state educational policies, be related to the spectrum of political conflict in civil society? Would a new adult education strategy be viewed as an effective mode of national integration of the masses that the ruling elite is using to mold the peo-ple and marginal groups into a nation-state? Or, instead, would this policy be viewed as an instrument that counteracts the decommodification of the labor force?

In this regard, to what extent would any new adult education policy in depen-dent societies represent—as is often argued by policymakers—some sort of re-sponse to new demands from the labor market for skilled labor? Or to what extent would it represent an expression of an educational bureaucracy acting in-dependently of the needs of capitalist development? Is there an inner bureau-cratic rationale for educational planning that can be thought of as part of a "law of motion of a bureaucracy"? Are there any other "laws" operating in public pol-icy formation that underpin adult education reforms?

Is the State a Problem-solving Agent?

A common thread that runs through Marxist and Marxist-influenced educational research is the analysis of education as part of the state-administered mechanisms for the reproduction of fundamental capitalist societal relations (Broady, 1981: 143; Youngman, 1986). Although the question of state–education relationships is at the core of the definition of the functions of education in capitalist societies, it has rarely been thoroughly analyzed in contemporary Marxist theory. A sound theoretical understanding and appropriate methodological procedures are still lacking for issues relating to the capitalist state, its class-based policies, and their impact on educational structures, practices, codes, and especially educational policy planning and policy making.

As Poulantzas argues, a particular function of the state is to serve as a factor in the cohesion of the levels of a social formation. However, in doing so, the state is also the structure or instance in which the contradictions between those various levels are condensed (Poulantzas, 1969). As several authors have emphasized, state intervention in civil society has become one of its crucial features, which takes different forms in different countries.

To organize a very complex and increasingly sophisticated literature, the main discussion topics can be identified as follows: (a) the articulation and/or independence of the capitalist state and the bloc in power (using the notion of bloc in power as developed in Poulantzas, 1969: 237–41), which is directly related to concrete configurations of social classes, their corporative organizations, and their leading role in commanding national politics; (b) the articulation of the state–subordinate classes relationship (sometimes labeling the latter as "popular movements"); (c) the degree of direct and indirect state action in the regulation of capital accumulation (the state's role in the economy); (d) the state–nation relationship, as a macrocosmic condensation of broader dynamics and strains built into this structural relationship (in the case of peripheral dependent states, the focus is primarily on the relationship between the dependent state and the metropolitan state); (e) the issue of consent legitimation and representation vis-à-vis the capitalist state, which in turn introduces the complex issue of state ideology.

In this literature, when analyzing the role of the state in contemporary societies, it has been emphasized that the function of various public institutions that maintain ideological hegemony has been modified. This in turn has had various consequences in the development of class consciousness. The increasing internationalization of capital has modified the framework in which state economic and social policy is implemented. The structure of the labor force and the relationships between classes have been changed by the enormous growth of the public sector. The bureaucracy has become a social force in itself, and the policymaking process within certain forms of the state has become subject to increasing bureaucratic encapsulation. At the same time, the bureaucracy is thought of as pursuing interests of its own. The interplay of interests among different factions of capital and different classes and strata in society determines domestic as well as international policies. These policies have been increasingly reinterpreted and appropriated by a capitalist state whose relative autonomy from civil society has become absolutely essential in maintaining the system as a whole, particularly under conditions necessary for consent and legitimacy enforcement.

In basing an analysis on these premises, it is possible to reject the notion that the capitalist state is a problem-solving agent, an approach that in general places too much emphasis on the analysis of policy content. The main assumptions of this latter approach to policymaking are the following: (1) that the state seems to be analyzing those processes which occur in the political arena, and through a diagnosis of the chief problems, organizes its political agenda for action; (2) from this standpoint, it is important for researchers to focus upon which interests are involved in the determination of policymaking; (3) as soon as this identification has been made, the corollary of the analysis will be to check those interests against the material outcomes and the distribution of tangible benefits that result from these policies and their implementation (Lindblon, 1968: 12–31). In general, these shared assumptions are used in the basic approaches to policyplanning in education in such areas as the estimation of social demand, manpower planning, and rate-of-return and cost-effectiveness analyses (Russel and Hudson, 1980: 1–15; Weiler, 1980; Simmons, 1980: 15–33).

Analytical Frameworks for Study of Nonformal Education Policymaking

It is evident that there is need for an organizational analysis of public policy against which decisions about adult education or any other field could be projected (Therborn, 1980: 37–48). In addition, it is of fundamental importance to know the different forms of functional interaction and interdependency within a bureaucratic organization—forms that can be analytically differentiated. Similarly, it should be noted that the form this interaction assumes will vary according to the type of political regime considered. For instance, Oscar Oszlak has presented, in analyzing the Latin American state, three main types of political regimes: (a) bureaucratic-authoritarian, (b) democratic-liberal, and (c) patrimonialist—corresponding to which are the three main types of bureaucratic interdependency, hierarchical, functional, and material or budgetary (Oszlak, 1980). To deal with these distinctions it will be helpful to avoid the common pitfall of considering the state as a neutral, problem-solving agent. An analysis of public policies along these lines will throw light on the process of policy formation and on some of its effects upon society.

Coming back to the role of educational practices in social reproduction, educational institutions have been viewed as a versatile apparatus that contributes to the political legitimation of the status quo, to the reproduction of the existing social relations of production and the political culture, and to nation building or to political consciousness raising. Education also has often been seen as a prerequisite for human capital formation and capital accumulation. Viewed in this light, it is important to point out that education, as an activity mandated, sponsored, and supervised by the state, is as much an apparatus of the state as is any other agency.

However, one can hardly understand education's function in capitalist society —educational plans and programs, codes, practices, and policies—unless one emphasizes that capitalist education, like the capitalist state, has a dual character. On the one hand, capitalist education is used to provide the means to contribute to the reproduction of the capitalist system, either as a tool to enlarge capital accumulation and labor force reproduction, or as an instrument to enhance political domination structures, practices, and codes. On the other hand, education expresses the notion of national sovereignty and the demands of civil society upon the state. That is, education is concerned with people's consciousness and their expectation of greater social mobility, the attainment of higher personal skills with which to achieve better positions in the labor market, or organized efforts that seek social, economic, and political democratization. Education is also concerned with knowledge construction, transmission, and reproduction; knowledge that constitutes in and of itself a gratifying experience of social and individual learning. And in these functions adult education is not different from the education provided for other age groups or by other institutional means for the remainder of the population.

At the same time that capitalist education strongly corresponds to the social organization of labor and to the social relations of production, it constitutes in itself a moral and empirical expression of democracy in capitalist societies. In this sense, almost every educational institution is far more democratic, open to change and innovation, and subject to potential community control than any other state apparatus, or the work place. Education is potentially, and in some sense actually, far more democratic than any other juridical and political instance of a capitalist mode of production.

Two examples are illustrative. Adult education had been provided in Latin America even before the state took over this particular field of educational activity after World War II. At the turn of the century, many outstanding programs for the political education of workers or peasants run by trade unions and small political parties were available in Latin America; in some cases these programs were at the center of the movement for creating cooperatives for the distribution of goods and credit, and the expansion and implementation of work legislation. In other cases, they were instrumental in the consolidation of some socialist parties, particularly in the Southern Cone. Similar trends have been identified in Canada from a "reconstructivist" perspective in analyzing the relationship between adult education and social movements, particularly the Antigonish Movement in Nova Scotia (Welton, 1987) or independent working-class organizations that use adult education as a center for social and political mobilization, as in Italy and England (Yarnit, 1981a, 1980b).

A second example is the close association of middle-class university students in Latin America with alternative projects of development or with radical political projects, particularly in the 1960s and 1970s. This political activism would show that even though the autonomous universities are financially supported by the state, the academic life is not necessarily tied to the dominant ideology of the ruling party or to the prevailing hegemonic culture. Thus, educational practices and institutions can be quite independent, politically and socially, from the dominant social classes. Similarly, public education has a relative autonomy that constitutes one of its principal features as an arena where social conflict is displayed.

Toward a New Research Agenda for Nonformal Education

In making the connection between the state's role and its adult education activities, it can be argued that to inquire into the reasons behind the growth of adult education programs, how they have been devised historically, by whom, for what purposes, and how they are related to their educational clientele is to ask for an explanation of the determinants of adult education policy formation in a way that is above and beyond the simplistic and perhaps misleading problem-solving approach. Expressed in more conventional terms, this inquiry means discovering which independent and intervening variables account for policy differences.

All in all, it can be claimed that it is necessary to inquire about policy formation in light of the following dimensions: (1) the main actors of policy formation, including the bureaucracy, administrative agents, and social constituencies and clienteles; (2) in terms of organizational studies, the main systemic elements found within a given setting of educational policy formation; (3) the main institutional phases, stages, and/or units of policy formation, that is, the levels of policy planning, policymaking, policy operation, and even policy outcome; (4) the intellectual, institutional, and ideological atmosphere in which those decisions are made (the policy framework). Additionally, it can be argued that those dimensions are offset or shaped by the general framework of organizational rules, which are, in turn, laid down and superimposed in an organization-structure. Following Stewart Clegg, the "organization-structure can be conceptualized as a structure of sedimented selection rules. Those prescribe the limits within which the organization-structure might vary" (Clegg, 1979: 97). Finally, it is important to identify the production rules of public policy with which to understand educational relationships between the political society and the civil society at a particular point in time.

CONCLUSION

The main concern of this chapter has been to critically assess the contradictory goals assigned to adult education, and to show some possible ways to deal with the process of adult education policy formation in a capitalist dependent state. As a preliminary attempt, it sets out distinct analytical dimensions, such as (1) the state's goals and policy targets, as revealed in the social history of the state apparatus; (2) the extent and type of bureaucratic organization; (3) the ideologies of the educational bureaucracy involved in policy planning, as internal determinants of policymaking; (4) material and nonmaterial policy outcomes; (5) the role of educational policy within the overall public policy of the state; and (6) the struggles by groups and social classes to resist the hegemonic practices of the capitalist state. However, if they are somehow inserted within the state apparatus, the task will then be to study how they have tried to consolidate or enlarge their positions.

Several questions and queries have been advanced, questions that call for concrete empirical research on adult education policies and programs in Third World societies. At the same time, this agenda for research points out the need for a dialectical theory of adult education in dependent societies, a theory that is still to be developed in order to overcome the analytical weakness of the conventional views on adult education and development. The next chapter will present an elaborated perspective on adult education policymaking.

In conclusion, it is suggested that the ambiguity of the field and its amorphous nature are not due to the lack of a precise definition of adult education's goals and social functions. Instead, it is due to the lack of a consistent historical and structural theorization of adult education policies and programs in the light of recent findings on the political economy of education and the newly emerging political sociology of education. Without theory, empirical research, and evaluation, adult education policies and programs will continue to have the dominant flavor of the conventional adult education literature: guesswork and wishful thinking. But, what is even worse, such educational research would continue to be instrumental only in advancing the interests and needs of policymakers without addressing the real needs of the communities and the subordinate social classes for whom such programs are supposed to be developed.

NOTES

I would like to thank M. Kazim Bacchus and R. S. Pannu from the University of Alberta, Thomas J. La Belle from the University of Pittsburgh, and Jorge Padua from El Colegio de México for their helpful comments on an earlier draft of this chapter.

Modified version of an article published in *Prospects*, No. 67, Vol. 23:3. ©UNESCO, 1988.

1. To this extent, it is instructive to mention that according to the Economic Commission on Latin America (ECLA), almost half of the total active economic population (ages 15–60) in Latin America should be considered functional illiterates, that is, with less than four years of schooling (CEPAL, 1976).

2. In Australia, Canada, Denmark, the Federal Republic of Germany, France, the So-

viet Union, Sweden, the United Kingdom, and the United States. (See Peterson et al., 1982).

3. For the dependency argument, see Cardoso and Faletto (1978). For the NIC's emergence, trade policies, and economic adjustment, see Frobel et al. (1980) and Turner and McMullen (1982). For a coherent argument on the notion of semiperipheral societies, see Wallerstein (1979).

7

ADULT EDUCATION POLICIES IN LATIN AMERICA AND THE CARIBBEAN: THEORETICAL-METHODOLOGICAL PERSPECTIVES

Educational planning is an exercise in optimism. The formulation of public policy is often understood in the context of a "black box" where inputs, processes, and outputs interact. This notion of an impenetrable "black box" impedes our learning in detail the origins, nature, objectives, dimensions, and dynamics of a specific policy. It is precisely the dissatisfaction with the "black box" approach that has led in recent years to attempts to explicate the processes of decision making and the formulation of policy on the basis of structural and historical analysis that has shed more light upon, and better elaborates, the empirical evidence in this domain.

There is a second aspect of this dissatisfaction that must be clarified. Various investigators (e.g., Offe, 1972b: 479–88; Oszlak and O'Donnell, 1976; Grindle, 1977; Weiler, 1983; Pescador and Torres, 1985) have confronted the idea that the public sector, government, or state always acts within the logic of the resolution of problems—a "problem-solving approach." Taking these as points of departure, I will discuss the object of investigation in adult education.

RESEARCH OBJECT IN ADULT EDUCATION POLICIES

Two dimensions define the object of study in adult education policies. On the one hand, we can include under the rubric "adult education policies" those in which the institutional origin of decision making, financing of the resulting programs, and the level of institutional formalization of the services and/or programs is linked to the state.

This analytical convention is still not sufficient for outlining this field of "state" operation. It is necessary to differentiate here the policies of adult education that are linked with the ministries of public education in their administrative authority from those carried out by other governmental agencies linked to social welfare policies but not directly to education (e.g., ministries of health, agriculture, etc.).

For all practical purposes, I would like to incorporate into the definition of "institutions for public (adult) education" any autarkic and decentralized parastate organization, oriented to the development of adult education as a priority activity, that could be functionally delegated to some subsecretary or agency of a ministry of education; it also would devote an important amount of its resources to this task (e.g., MOBRAL in Brazil until its dissolution in 1983 and the National Institute of Adult Education in Mexico).

A second research dimension is concerned with alternative policies of adult education that have their origins in and are initiated, administered, financed, and evaluated by institutions in civil society. Reference here is to the myriad "popular" education projects (Morales Jeldes, 1986) carried out in this region by churches or evangelical groups, by political parties or trade unions, or by groups of individuals linked to distinct social movements (environmental and ecological defense, human rights, women's rights, and ethnic group defense).

Two factors impede "closing" this descriptive framework. On the one hand, given the growing complexity of Latin American civil society, there are endless exchanges between administrative units whose roots are clearly based in civil society and administrative units of political society; this is particularly relevant with respect to the financing of educational activities developed by "private" institutions with public funds. Here there is a limit to what can be established on the basis of juridical arguments about the private/public distinction. Perhaps there remains no alternative, in such cases, to an ad hoc analysis attempting to show the degree of control the political society has over civil society in the context of financing, and reclassifying the institution in question.

On the other hand, there is a very important camp, which has been brought to attention by Thomas La Belle, linked with the presence of the international system in adult education. In this camp are the institutions linked to the ostensibly liberal philanthropy of the countries of the advanced industrial world. Nevertheless, on occasions, the United States and the practices of its best representative in this area, the U.S. Agency for International Development, appear to give evidence that this supposed philanthropy is linked with the interests of U.S. national security and interventionism in Latin America (Arnove, 1980).

In addition, there is a large amount of financial support by foundations and governments with fewer interests in the region (e.g., Nordic foundations and Canada) or institutions like UNESCO and the World Council on Adult Education, which have contributed to making even more complex the range of the linkages between civil and political society in Latin America nonformal education. The intervention of these aid agencies and projects supported by international funds implies the delimitation of a new arena, international nonformal education policy, which modifies the spectrum of forces interacting in the region.

To summarize, the first analytical convention consists in identifying the aspect of nonformal education that emerges from political society, that which emerges from civil society, and—crossing both camps—that emerging from the international system. To delimit the origin of financing, the juridical–administrative dependence of the institution or agency, the level of institutional formalization of the programs, and perhaps—particularly for state adult education—its massive and national, or restricted and regional, character could be very fruitful in research on the formation of educational policy.

The limitation of this "state–institutional" approach is obvious: left outside the object of analysis are the nonformal education policies initiated in civil society, with or without intervention by the international system. Practically speaking, it is perhaps more appropriate to gain experience in the analysis of state policies in order to attempt to systematize and analyze the policies of nonstate institutions at a later time. It is also appropriate to note the value of undertaking the analysis of public policy in adult education from the perspective of comparative education. We will return to this point.

THE SCOPE OF INVESTIGATION

The challenge is to understand the process of forming adult education policy in Latin America and the Caribbean on the basis of identifying the reasons for, the actors involved in, and the mechanisms of decision making; the rationality of educational planning; and the mechanisms, actors, dynamics, and institutions of implementation and evaluation of policy.

As a consequence, the problem of research consists of knowing why a decision in adult education is made; how is it articulated, planned, and carried out; the most relevant actors in the formulation and operationalization of policy—and perhaps we should add the "repercussions of the policy"; and the fundamental systemic processes from the origins to the implementation of policy.

To be able to design a general model for the analysis of public policy in adult education, it would perhaps be appropriate to begin with the following premise: Every analysis of public policy requires historical-structural discussion and understanding of the "nature" of the state and political regime in question. This discussion of the state as a problem-solving agent shows that the liberal-pluralist conception of the state is not easy to sustain, especially in the context of dependent Latin American capitalism (Cardoso, 1974; O'Donnell, 1978a; Boron, 1981; Carnoy, 1984).

A more precise and useful characterization for our purposes must be based on a definition of the state. In purely indicative terms, the state is "the totality of the political authority in a given society (governmental or otherwise) regardless of the level—national, subnational or local —at which it may operate" (Weiler, 1983: 259). Political authority implies the capacity to impose a political voluntarism—elaborated on the basis of perceptions of the fundamental determinants for the continuation of the accumulation of capital and the imperatives of the political legitimation of the nation-state—by means of a system of decisions in a social formation that is highly heterogeneous and characterized by very contradictory interests. In analytical terms, therefore, the state can be considered as a pact of domination and as a self-regulated administrative system that constitutes itself in an arena of struggle—and at the same time is an important actor—in the confrontation between alternative political projects (C. Torres, 1984a: 279–84; 1988b).

As for a "pact of domination," Cardoso has noted that the state represents the basic pact of domination that exists between social classes or fractions of the dominant class and the norms that guarantee its domination over the subordinate strata (Cardoso 1979: 38). Nicos Poulantzas argues that a specific function of the state is to serve as a factor of cohesion between the different levels of a social formation. Nevertheless, in constituting itself as this factor of cohesion, the state is also the structure or instance where the contradictions between these distinct levels are condensed (Poulantzas, 1969). As a factor of cohesion, the capitalist state, as such and as reflected in public policy, utilizes long-term planning (and emergency or conjunctural policies in moments of crisis) for synthesizing the economic objectives and social reproduction of capitalism, despite the short-term imperatives and sectoral disputes of individual capitalists (Skocpol, 1982: 7–28; Altvater, 1973; Jessop, 1982; O'Connor, 1981).

This relative autonomy of the state and the contradictions emerging in it bring forth state interventionism, as a "pact of domination"; these are decisive characteristics for the regulation of the economic, political, social, symbolic, and cultural life of society. In this manner, in liberal-democratic capitalism the state at the same time constitutes an arena of struggle and a democratic space for the confrontation of ideologies, beliefs, and social movements. Still, as a materialization and condensation of class relations (Poulantzas, 1978), the state is not a monolithic bloc but a terrain of struggle and confrontation. The formation of public policy will necessarily reflect the conflicts, agreements, and negotiations of this theater of operations, as is confirmed by various analyses of the formation of educational policy (Carnoy and Levin, 1985: 26–51; Pescador and Torres, 1985: 3–6, 66–78).

It can be argued, following Claus Offe, that the state, as a "self-regulating administrative system," is organizationally a system of selective and self-regulating rules, a process of continuous discrimination generated by the state structure. In this way, the state creates the institutional apparatus and bureaucratic organizations—often defined as the institutions of the public sector—and the norms and formal and informal codes that constitute and represent the public spheres of social life.

Without pretending to outline the whole of such a complex conceptual framework as that of Offe, it is useful to indicate descriptively and generally that there would be (1) patterns of selectivity of state action that, following Offe, can be divided into patterns of exclusion, maintenance, dependence, and legitimation; (2) modes of state intervention (where distributive and productive modes can be distinguished) that depend on the appropriation and modification of the use of resources; (3) means of state intervention, which as a general rule can be grouped in three main types (fiscal, administrative rationality, and mass loyalty); (4) distinct methods of state intervention, including state regulation—which can encompass the repressive intervention of the state, but Offe has not sufficiently stressed this, and limits himself to indicating those regulative and legal aspects of state action—infrastructural investment, and participation (Offe, 1972, 1975b; C. Torres, 1984a: 21–70).

Following this analysis, two sources of the determination of public policy emerge: determinations and contradictions resulting from the structure of the state apparatus and class biases in its administrative-organizational forms, and determinations and contradictions originating in the state as a condensation of political power. To understand the formulation of educational policy, it is crucial to consider (a) the changing character of class alliance that underlies the constitution of a specific political regime and/or governmental administration—this alliance can be characterized basically by the predominant modality of recruitment or access to the highest positions and roles within the state and the basic process of political representation (O'Donnell, 1978a, 1982; C. Torres, 1988b); (b) the historical and administrative characteristics of the state apparatus (Clegg, 1979; Oszlak, 1981; C. Torres, 1984b); and (c) the socioeconomic and political characteristics of the educational clientele (La Belle, 1986: 89), as well as the role of education in its modes of social survival.

THE COMPARATIVE ANALYSIS OF EDUCATIONAL POLICY: THEORIES AND AGENDAS

At times elucidating the basic theories in comparative nonformal education may contribute to situating with greater clarity the research agenda one hopes to initiate. In comparative politics, texts like those of Chilcote (1981) or Carnoy (1984) allow ordering—though not without analytical costs—a very fertile and continually expanding field of analysis.

With the objective of bringing experiences stemming from comparative politics or political sociology to the question of education, the following will succinctly present four possible agendas of comparative research that can be used to illustrate how to establish a theoretical demarcation: the agenda centered on the political culture of the social actor; the agenda centered on the link between inputs and systemic outputs; the agenda centered on the legitimation of the sociofunctional system and emergent bureaucratic dynamics; and the agenda centered on the production of educational policy as a result of class conflict and social movements.

Agenda Centered on the Political Culture of the Social Actor

At the heart of structural functional analysis lies a fundamental conviction: the social actor continuously organizes his or her actions and conduct—whether covertly or manifestly—by means of basis patterns of reference. This discriminating activity implies continuously taking positions with respect to attitudinal components (e.g., the Parsonian tension between evaluative affectivity and neutrality or that between specific and diffuse relations), modes of categorization of social objects (e.g., universalism versus particularism), judgments about the nature of social action (whether based on the ascriptive characteristics of a social object relation or on a complex individual enactment of a role-status complex), and the meaning and origin of the action of a subject (e.g., in the tension between self-oriented action versus action oriented toward and centered in the community).

For the study of educational policy, one of the most stimulating and widely used aspects of this approach is the study of the political culture of the agents who participate in decision making. Analyzing this perspective elsewhere, we have noted that "the concept of political culture has been used to identify the complex of ideological norms, values and presuppositions, as well as theories and scientific instruments, obtained by any agent through a systematic or nonsystematic process of political socialization" (Pescador and Torres, 1985: 112).

In the words of one of the best-known pioneers of the concept, "the term political culture thus refers to the specifically political orientation—attitudes toward the political system and its various parts, and attitudes toward the role of the self in the system. . . . It is a set of orientations towards a special set of social objects and processes" (Almond and Verba, 1965: 13). The application of the concept to the study of educational processes has a certain history. For example, Parsons and Platt, using a descriptive approach, utilize political culture notions especially to study the implications of the student political movements at Harvard University during the Vietnam crisis, and to offer prescriptions for a modification of postsecondary education in this period (Parsons and Platt, 1973).

An approach like that of political culture is the basis of a much more sophisticated analysis, such as that presented by Pierre Bourdieu with his postulation of notions of "cultural capital" and social reproduction. From this perspective, the confrontation of differentiated forms of cultural capital in the educational arena—one subordinate, the other dominant—would explain the failure and social differentiation—mediated by the symbolic violence characteristic of educational settings—of the majority of the children and youth from the subordinate sectors. Similarly, this explains the success and social mobility of those who come from families with the appropriate cultural capital (heredity and environment) and the formal codes, and those who, lacking this, produce a sociocultural change in their aspirations, expectations, and codes in order to survive in the educational system.

For example, in the study of the formation of administrative elites in Mexico, Roderic Ai Camp notes, given the highly personalized character of decision making, requires an effort to develop a sophisticated model that will predict policy outcomes by accounting for the factors or characteristics most evident in the political culture of the Mexican political elite. Among these, Camp notes the following: the sense of "confidence" between politicians who create a lobby (*camarilla*), a politics centered on the personalization of decisions, the presence of "bureaucratic families," and the practice of co-optation. After analyzing the configuration of these elements, Camp concludes that they are much more important than the ideological orientation of a given functionary, and illustrates how personal loyalty is an essential characteristic of the process of the recruitment of leaders and decision making in Mexico (Camp, 1980).

In nonformal education, an agenda or research centered on systems of significations, cultural capital, and the ideology and expectations of the actors intervening in the decision-making process and the operation of services would prove fruitful. This is particularly the case when at least three fundamental types of systemic actors are differentiated, following Claus Offe: those who intervene in the making of decisions ("decision-makers" and "policy brokers"), those who operationally implement such decisions ("policy implementers"), and the educational clients who constitute, at least nominally, the fundamental factor of educational administration ("policy-takers").

This type of agenda does not necessarily has to rest on structural functionalist assumptions. The selection of individuals as the unit of observation and analysis, and the adoption of survey methods or the elaboration of indices, as in the case of the interesting work by Geert Hofstede (1980), perhaps show affinities with a positivist and functionalist logic of analysis.

Agendas Centered on Linkages Between Inputs and Outputs

These approaches reflect the typical preoccupation of economists seeking to measure and evaluate educational systems using techniques applicable to production functions, and thus producing recommendations for educational policy (Hanushek, 1986: 1141–77). At the most general level, Therborn (1980: 37–48) outlines some of the principal dimensions of this approach to research:

1. Input mechanisms: (a) the principles that regulate the tasks to be developed by the state, (b) criteria for the recruitment of state personnel, (c) mechanisms that assure the financial income of the state.

2. Processes of transformation: (a) modes of decision making and the management of tasks, (b) heads of organizations and the relations between those positions, (c) modes of assigning and utilizing material resources.

3. Output mechanisms: (a) decision makers and practices of the state, toward other states and toward the society of which they are part; (b) organizers of relations between the personnel of the state, with the personnel of other states, and with other members of the society; (c) modes of distributing the material resources of the state.

This input-output process can be used sociologically by considering the state institutions of adult education as a subsystem in the context of educational policy, and thus studying the linkages with other state agencies and with clienteles, the different interbureaucratic spaces, and the interactions (functional and budgetary hierarchies) between bureaucratic divisions, showing their processes of negotiation and confrontation. Similarly, such a model allows us to study the linkages between adult education and the overall flow of state resources into education and other social welfare policies.

Levin (1980), for example, utilizes this input–output approach to provide an essentially descriptive analysis of educational reform and planning in the government domain of the United States. The model is illustrated in Figure 7.1.

Figure 7.1
A Model for Policy-Planning Analysis

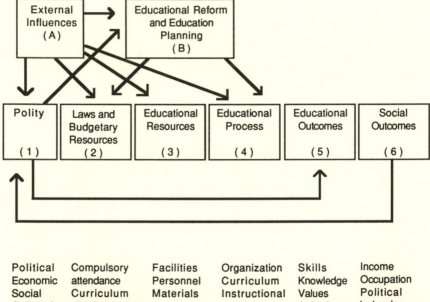

Political	Compulsory	Facilities	Organization	Skills	Income
Economic	attendance	Personnel	Curriculum	Knowledge	Occupation
Social	Curriculum	Materials	Instructional	Values	Political
Cultural	requirements		methods	Attitudes	behavior
Religious	Funding			Grades	Child-Rearing
Historical				Certificates	behavior
					Cultural
					attributes
					Literacy
					Alienation
					Competition

Source: Henry Levin (1980, p. 16). Reprinted with permission from UNESCO.

Social and economic factors influence educational transformations in a decisive manner—reforms never result exclusively from endogenous processes of the educational system. Nevertheless, once carried out, educational reforms may alter the composition and dynamics of society. There also are influences "external" to the political arena where actors carry out educational reforms (national, regional, local) that can become a new input into the process of educational reform in a subsequent phase. Every process of educational reform implies cognitive outcomes at the general level of social actors and social outcomes dispersed throughout society, and therefore is difficult to measure. Finally, every educational reform presupposes a specific legal framework (which constrains actions and the appropriation of resources); a complex of human, material, and financial resources; a context; a process; and specific educational resources (e.g., at the curricular level).

Decision making will still be the result of the complex interaction of these variables and institutional processes, but no decision is exclusively contingent upon the educational system; rather, it is always remodeled in the context of the interaction of these variables, and however significant a governmental initiative may be (as a global educational reform), it acquires its specificity only in the interaction of inputs, processes, and outputs.

Some criticisms of this input–output notion as a research strategy have been advanced. As a general rule, it is a question of an ex post facto reconstruction of a decision-making process, and even if at the descriptive level this may be relatively complete, at the analytical level it runs the risk of formalizing "rationalities" operating in decision making that do not necessarily correspond to the dynamics of confrontation and negotiation, which, as Levin has noted, are crucial to any process of educational transformation (Carnoy and Levin, 1985).

On the other hand, in applying this type of "external"/"internal" analysis to an educational system, it is difficult to control the collinearity of the intervening variables; as a consequence, one may lose sight of the specific weight of the basic factors that underlie decision making in educational systems. The "additive" character of the model does not appear to be fully justified, and inevitably the dynamics of change may jump out of the flow chart, requiring a historical interpretation to become comprehensible. Finally, an analytical model like this does not at first sight offer a hierarchical ordering of the units (and/or social actors) that intervene in distinct processes on the basis of the relative weight of the intervention (which may be modified by the type of state, political regime, sociohistorical circumstances, characteristics of the bureaucracy, etc.).

Agendas Centered on the Legitimacy of the Social System and Emergent Bureaucratic Dynamics

Claus Offe has developed a very sophisticated model for studying late capitalism and the processes of public policy formation. Regrettably, on only one occasion, in collaboration with Gero Lenhardt, has he systematically studied a

process linked to educational policy (Offe, 1985: 88–118) or given some attention to understanding the rationality of educational reforms (Offe, 1975b). The
focus of his analysis is the contemporary advanced capitalist state. He is concerned neither with interpersonal links between governmental and social elites
nor with the study of the processes of governmental decision making per se.

One of Offe's analytical premises is that the class character of the (capitalist)
state does not reside in the social origins of those who make decisions, or of the
state elite, bureaucracy, or dominant class. On the contrary, this class character
of the state (which is projected subsequently in the formulation of public policy)
resides in the structure of the state apparatus and political institutions; this
structure will select the type of policies permissible, according to the activating
rules of the social system.

This institutional "selectivity" of the state apparatuses and political institutions gives public policy an internal rather than an external "determination" in
the production of policy. That is, there is no need to look for the key to state behavior in the presence of a given elite commanding it or in the influence of a
pressure group or segment of the dominant class "external" to the state; rather,
it is necessary to explore the state itself.

Offe attempts to establish "laws of public policy formation in the capitalist
state." Generally speaking, state domination is secured by (a) extracting a
general class interest from the multiple and divided fractions of capital in society, and (b) by opposing or suppressing any anticapitalist interest (Offe,
1975b: 125–44). On the basis of these fundamental principles, Offe distinguishes the four basic patterns of state action: exclusion, maintenance, dependency, and legitimacy.

The pattern of exclusion implies that the state does not have complete authority for ordering and controlling economic production. The state is relatively divorced from the accumulation of capital, to the extent that production
and accumulation are inseparable, and the production of goods is essentially
private. The pattern of maintenance implies that though the state does not
have the authority to control production, it has the mandate to create and sustain the conditions necessary for the accumulation of capital and for avoiding,
regulating, or suppressing social "threats." These "threats" can arise from
these same imperatives of accumulation (e.g., at the level of interindustry ri-
valry), from noncapitalist sources (e.g., demands of the working class), or from
criminal or "deviant" behavior (e.g., export of capital as disinvestment). The
pattern of dependency implies that the relations of power and decision making
in the capitalist state depend on the presence and continuity of the process of
capital accumulation (Offe, 1975a: 126). Finally, the pattern of legitimacy implies that the state can function as a capitalist state only by calling on the symbols and sources of support that "obscure" its true source and purpose from
the general population.

This last aspect is fundamental. For Offe there exists an increasingly pro-
nounced discrepancy between work and social forms linked to abstract labor,

which generates exchange value, and work and social forms linked to concrete labor, which produces use value. Only the presence of a system of legitimating beliefs assures a minimal loyalty of the population, giving the system the opportunity to continue to integrate and moderate this legitimation crisis, but not resolve it over time.

As Offe's analytical framework suggests, the contradictions of public policy cannot be attributed only to class "antagonisms," but also must be considered as subproducts of an integral system of control. From this come some of Offe's "fundamental laws of the formation of public policy." First, any mode of state intervention will be linked to a pattern or process (potential or active) of social threats, structural problems that emerge from the capital accumulation process. Consequently, all state public policies seek to reproduce the abstract "systemic" interest of the public sector and the social formation, without representing, necessarily, the interests of a pressure group or specific social segment. Hence it is necessary to distinguish between the form of a public policy and its content. Finally, the adoption of a specific means implies the appropriation of increasingly scarce financial means, given the fiscal crisis of the state. Particularly in the case of social welfare policies, public investment sometimes implies a collision of interests with public policies oriented toward the accumulation of capital.

The state thus remains trapped in a dead-end street: it must produce (increasingly costly) welfare policies that promote and reinforce the legitimacy of the system and the state itself, while simultaneously diverting resources from the general promotion of capital accumulation (from which it obtains fiscal resources and without which the state could not operate); at the same time, without a base of legitimacy, potential or real social threats could culminate in interruption of the process of accumulation itself, putting at risk the existence of the state and social system.

In the context of this state dilemma between accumulation and legitimation, and the difficulty of establishing a balance, given fiscal crises and subsequent austerity policies, there is an aspect that makes the formation of public policy even more difficult: despite not its having power as such, there does exist a state bureaucracy that, by virtue of the mandate of the state, utilizes resources on the basis of a concentric system of interests that may end up departing from the necessities of the model of development.

Therefore, there may be a "law of the development of bureaucracy." The bureaucracy may promote public policies seeking (apparently) to gain legitimacy for the system but still operating with an internal rationale and a dynamic that may derive more from the imperatives of the survival of the bureaucracy and its search for legitimation than from social and systemic demands.

Nevertheless, despite the "expensive" character of the bureaucracy, the state cannot do without it, even though it may seek to reduce its size. The framework of bureaucratic action may constrain state action and its difficulties with the accumulation process. To confront the crisis of legitimation, the state calls upon the state bureaucracy (in the context of Weberian rational and legal domination) by (a) making use of scientific and technical knowledge (expertise), a strategy that in education is expressed most strongly in the ideology of educational planning; (b) the promotion of policies of participation that link all of those social sectors which have difficulty in exchanging goods at the level of the market; and (c) the use, in the last instance, of the ultimate recourse for legitimation in advanced capitalism: compensatory legitimation, which remains in the hands of judges and the judicial system, and may even serve to modify the substance of decision-making processes (Weiler, 1983).

An approach like this may be very useful for studying adult education policy, especially if one accepts the assumption elaborated by Offe that any public policy (e.g., education) shows that texture and general dynamics of state action. Such policies are inserted in the dilemma of accumulation versus legitimation, and operate with laws of "development" similar to those which can be verified in the larger context of public policy, including the activity of the bureaucracy within the range of its specific competence.

The difficulties of such an approach are, however, numerous. In general terms, as mentioned previously, it is not easy to apply an analytical model elaborated for advanced or late capitalism to peripheral capitalism. Nor is it clear that the model of Latin American state domination would be strongly or primarily rational-legal, as the analysis presupposes. One of the characteristics of Latin American bureaucracies and states is the practice of "political clientelism," which substantively modifies the processes of legitimation vis-à-vis systems of electoral representation.

Finally, with respect to adult education, however attractive the notion of compensatory legitimation may be, its heuristic value depends on the magnitude of state operations in adult education and the position the latter occupies in the hierarchy of educational policy generally. To judge its role in legitimation, it would be useful to know the effective impact (nature, magnitude, and duration) an adult education policy may have on educational clienteles.

Agendas Centered on the Production of Educational Policy as a Result of Class Conflict and Social Movements

The most recent work of Carnoy and Levin in the political economy of education (1985) clearly illustrates this agenda. Three aspects are fundamental for this research approach: (1) the advanced capitalist state appears as a terrain of social struggle, and the future of democracy will depend on the effective balance of this struggle; (2) it is impossible to understand the dynamics of transformation of education without simultaneously knowing the dynamics of transformation of the labor process, and how they mutually condition each other in a dialectical relation; and (3) the basic social conflict will be between social movements that defend the liberal capitalist ideology and those which promote the development of radical democracy to the greatest extent possible (Carnoy and Levin, 1985: 76–110; Bowles and Gintis, 1986).

The model of educational change that these authors develop refers explicitly to formal education. The dynamics of transformation in the educational system of the United States are best understood as part of a larger social conflict resulting from the nature of capitalist production with its inequalities of income and social power (Carnoy and Levin, 1985: 24). The authors classify what they term educational reforms (1985: 216–29) and reforms in the labor market (183–97) into four large groups: micro- and macrotechnical changes, micro- and macropolitical changes, and associate these changes with the larger processes of social conflict. This notion of conflict is held to be the fundamental motor for transforming contemporary capitalist societies, and presupposes that a struggle over the appropriation of resources and definitions of social values will be expressed in the state as a privileged arena, taking place in the educational system and schools as state institutions.

The notion of public policy as a product of basic social conflict and the state as a terrain of struggle is the immediate outcome of this agenda of research. Along with this, it suggests studying any changes in the educational models by searching for their counterparts in labor markets. In the third place, many (but not all) of the bureaucratic confrontations in the capitalist state could be contrasted with alternative ideological models and projects of social development linked, ultimately, with models of social organization. The identification of these models and their expression in public policy would be of fundamental importance.

Despite the analytical value of this agenda of research—presented, once again, in a simplified manner—it would probably not be sufficient for the purposes at hand. This type of analysis is very abstract and does not pretend to understand the formulation of educational policy per se; rather, it is concerned with the political economy of education.

This approach is strongly institutional and refers more clearly to processes in the academic system (in La Belle's terms, the formal system) than to processes that may take place in the nonformal system. Finally, the Latin American democracies differ—often drastically—from those in advanced capitalism. The homogeneity of advanced capitalism cannot be compared with the social and economic heterogeneity characteristic of Latin America.

Considering the politics of adult education, this research approach could be useful for various purposes. On the one hand, because it so strongly emphasizes the correspondence between the social organization of work and capitalist education, education also constitutes an expression of and terrain for democratic struggle. Many of the demands for systems of adult education rest on the logic of equality and equity promoted by the capitalist state itself. In this sense, any educational institution could be much more democratic, open to change and innovation, and more subject to the potential control of communities and social movements than other state apparatuses or labor markets. On the other hand, this perspective is useful because it complements the notion of correspondence between the social relations of production and educational social relations with that of contradictions that arise as much from the functioning of the state educational apparatus as from the structure of social power and production.

Finally, because it links the production of public policy with alternative social movements, this approach is particularly important in conjunctures of political crisis. At the same time, the social movements approach is different from focusing on social actors, where it is a question of a specific group making decisions (policymakers, politicians, bureaucracies, their linkages, conflicts, political culture, etc.), thus constituting the overwhelming focus of attention in the study of public policy. However, the understanding of educational policy formation from the larger perspective of political conflict, along with the most significant collective positions that may influence policies, would be of much use for studying Latin American societies, states, and politics.[1]

CONCLUSION

A great number of questions remain. In the first place, can the exposition developed to this point take into account all of the possible agendas of research, or would it have to include others or refine even further those presented here? Reviewing the alternative agendas, to what extent is it feasible to establish a combination of approaches for an integrated study of educational policy, without excessively forcing the epistemological principles demarcating different social theories?

Likewise, if it were feasible to study adult education policies following these approaches, would such a study be done in stages? That is, would it be feasible to begin with an approach based on the social actor and end up by understanding the formation of adult education on the basis of an approach based on conflict and social movements? At another level of analysis, are the questions of research noted above useful for, adequate to, and complete enough for the study of adult education policy?

The panorama is even more complicated if we think that every study of educational policy that claims to move beyond the case study (local, regional, or national), and seeks to reach conclusions that are sufficiently rigorous to be of use in the regional context of Latin America and the Caribbean, must be carried out in a comparative manner. The work of Thomas La Belle (1986), including a historical and structural approach, constitutes a very valuable example here. In these terms many of the most significant studies that adopt a strongly quantitative approach by means of surveys—for example, the classic work of James Coleman et al. (1966, 1982)—however suggestive for knowing the relation between inputs and outputs in education, have been amply criticized, as much for intrinsic problems of measurement as for problems in the data analysis (e.g., Bowles and Levin, 1968; Jencks et al., 1972).

For the reasons noted, the predominant use of quantitative methodologies and inferential statistical analysis for studying adult education policy in Latin

America may not be very fruitful for policy analysis. On the contrary, we need to take very seriously into account the appropriateness of initiating qualitative analysis, drawing upon some of the most suggestive methodological or technical innovations in this field (Miles and Huberman, 1984; Gajardo, 1974: 29–55).

Perhaps it would be useful to understand the principal dimension of the processes of adult educational policy formation in institutions of public education as a complex of spirals, with specific arenas of administrative and political competence that, as much as they are inevitably linked to the more general problematics that confront capitalist states (accumulation versus legitimation), are also differentiated by levels of bureaucratic competence, administrative functionality, technical specialization, organizational schemes and routines, use of and access to resources, and distinct rationalities (bureaucratic, ideological, and political) operating in the design and implementation of systems (C. Torres, 1988b).

The inductive-deductive interaction between these levels could constitute a process of decision making, educational planning, and evaluation, and at the same time allow initiatives in the study of policy impacts (social, political, cognitive, etc.). The inductive-deductive diagram presented in Figure 7.2 is based on my previous theoretical work (C. Torres, 1984a, 1989a) and attempts to show the main dimensions of this research process.

At the most abstract level, it can be argued that public policy formation cannot be understood without a consistent theory of the capitalist state and politics. Expanding capital accumulation and increasing the legitimation of the entire mode of production seem to be the principal roles of the capitalist state; a role that is in perpetual tension.

I have argued elsewhere (C. Torres, 1989a) that the capitalist state follows basic production rules of public policy. In my framework of analysis, the capitalist state is defined as an arena, a product, and a determinant of class, gender, racial, ethnic, and social conflict. However, I must point out that at the most abstract level, the main determinants of public policy formation are not the pursuit of any particular interest but an abstract systemic interest—hence the importance of an institutionalized set of selectivity rules that can alter the intensity, degree, level, and character of class and social struggles. These selectivity rules are built into the very same structure of the state (and are expressed in nonformal education policies) and, to a certain extent, constrain human agency. As such, modes and methods of state intervention and guiding patterns of state activity are affected by a perpetual tension in state policies between protecting, guiding, and expanding capital accumulation and, at the same time, increasing and reinforcing the political and symbolic legitimation as well as the role of liberal democracy in capitalist social formations (Offe, 1984; Offe, 1985: 1–10, 259–317; Carnoy, 1984; Welton, 1987; C. Torres, 1984a, 1989a, 1989b).

In looking at determinants of educational policy formation, I have distinguished between long-term, organic determinants à la Gramsci or à la Braudel,

Figure 7.2
Adult Education as Public Policy: An Interconnected Set of Circles
with a Deductive-Inductive Dynamic

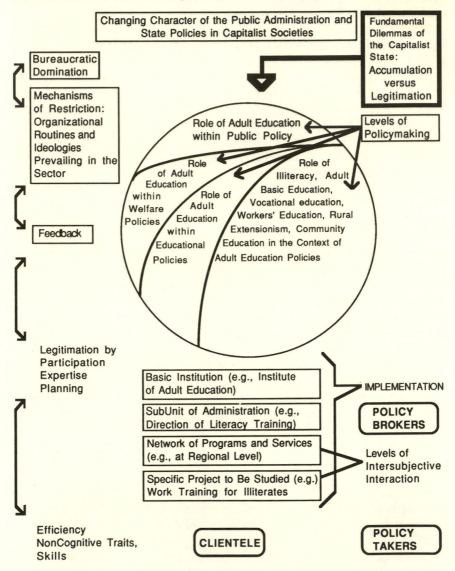

and short-term, conjunctural determinants. Similarly, at the highest level of generalization, I have emphasized that public policy in education is mainly a response to or anticipation of social threats (a pattern that cannot, however, be taken mechanically); that regulation, infrastructure investment, and mass participation are methods of state intervention addressing problems of economic growth and political stability; that form and content of policymaking are not two distinct dimensions when the state is considered as something else than a problem-solving agent; that functional interaction and interdependency of diverse educational agencies can be differentiated according to the form of the state and the type of political regime; and that social control is built into the selectivity rules of state operation. Adult education policy formation as part of the state's public policies cannot escape these dynamics of state operation.

A strategy of research on the politics of nonformal education in Latin America should begin with (1) an analysis of the state and adult education policies designed by public educational institutions in order to initiate (2) an analysis of nonformal education policies of nongovernmental organizations and social movements (especially institutions and groups linked to the church, trade unions, and political parties in Latin America). The study of nongovernment organizations' policies permits one to understand governmental policies. The institutions of civil society often advance reactive educational projects, attempting to establish alternative programs to state policies—and by implication they may constitute a critique of the state's policy rationale. The third state of a research strategy on the politics of nonformal education should include an analysis of international adult education and the explicit agendas as well as hidden curriculum of aid agencies and/or international institutions giving educational financing, providing technical expertise, and promoting educational innovations. A comparative analysis of these levels or fields of nonformal educational policy formation based on an explicit theory of the state is a prerequisite to understanding the relationships between public policies and private initiatives in Latin America.

It is crucial to define clearly the theoretical-methodological agenda that may support comparative research in nonformal education, thus revealing in greater detail its possibilities and limitations. Regrettably, experience shows that much of the research in adult education lacks a solid theoretical-methodological foundation. As a consequence, these studies are often merely descriptive and mixed with normative prescriptions and ideological convictions, including flippant evaluations and political affirmations about the value (or lack of value) of programs and services that, by and large, are directed to the poorest of the poor in Latin American societies.

In capitalist Latin America, in the absence of a substantial transformation of the political processes of representation and participation, and of the social relations of production, or without integrating popular social movements into the political process, the subordinate social sectors will remain on the margins of political power. They will be without the capacity to participate in the determination of their own collective welfare, let alone their nonformal education.

NOTE

1. A culturalist elaboration on social movements is presented in Jelin's article (1987). In Argentina, Jelin identifies the following as contemporary social movements: human rights movement, youths' rock-and-roll ('rock nacional') movement, the neighboring movements in marginal barrios ("sociedades de fomento"), women movement, and new trade-union movement. Her interpretation opposes Brandão's perspective (referred to in footnote 6, chapter 4) inasmuch as those social movements: "should not be interpreted in political terms (if for politics we understand a struggle for power), but as practices centered on the construction of collective identities, and the recognition of spaces of social relations" (Jelin, 1987: 30, our translation). This interpretation is culturalist or societal, following the European analysis of Alberto Melucci and Alan Touraine, and incorporates the dimension of everyday life as an area of reflection and investigation in which the structures and mechanisms of political and social life are condensed and manifested (Jelin, 1987: 30–31). Indeed, a bridge between an analysis centered on relations of production and on moral concerns (or social relations) should be found, and a discussion on the relationships between popular movements and social movements will be very useful in characterizing the relationships between adult education and social and political movements in the new, fragile democracies of the Southern Cone.

8

THE POLITICS OF NONFORMAL
EDUCATION IN LATIN AMERICA:
SUMMARY AND CONCLUSIONS

This book is more a research program than a research report. The strategy adopted is to give each chapter a life of its own instead of its being tied to the overall logical sequence and structure of the book. In many respects, this strategy reflects the way this book has been written: as a series of progressive reports of my ongoing research agenda, which is far from being completed. However, this strategy also will account, on occasions, for some recapitulation of concepts while organizing a theoretical or historical background for each of the chapters. If there is any slight repetition, the gains, I think, outnumber the losses. Overall, there is a coherent argument informing the different chapters while each individual chapter, or a selection thereof, can be used for different purposes in policy planning, research, and teaching. A comprehensive analysis and application of the research model outlined here, but with a lesser degree of generalization allowing for empirical investigation, can be found in Morales-Gómez and Torres (1990).

The theoretical perspective in understanding the politics of nonformal education is based on a political sociology informed by political economy analyses. The relationship between state theory and adult education policies has a prominent role in the theoretical framework of this study. Basically, it is argued that without a consistent theory of the state and politics, it will be impossible to understand the politics of nonformal education and nonformal education as politics in Latin America, and in the industrialized world as well (Block, 1987: 3–35). In this regard, Martin Carnoy's preface set the stage for a discussion of adult education and social policy, with a focus on the state.

If there is any merit in this book, it is the attempt to single out the process of policy formation in adult education as a specific field for educational research and participatory policy planning. In so doing, many theoretical aspects are emphasized in Chapter 1, discussing paradigms of nonformal education. With-out attempting to add another taxonomy to the prevailing ones, Chapter 1 calls attention to a main distinction: programs and policies inspired by incrementalist perspectives of policymaking, and those inspired by structuralist criticisms. There is no claim, however, to reduce all increment-alist perspectives to the logic of functionalism or technocratic approaches. Incrementalism may be treated as a strategy (and logic) of policymaking that is functional to the needs of capitalism and the prevailing political regime, by and large holds no critical assumptions, and utilizes the mainstream planning and research techniques. Alternatively, it could be analyzed as a strategy that fol-lows a logic of the possible in the context of the capitalist states. This "logic of possibility" may be informed by radical politics, but it may have accepted, on the one hand, the rules of the game prevailing within the state structures and, on the other hand, the all-embracing notion that occupying positions in politics is the key element in building a progressive outlook in public policy. Hence, politics becomes the science and art of the possible instead of the science and art of the probable. Debates on what alternative strategy of development is possible in education have been under way in Latin America for quite some time, including debates on nonformal education (CEE, 1982: 363–83; C. Torres, 1982d; Muñoz Izquierdo, 1982b, 1982c). In many respects, these de-bates mirror the structuralist-instrumentalist debates in radical political sci-ence during the 1960s (C. Torres, 1984a: 24). Ultimately, the structuralist-instrumentalist debate has not been a fruitful one, leaving a deadlock scenario. However, in revising state theory and looking at business dominance theories, Fred Block duly cautions us—and this could be applicable to the analysis of state-sponsored nonformal education policies, that:

> It appears that even when the business community is not able to influence the state in the traditional ways, policy outcomes tend to be favorable to business con-cerns. This suggests that there are "structural" factors that operate at a different level from the exercise of personal influence. These "structural" factors are still the consequence of behavior of real human beings, but it is not necessarily the kind of purposive, instrumental action that business dominance theorists empha-size. (Block, 1987: 8–9)

In light of Block's comments, the distinction proposed in Chapter 1 between rationalities and practices in adult education seems to be useful. This distinction points out that normative ideologies, practical measures (or working philoso-phies, as described in Apps, 1973), and theoretical rationales blend together and the policy realm becomes opaque. Therefore, the analysis of policy, practices, and programs needs not only research but also metatheories and theories.[1] It is the reason why in a field such as nonformal education, which is undertheorized, many have succumbed to the seduction of creating typologies that, in the last analysis, replace real analysis of concrete situations. Hence, instead of using a typology as a heuristic device in exploring the research object, some studies have looked for evidence to support the existence of the typology. In contrast, the typology suggested in this book is merely a heuristic device. The notions of modernization–human capital theory, pedagogy of the oppressed–popular education, pragmatic idealism, and social engineering–corporatism approaches are offered simply as a way to classify theoretical rationales in the field. However, since the state is an arena of struggle, many of them may be present simultaneously, in a contradictory array, in public policymaking. Finally, it is emphasized in Chapter 1 that there is a contradiction between adult education as a state practice and popular education as a practice that emerges from institutions of the civil society. This contradiction is further reflected in the alternative strategies for literacy training and adult education.

In Chapter 2, the capitalist state in Latin America is analyzed. Two aspects are emphasized. First is the need to come back to the analyses of Gramsci in order to understand adult education as a field of practice. Moreover, some forms of popular education clearly can be understood in relationship to the Gramscian notions of hegemony and war of position. Second, since the basic goal of this chapter is not to produce a comprehensive account of theory of the state but to single out the main roles and functions of the state in Latin America, the dual character of the capitalist state is stressed: a state that is at the same time a pact of domination and a self-regulated administrative system, a state that must contribute to the reproduction of the capitalist relations of production but at the same time must satisfy, within limits, the democratic aspirations of its citizens. This dual character has enormous implications for educational policy formation and nonformal education.

Chapter 3 offers a political economy approach to adult education . The relationships among social structure, policy-planning ideologies, and educational expansion, and the role that adult education has played in Latin America are briefly analyzed. Two basic lessons are learned. First, as Machiavelli pointed out long ago, in politics, the weaker the clientele, the lesser the resources in a society marked by competing political forces in permanent conflict (Rogowsky and Wasserspring, 1971). Adult education policies are no exception to this rule. Second, the dilemmas of the capitalist state in promoting capital accumulation while attempting to sustain the legitimation of the entire mode of production are introduced in producing nonformal education policies, particularly in regard to the supposed economic returns of adult education and labor force training.

Chapters 4 and 5 discuss adult education in the context of a fairly successful experience of capitalist dependent development (Mexico) and in the context of transitional, socialist societies (Cuba, Nicaragua, and Grenada). Perhaps the unifying theme in the comparison, besides the importance of the state's policies, is the need to explore in more detail how adult education as social policy is formed in dependent states, and what lessons can be learned from radical experiences.

Chapters 6 and 7 identify the object of research in nonformal education, and the main lines of demarcation of theories and agendas. Four main agendas are presented, with some of their analytical strengths and limitations. Chapter 7 concludes by emphasizing the need to carve out the study of the politics of non-formal education (and practices, programming, curriculum), using a theory of the state and politics, a historical-structural approach, and more qualitative than quantitative research methodologies.

This summary of the book, as a research program, brings us, in closing, to several main concerns for future research. First, the role of the state in policy-making needs to be revisited in terms of the challenge of scale, including the challenge of micro versus macro experiences; second, the notion of legitimation of educational policy needs to address the challenge of change in models of political domination; third, the amorphousness of the field of adult education needs to be confronted by the challenge of emancipatory and critical theories.

Nonformal education in Latin America and elsewhere is very rich in micro experiences of educational innovation at the level of communities where, due to the peculiar historical and structural conditions of their production or emergence, and the quality, amount, and diversity of resources used (and whose impressive enthusiasm and commitment of their promoter agents is not a minor asset), the experiences usually are such that they cannot be im-plemented at the national level. Similarly, the challenge of scale applies be-tween small and big nation-states (Bacchus and Brock, 1987). It is obviously easier to develop a policy of popular education in the context of a small state, such as Nicaragua or Grenada, than to attempt the same type of policy, the political conditions being the same, in a comparable demographic municipal-ity, say Coyoacán in Mexico City.

A main hypothesis explored in this book is that adult education policies in Latin America have been promoted more as part of a package of legitimation policies of a dependent state (in Carnoy's terminology, a "conditioned State"; see Carnoy and Samoff, 1989) than as part of policies attempting to commodify and/or recommodify the labor force. This hypothesis needs to be addressed, considering the type of state and political regime in turn: Is compensatory legiti-mation a possible rationale and strategy pursued in both capitalist and socialist experiments? To approach this question, a metatheoretical discussion of the re-lationships between hegemony (a concept clearly located within the Marxist framework) and legitimation (a concept more clearly located within the Weberian framework) needs to be undertaken. Similarly, at the level of theory, the relationships between the theory of compensatory legitimation as formu-lated, for instance, by Weiler (1983) needs to be confronted with the theory of monopoly capitalism and the structural dilemma for capitalist states as ex-pressed in O'Connor's work (1973) or the theory of disorganized capitalism as analyzed in Offe's work (1974, 1985). In short, is compensatory legitimation re-lated to, or a necessary outcome of, the dilemma that every capitalist state faces between accumulation and legitimation practices?

Nonformal education has to confront the challenge of theory (of any kind, I must say at the outset). Obviously, to say that adult education is undertheorized does not mean that there are not competing theories in adult education. What is meant is that there is a poverty of theory among those so-called adult education theories which tend to compete for mainstream recognition; that the threshold between theories and ideologies is not only very thin but, in this field, sometimes nonexistent; and that there is a tremendous amount of labeling while very little serious theorizing is done in the field.

On top of that, adult education, in particular, has to face the challenge of emancipatory education and critical theory. It is fair to say, however, that emancipatory theories have been plagued by contradictions, and some of their normative underpinnings have not been completely elaborated (Antonio, 1989). Similarly, the theory of argumentation à la Habermas may not be an easy dish to digest for nonformal educators who are, in principle, practitioners, in many cases working with culturally rich but economically dominated and oppressed populations. Needless to say, these are social sectors that cannot engage in philosophizing about their own existence, but they need to find ways to cope with it—better yet, to overcome those oppressed structures. Obviously, a bridge between critical theory and tragic educational practices has to be found to articulate a more coherent and comprehensible discourse in critical theory for nonformal educators.

The challenge to and criticisms of pragmatism, evolutionary normative arguments, shortsighted pedagogical functionalism, and empirical activism have been brilliantly advanced by Freire and the pedagogues for liberation; and these challenges are well entrenched in the growing tradition of popular education. However, in many respects, the main thrust of the Freirean argument still remains at the level of metatheory. This is perhaps the greatest strength of Freirean analysis, and what has made his message not only long-lasting but also a watershed division in education. With few exceptions, however, his contribution has not always entirely reached the level of educational theory.[2] Morrow is right when he states that Freire can complement Habermas' analysis while Habermas can help Freire to redefine some major themes and arguments (Morrow, 1989).

Morrow has attempted to demonstrate the fundamental convergence of the theories of Freire and Habermas viewed as variants of a critical social psychology. At the ontological level, Morrow identifies the convergence between both authors in that Habermas' critique of the production paradigm, and the reductionism inherent in this paradigm in attempting to generalize the category of labor as a model of all human action, is compatible with Freire's critique of the subject-object paradigm, inasmuch as Freire always subordinates instrumental to symbolic action (Morrow, 1989: 21). At the epistemological level: "Both approaches are grounded in a critique of positivism (whether in its logical empiricist or historical materialist forms); both privilege a hermeneutic conception of knowledge as decisive for the human sciences; both seek to ground the validity of knowledge in processes of rational (dialogical) discourse or ideal speech in which critical reflection becomes the basis of a critique of domination and a vision of transformation" (Morrow, 1989: 22). Finally, at the methodological level, while Habermas sought to move from reconstructive sciences to critical reflection, Freire, due to his practical concerns, grounds the process of critical reflection in everyday existence of individuals.

For Morrow, both Freire and Habermas base their own theories on a developmental anthropology, a theory of domination and a theory of emancipation. They are, then, complementary. Habermas can provide Freire with a better epistemological grounding, with a more comprehensive and systematic treatment of philosophy of science literature and a theory of knowledge interest. Similarly, the theory of communicative action and the normative grounding of Habermas can improve the limitations of Freire's theory of dialogical cultural action. Freire, on the other hand, with his theory of dialogue as cultural action can anticipate, with "here and how situations of transformation" the ideal speech situation in Habermas—which is at the same time an epistemological concept and an utopian construct for understanding the preconditions for unconstrained communication (Morrow, 1989: 44). Also Freirean thinking can prevent the problem of Eurocentric bias in critical theory and its almost exclusive preoccupation with issues of advanced capitalism. Similarly, Freire's emphasis on the utopian dimension of praxis theory can transform Habermas's ethical formalism. Finally, I shall add to Morrow's formulation that Freire's more Gramscian underpinings could improve Habermas' vision of politics as social transformation. In this regard the pedagogy of the oppressed, as a concrete response to a psychology of the oppression, is one of the few approaches that can combine successfully a theory of domination and social change (a theory of hegemony) with a practical human domain such as literacy training as cultural politics in the current situation of Latin America.

There is a second theme in which emancipatory theory has yet to produce a breakthrough. The same is true for the practical importance of the "Freire's method" (the psychosocial method) for literacy training.[3] Emancipatory education still has to move from a "discourse of criticism" to a "discourse of possibilities," to paraphrase H. Giroux. In emancipatory education, this transition has to be at the level of theory, and not just at the level of metatheory, and should be informed by concrete empirical and historical research.

In this regard a solid approach is provided by critical transformation theory as developed by Jack Mezirow (1979, 1981, 1985). He attempts to develop a comprehensive theory of adult education and learning by differentiating the primary domains of learning following Habermas, and linking to a foundational triad of functions for adult education (e.g., work and effective control, the practical domain and communicative action, and emancipatory action, the knowledge of self-reflection), each with its own goals, designs and methods of research and program evaluation. By drawing from Freire's emancipatory theory, Mezirow identifies the notion of perspective transformation: "the process central to the third learning domain, involves other educational approaches. Here the emphasis is on helping the learner identify real problems involving reified power relationships rooted in institutionalized ideologies which one has internalized in one's psychological history. Learners must consequently be led to an understanding of the reasons imbedded in these internalized cultural myths and concomitant feelings which account for their felt needs and wants as well as the way they see themselves and their relations" (Mezirow, 1979: 28).

Indeed, the last—and a crucial—aspect of a theoretical program in emancipatory education and critical theory is to refine the linkages and metatheoretical and theoretical bridges between this tradition and postpluralist theories of the state.

These challenges cannot wait too long to be addressed, particularly at the level of planning. Morales-Gómez is right when he affirms that "efforts to plan education have been framed in a technocratic rationale of neo-classical economic efficiency . . . and a naive rhetoric about reaching and benefiting the poor, without taking into account the inherent ideological contradictions that this implies" (1989: 198). Indeed, the above challenges are an even more pressing demand in the context of Latin American societies that are experiencing, in the words of Norberto González, executive secretary of the Economic Commission of Latin America:

> The most severe and prolonged crisis of the last fifty years, which has forced us to undertake a thorough reassessment of many of our long-standing assumptions concerning development. This reassessment covers both long-term development strategies and short-term economic policies on the one hand, and the role of economic agents and the manner in which they operate, on the other. (in Morales-Gómez, 1989: 204 n.16)

The politics of nonformal education in Latin America have to be viewed in the context of these pervasive economic and social crises, but also in the context of the theoretical impasse that seems to prevail in the sociology of development (Vandergeest and Buttel, 1988; Sklair, 1988) and eventually in the sociology of education (Whitty, 1985). A main disadvantage of the situation as it is, is the lack of resources of any kind, even at the level of sociological imagination. The advantage is that at times of crisis, new research programs may emerge. New research programs can produce a new, fresh look at all these conflicting scenarios. It may perhaps be too naive to hope that these new research agendas will be developed from, and be informed with, theoretical rigor, progressive politics, and human compassion.

NOTES

1. In spite of some positivist overtones, I basically agree with Leslie Sklair's argument that "metatheory is a set of assumptions about the constituent parts of the world and about the possibility of knowledge of them" (1988: 697), while theory, which can logically be deducible from a metatheory, "is a set of propositions derived directly or in-

directly from a metatheory not logically incompatible with it" (1988: 698). Finally, empirical research "is the practice of manufacturing explanations and predictions about real objects" (1988: 698). However, I should add, following Habermas, that the pursuit of knowledge in the human sciences can be better understood as guided by three fundamental knowledge-guiding interests rather than a single explanatory one. There is empirical-analytical knowledge in the sense described by Sklair, but there are also historical-hermeneutic interests and critical emancipatory knowledge. Habermas' guiding knowledge interests can be used to articulate these three levels of inquiry in social science. Distinctions among metatheory, theory, and empirical research will remain, although in the theory of argumentation the criteria of evaluation will differ (Morrow, 1983, 1989; Ureña, 1978: 92–105).

2. Gottlieb and La Belle (1988) have correctly identified this problematic when they argue that Freire is working in the realm of metalanguage.

3. However, as is well-known, Freire does not agree with the characterization in vogue of a psychosocial method for literacy training. Nor is he happy with the idea that he has created a method or a set of techniques for literacy training. Freire seems to feel more comfortable identifying his own contribution as methodological indications in literacy training (Freire, 1968a, 1979b, 1984).

BIBLIOGRAPHY

Alberta Journal of Educational Research (AJER). (1988). "Adult Education in International Perspective" (Carlos Alberto Torres, Guest Ed.). 34, no. 3 (September).

Almond, Gabriel, and Sydney Verba. (1963). *The Civic Culture*. Princeton, NJ: Princeton University Press.

Althusser, L. (1971). *Lenin y la filosofía*. México, DF: ERA.

Altimir, O. (1975). "La medición de la población económicamente activa en México, 1950–1970." 73/15. México, DF: CEPAL.

Altvater, Elmar. (1973). "Notes on Some Problems of State Interventionism, (I)." In *Working Papers of the Kapitalistate*. 1: Palo Alto, CA. 96–108.

———. (1979). "Some Problems of State Interventionism." In J. Holloway and S. Piccioto (eds.), *State and Capital. A Marxist Debate*, pp. 40–42. Austin: University of Texas Press.

Anderson, Perry. (1978). *Las antinomias de Antonio Gramsci*. Barcelona: Fontanella.

Antonio, Robert J. (1989). "The Normative Foundations of Emancipatory Theory: Evolutionary Versus Pragmatic Perspectives." *American Journal of Sociology* 94, no. 4 (January): 721–48.

Apple, Michael W. (Ed.). (1982). *Cultural and Economic Reproduction in Education. Essays on Class, Ideology and the State*. London and Boston: Henley, Routledge & Kegan Paul.

Apps, Gerald. (1973). *Towards a Working Philosophy of Adult Education*. Syracuse, NY: Syracuse University Publications in Continuing Education.

Arnove, Robert. (1986). *Education and Revolution in Nicaragua*. New York: Praeger.

———. (Ed.). (1980). *Philanthropy and Cultural Imperialism. The Foundations at Home and Abroad*. Boston: G. K. Hall.

Arnove, Robert, and Harvey Graff. (1987). *National Literacy Campaigns. Historical and Comparative Perspectives*. New York and London: Plenum Press.

Aronowitz, Stanley, and Henry Giroux. (1986). *Education Under Siege. The Conserva-*

    tive, Liberal and Radical Debate over Schooling. Amherst, MA: Bergin &
    Garvey.
Avalos, Beatrice. (1987). "Moving Where? Educational Issues in Latin American Con-
    texts." *International Journal of Education Development* 7, no. 3. 151–72.
Bacchus, M. K. (1976). "Some Observations on Social Structure and Craft Training in
    Economically Less Developed Countries." *Canadian and International Educa-
    tion* 5, no. 2 (December): 109–23.
Bacchus, M. K., and Colin Brock (Eds.). (1987). *The Challenge of Scale. Educational
    Development in the Small States of the Commonwealth.* London: Common-
    wealth Secretariat.
Bacchus, M. K.; Raj S. Pannu; and Carlos Alberto Torres. (1988). "The Sociology of Ed-
    ucational Expansion and Development Revisited." Paper presented at the mid-
    term conference of the Sociology of Education Research Committee,
    International Sociological Association, Salamanca, Spain, August 23–27.
Barreiro, Julio. (1974). *Educación popular y proceso de concientización.* Buenos Aires:
    Siglo XXI.
Bee, Barbara. (1981). "The Politics of Literacy." In Robert Mackie (ed.), *Literacy and
    Revolution,* pp. 39–56. New York: Continum Publishing.
Bhola, Harban S. (1981). "Why Literacy Can't Wait: Issues for the 1980s." *Convergence*
    14, no. 1:6–22.
———. (1984). *Campaigning for Literacy: Eight National Experiences of the Twenti-
    eth Century.* Paris: UNESCO.
Bishop, Maurice. (1982). *Forward Ever! Three Years of the Grenadian Revolution.
    Speeches of Maurice Bishop.* Sydney: Pathfinder Press.
———. (1984). *In Nobody's Backyard: Maurice Bishops Speeches 1979–1983. A Me-
    morial Volume.* Edited by Chris Searle. London: Zed Books.
Blaug, Mark. (1966). "Literacy and Economic Development." *The School Review,* 74, no.
    4 (Winter): 393–415.
Block, Fred. (1987). *Revising State Theory: Essays in Politics and Post-Industrialism.*
    Philadelphia: Temple University Press.
Bock, John, and George Papagianhis. (1983). *Nonformal Education and National De-
    velopment.* New York: Praeger.
Borón, Atilio. (1981). "Latin America: Between Hobbes and Friedman." *New Left Re-
    view* no. 130 (November–December): 45–66.
———. (1982). "The Capitalist State and Its Relative Autonomy. Arguments Regard-
    ing Limits and Dimensions." Mexico, DF: CIDE. Mimeographed.
Bowles, Samuel. (1975). "Unequal Education and the Reproduction of the Social Divi-
    sion of Labor." In M. Carnoy (ed.), *Schooling in a Corporate Society,* 2nd ed., pp.
    38–66. New York: David McKay.
———. (1980). "Education, Class Conflict, and Uneven Development." In John
    Simmons (ed.), *The Educational Dilemma. Policy Issues for Developing Coun-
    tries in the 1980s,* pp. 205–23. Oxford: Pergamon Press.
Bowles, Samuel, and Herbert Gintis. (1981). "Education as a Site of Contradictions in
    the Reproduction of Capital-Labor Relationship: Second Thoughts on the Corre-
    spondence Principle." In *Economic and Industrial Democracy,* Vol. 2, pp. 223–
    42. London and Beverly Hills, CA: Sage.
———. (1986). *Democracy and Capitalism.* New York: Basic Books.

Bowles, Samuel, and Henry Levin. (1968). "The Determinants of Scholastic Achievement: An Appraisal of Some Recent Findings." *Journal of Human Resources* 2, no. 1 (Winter): 3–22.

Braverman, Harry. (1974). *Labor and Monopoly Capital: The Degradation of Work in the Twentieth Century.* New York: Monthly Review Press.

Brizan, George. (1984). *Grenada: Island of Conflict. From Amerindians to People's Revolution, 1498–1979.* London: Zed Books.

Broady, D. (1981). "Critique of the Political Economy of Education: The Prokla Approach. Apropos of a Tenth Anniversary." In *Economics and Industrial Democracy,* Vol. 2, pp. 141–89. London and Beverly Hills, CA: Sage.

Bruno-Jofre, Rosa. (1984). "Popular Education in Latin America Today." In *Progressive Education. Past, Present and Future,* pp. 25–44. Proceedings of the Alberta Universities Educational Foundations Conference, Edmonton: University of Alberta, April 26–28.

Bruss, Neal, and Donaldo P. Macedo. (1984). "A Conversation with Paulo Freire at the University of Massachusetts at Boston." *Boston University Journal of Education* 166, no. 3: 215–25.

―――. (1985). "Toward a Pedagogy of the Question: Conversations with Paulo Freire." *Boston University Journal of Education* 167, no. 2: 7–21.

Burke, R., and M. Chiappetta. (1978). "Characteristics of Illiterates and Programme Hypotheses." Final Report AID/TA-C-1203. In IDRC-MR1, *Literacy: A Summary Review,* pp. 46–48. Ottawa: IDRC.

Camp, Roderic Ai. (1980). *Mexico's Leaders. Their Education and Recruitment.* Tucson: University of Arizona Press.

Campusano, Felipe. (1981). "Althusser, la sociología y la educación." In G. González R. and C. A. Torres (eds.), *Sociología de la educación: Corrientes contemporáneas,* pp. 229–46. México, DF: CEE.

CAN *Cruzada Nacional de Alfabetización.* (1982). Managua: Ministry of Education.

Cardenal, Fernando, and Valerie Miller. (1982). "Nicaragua: Literacy and Revolution." *Prospects* 12, no. 2: 201–12.

Cardoso, Fernando H. (1974). "Las contradicciones del desarrollo asociado." *Desarrollo económico* 14, no. 53 (April–June): Selected pages.

―――. (1979). "On the Characterization of Authoritarian Regimes in Latin America." In D. Collier (ed.), *The New Authoritarianism in Latin America,* pp. 33–60. Princeton, NJ: Princeton University Press.

―――. (1981). "Political Regime and Social Change: Some Reflections Concerning the Brazilian Case." Stanford-Berkeley Joint Center for Latin American Studies, *Occasional Papers in Latin American Studies* no. 3 (Fall): selected pages.

Cardoso, F. H., and E. Faletto. (1978). *Dependency and Development in Latin America.* Berkeley and Los Angeles: University of California Press.

Carnoy, Martin. (1977). "Economics and Education." In Nash Manning (ed.), *Essays on Economic Development and Cultural Change in Honor of Bert Hoselitz.* Chicago: University of Chicago Press.

―――. (1982). "Education, Economy and the State." In M. Apple (ed.), *Cultural and Economic Reproduction in Education,* pp. 79–126. London and Boston: Routledge and Kegan Paul.

————. (1984). *The State and Political Theory.* Princeton, NJ: Princeton University Press.

————. (Ed.). (1975). *Schooling in a Corporate Society,* 2nd ed. New York: David McKay.

Carnoy, Martin, et al. (1979). *Can Educational Policy Equalize Income Distribution in Latin America?* London: Saxon House.

————. (1982). "The Political Economy of Financing Education in Developing Countries." Paper presented at the annual meeting of the Bellagio Group, Ottawa, May 19–21. Published in *Financing Educational Development,* IDRC 206, pp. 39–68. Ottawa: IDRC.

Carnoy, Martin, and Henry Levin. (1985). *Schooling and Work in the Democratic State.* Stanford, CA: Stanford University Press.

Carnoy, M., and J. Samoff (Eds.). (1990). *Education, Social Transformation and the State in the Third World.* Princeton, NJ: Princeton University Press.

Carnoy, Martin, and Carlos Torres. (1989). "Education and Social Transformation in Nicaragua." In M. Carnoy, and J. Samoff, (eds.), *Education, Social Transformation and the State in the Third World.* Princeton, NJ: Princeton University Press.

Carnoy, Martin, and Jorge Werthein. (1979). *Cuba: Economic Change and Educational Reform.* Washington, DC: World Bank.

————. (1980). *Cuba: Cambio económico y reforma educativa (1955–1978).* México, DF: Nuevo Imagen.

Carr, W., and Stephen Kemmis. (1986). *Becoming Critical. Education, Knowledge and Action Research,* pp. 179–213. London and Philadelphia: Falmer Press.

CEDES. (1963), "Final Report." *La educación* (Panamerican Union) 7, no. 25/26 (January–June): 73–81.

CEE (Centro de Estudios Educativos). (1982). *La educacíon popular en América Latina: ¿Avance o retroceso?* México, DF: CEE.

CENIET (Centro de Investigación y Estadísticas del Trabajo). (1976). Encuesta realizada para evaluar el sistema nacional de educación para adultos. México, DF: Secretaría del Trabajo. Mimeographed.

CEPAL. (1963). "Desarrollo económico y educación en América Latina." *La educación* (Panamerican Union) 7, no. 25/26 (January–June): 119–27.

————. (1976). *La evolución económica de América Latina.* Santiago de Chile: CEPAL.

————. (1977). "Antecedentes y orientaciones para los censos de población de 1980." 77–10/2864. Santiago de Chile: CEPAL, Division of Statistics. Mimeographed.

CEPAL/PNUD/UNICEF. (1984). "La Superación de la pobreza; Una tarea urgente y posible" Santiago de Chile: CEPAL/G 1308–9, Mimeographed.

Cerroni, H. (1976). *Teoría política y socialismo.* México, DF: ERA.

Chilcote, R. (1981). *Theories of Comparative Politics. The Search for a Paradigm.* Boulder, CO: Westview Press.

Chonchol, Jacques. (1973). "Prefacio." In Paulo Freire, *Extensión o comunicación. La concientización en el medio rural.* Buenos Aires: Siglo XXI.

Cirigliano, Gustavo F. J. (1976–1977). "Perspectiva en educación de adultos." *La educación: Revista latinoamericana de desarrollo educativo* nos. 75–77.

Cirigliano, Gustavo, and Carlos Paldao. (1978). "Educación de adultos: Hipótesis interpretativa y perspectivas." *Revista interamericana de educación de adultos* 1, no. 2.

Clegg, Stewart. (1975). *Power, Rule and Domination.* London and Boston: Routledge and Kegan Paul.

———. (1979). *The Theory of Power and Organization.* London and Boston: Routledge and Kegan Paul.

CNTE-PRONALF. (1982). *Investigación de evaluación interna del PRONALF,* 4 vols. México, DF: CNTE-PRONALF.

CNTE-UNESCO. (1982). *América Latina y el proyecto principal de educación.* México, DF: CNTE-UNESCO.

Cole, Mike (Ed.). (1988). *Bowles and Gintis Revisited. Correspondence and Contradiction in Educational Theory.* London: Falmer Press.

Coleman, G. et. al. (1966). *Equality of Educational Opportunity.* Washington, DC: U.S. GPO.

———. (1982). *High School Achievement: Public, Catholic, and Private School Compared.* New York: Basic books.

Comisión de Recursos Humanos del Sector Público Federal. (1975). *Censo de recursos humanos del sector público federal.* México, DF: Comisión de Recursos Humanos del Sector Público Federal.

Coombs, Phillips. (1968). *The World Educational Crisis: A System Analysis.* New York: Oxford University Press.

———. (1985). *The World Crisis in Education: The View from the Eighties.* New York: Oxford University Press.

Coombs, P. W., and M. Ahmed. (1974). *Against Rural Poverty.* Baltimore: Johns Hopkins University Press.

Coombs, P. W., et. al. (1973). *New Paths to Learning for Rural Children and Youth.* New York: ICED for UNICEF.

COPLAMAR. (1982). *Necesidades esenciales en México: Situación actual y perspectivas,* vol. 2, *Educación.* México, DF: COPLAMAR–Siglo XXI.

Cornwall, Valerie. (1981). "Report on the Adult Literacy Campaign. Grenada, July 1980–March 1981." Paper presented at the Seventh Technical Meeting of Integrated Adult Education, Bogotá, Colombia, October 26–November 4.

Cuéllar, Oscar. (1981). "El sistema nacional de educación de adultos (SNEA): Evolución del registro y características de la población inscrita (1975–1978)." Documento de Trabajo no. 1. México, DF: Universidad Iberoamericana. Mimeographed.

Dale, Roger. (1983). "The Political Sociology of Education." *British Journal of Sociology of Education* 4, no. 2: 185–202.

Darcy de Oliveira, Rosiska, and Pierre Dominice. (1975). "Illich-Freire: Pedagogía de los oprimidos. Opresión de la pedagogía. El debate pedagógico." *Cuadernos de pedagogía* (Madrid) no. 7–8 (July–August): 4–16.

De Anda, María. (1983). *Educación de adultos: Nuevas dimensiones en el sector educativo.* México, DF: CEE.

De Lella, Cayetano. (1982). "Evaluación del proceso de alfabetización por los alfabetizadores." México, DF: PRONALF. Mimeographed.

De Santa Ana, Julio, et al. (1970). *Conciencia y revolución.* Montevideo: Tierra Nueva.

DEALC-UNESCO-CEPAL-PNUD. (1981). *Desarrollo y educación en América Latina, Síntesis General,* Vol. 3. Buenos Aires: DEALC-UNESCO-CEPAL-PNUD.

Deutsch, Karl. (1963). *The Nerves of Government: Models of Political Communication and Control.* Glencoe, IL, and London: The Free Press.

Dewey, John. (1899). *The School and Society.* Chicago: University of Chicago Press.
————. (1926). *What Mr. Dewey Thinks of the Educational Politics of Mexico.* México, DF: Secretaría de Educación Pública and Talleres Gráficos de la Nación.
DGAC (Dirección General de Acreditación y Certificación). (1978a). "Características de los educandos del sistema nacional de educación para adultos. Mexico City. Mimeographed.
————. (1978b). "Organización de los educandos del sistema nacional de educación abierta." Mexico City. Mimeographed.
————. (1979). "Información obtenida de la muestra aplicada a los estudiantes de 1° año de secundaria abierta en junio de 1979." Mexico City. Mimeographed.
DGAC-CEE. (1979). "El proceso de enseñanza-aprendizaje y la eficiencia interna del sistema nacional de educación abierta." Mexico City. Mimeographed.
Dominguez, Jorge. (1980). *Cuba: Order and Revolution.* Cambridge, MA: Belknap Press of Harvard University.
Dore, Ronald. (1976). *The Diploma Disease. Education, Qualification and Development.* Berkeley and Los Angeles: University of California Press.
Duke, Chris (Ed.). (1985). *Participation Research.* Canberra: Australia University, Centre for Continuing Education.
ECLA. (1963). "Desarrollo económico y educación en América Latina." *La educación* (Washington, DC) 7, no. 25/26 (January–June): 119–27.
Eisenstadt, S. N. (1971). *Political Sociology.* New York: Basic Books.
Evans, Peter. (1979). *Dependent Development: The Alliance of Multinationals, State, and Local Capital in Brazil.* Princeton, NJ: Princeton University Press.
Fagen, Richard. (1969). *The Transformation of Political Culture in Cuba.* Stanford, CA: Stanford University Press.
Fagerlind, Ingmar. (1975). *Formal Education and Adult Earnings.* Stockholm: Almqvist and Wicksell.
Fagerlind, Ingemar, and Lawrence Saha. (1984). *Education and National Development. A Comparative Perspective.* Oxford: Pergamon Press.
Farrell, Joseph P. (1986). *The National Unified School in Allende's Chile. The Role of Education in the Destruction of a Revolution.* Vancouver: University of British Columbia Press.
Faure, Edgar, et al. (1972). *Learning to Be.* Paris: UNESCO.
Feijoó, Samuel. (1959). "Situación de la escuela rural cubana." *Revista Revolución* (November 5).
Fernández, Hugo. (1978). "La educación de adultos y los modelos alternativos de organización social de la producción en el medio rural." Paper presented at Reunión Técnica Internacional sobre Educación de Adultos y Empresas Comunitarias en el Desarrollo, San José, Costa Rica, July 3–6. Mimeographed.
Fiori, Giuseppe. (1970). *Antonio Gramsci. Life of a Revolutionary.* London: New Left Books.
Fletcher, Philipe R. (1982). "National Educational Systems as State Agencies of Legitimation." Paper presented to the Western Regional Conference of the Comparative and International Education Society, Stanford University, October 22–24.
Flores, Luis. (1982). "Estrategias nacionales para programas de alfabetización." In UNESCO/CNTE, *Dimensión cuantitativa de la situación del analfabetismo en América Latina.* México, DF: UNESCO-CNTE.

Freire, Paulo. (1968a). *Acción cultural para la libertad.* Santiago de Chile: ICIRA.
————. (1968b). "Reporte sobre las actividades del ICIRA." Santiago de Chile: ICIRA. Mimeographed.
————. (1977). "Concientizar para liberar (nociones sobre la palabra concientización)." In C. A. Torres (ed.), *La praxis educativa de Paulo Freire,* pp. 107–20. México, DF: Gernika.
————. (1979a). "Educação para o despertar de la consciencia: Conversa com Paulo Freire." In Carlos A. Torres (ed.), *Diálogo com Paulo Freire,* pp. 29–39. São Paulo: Ediçoes Loyola.
————. (1979b). "Entrevista com Paulo Freire." In Carlos A. Torres (ed.), *Diálogo com Paulo Freire,* pp. 41–62. São Paulo: Ediçoes Loyola.
————. (1980a). "La conciencia desmitificada." In C. A. Torres (ed.), *Paulo Freire: Educación y concientización,* pp. 43–49. Salamanca: Ediciones Sigüeme.
————. (1980b). "Desmitificación de la concientización." In C. A. Torres (ed.), *Paulo Freire: Educación y concientización.* pp. 60–72. Salamanca: Ediciones Sigüeme.
————. (1981). "Paulo Freire debate com os professores mineiros" Minas Gerais, Brazil: Departamento de Educação do Sindicato dos Professores MG/Departamento Pedagógico de UTE. Mimeographed.
————. (1985). *The Politics of Education. Culture, Power and Liberation.* Amherst, MA: Bergin & Garvey.
Freire, Paulo, et al. (1980). *Vivendo e aprendendo. Experiences do IDAC en educação popular.* Sao Paulo: Livraria Brasilense Editora.
Freire, Paulo, and Donaldo Macedo. (1987). *Literacy. Reading the Word and the World.* Amherst, MA: Bergin & Garvey.
Fritzell, Christer. (1987). "On the Concept of Relative Autonomy in Educational Theory." *British Journal of Sociology of Education* 8, no. 1: 23–35.
Frobel, F., et al. (1980). *The New International Division of Labour.* Cambridge: Cambridge University Press.
Fuller, Bruce. (1984). "Can Literacy Spark Economic Growth?" Washington, DC: World Bank. Mimeographed.
Furter, Pierre. (1966a). *Educação e vida.* Rio de Janeiro: Vozes.
————. (1966b). *Educação e reflexão.* Rio de Janeiro: Vozes.
————. (1970). *Venezuela: Alfabetización de adultos (perspectivas y problemas de la educación de adultos en la situación actual de Venezuela).* Paris: UNESCO.
————. (1972). "Adult Education: Its Clienteles." *Prospects,* 2, no. 3: 314–20.
Gadotti, Moacir. (1983). *Educação e poder. Introdução a pedagogia do conflito.* São Paulo: Cortes Editora-Autores Associados.
Gajardo, Marcela. (1974). "Capacitación sindical y conciencia campesina." *Revista del Centro de estudios educativos* 4 no. 2: 29–55.
————. (1982). *Evolución, situación actual y perspectivas de las estrategias de investigación participativa en América Latina.* Santiago de Chile: FLACSO.
————. (Ed.). (1985). *Teoría y práctica de la educación popular.* Michoacán, Mexico: PREDE/OEA/CREFAL/IDRC.
García-Huidobro, Juan Eduardo. (1983). "En torno al sentido político de la educación popular." Santiago de Chile: CIDE. Mimeographed.
————. (1985a) "La educación popular." In P. Latapí and Alfonso Castillo (eds.),

Lecturas sobre la educación de adultos en América Latina. México, DF: CREFAL.

―――. (1985b). "La relación educativa en proyectos de educación popular. Análisis de quince casos." In M. Gajardo, (ed.), *Teoría y práctica de la educación popular.* Michoacán, Mexico: PREDE/OEA/CREFAL/IDRC.

Gee, James Paul. (1986). "Literate America on Illiterate America." *Journal of Education* 168, no. 1: 126–40.

Gerhardt, H. Peter. (1985). "Brazil's Popular Education in the Eighties. Essentials, Fundamentals and Realpolitik." Paper presented to the SIDEC 20th Anniversary and CIES Conference, Stanford University, April 15–20.

Giroux, Henry. (1981). *Ideology, Culture and the Process of Schooling.* London and Philadelphia, Sussex: Falmer Press.

―――. (1983a). *Theory and Resistance in Education: A Pedagogy for the Opposition.* South Hadley, MA: Bergin & Garvey.

―――. (1983b). *Pedagogía radical. Subsidios.* São Paulo: Cortez Editora.

Gonzalez R. G., and C. A. Torres, (Eds.). (1981). *Sociología de la educación: Corrientes contemporáneas,* México, DF: CEE.

Gottlieb, Esther and Thomas La Belle. (1988). "Consciousness Raising, Theory and Practice: How Discourse Constructs Knowledge." Paper presented at the annual meeting of the American Educational Research Association. New Orleans: April. Mimeographed.

Gramsci, Antonio. (1975). *Quaderni del carcere.* Critical ed., Valentino Gerratana, ed. Turin: Giulio Einaudi Editore.

―――. (1980). *Selections from the Prison Notebooks.* New York: International Publishers.

Grindle, M. S. (1977). *Bureaucrats, Politicians and Peasants in Mexico. A Case Study in Public Policy.* Berkeley: The University of California Press.

Guevara, Ernesto (Che). (1967). *Episodes of the Revolutionary War.* Havana: Guairas Book Institute.

Hall, B., and Y. Kassam. (1985). "Participatory Research." In *International Encyclopedia of Education: Research and Practice,* Vol. 7, pp. 3795–3800. London: Pergamon Press.

Hamilton, N. (1982). *The Limits of State Autonomy. Post Revolutionary Mexico.* Princeton, NJ: Princeton University Press.

Hanushek, Eric A. (1986). "The Economics of Schooling: Production and Efficiency in the Public Schools." *The Journal of Economic Literature* 24, no. 3: September, 1141–78.

Hargreaves, Andy. (1982). "Resistance and Relative Autonomy Theories: Problems of Distortion and Incoherence in Recent Marxist Analysis of Education." *British Journal of Sociology of Education* 3, no. 2: 107–26.

Harris, W. J. A. (1980). *Comparative Adult Education. Practice, Purpose and Theory.* London and New York: Longman.

Hayden, Robert. (1982). *Culture and Adult Education. A Study of Alberta and Quebec.* Edmonton: University of Alberta Press.

Hernández, Isabel, and Ana M. Facciolo. (1983). "La educación de adultos en la Argentina de la última década." São Paulo: Instituto Interdisciplinario de Docencia e Investigación en Artes y Ciencias. Mimeographed.

Hofstede, G. (1980). *Culture's Consequences. International Differences in World-Related Values.* Beverly Hills and London: Sage.

Hopkins, P. G. H. (1985). *Workers' Education. An International Perspective.* Milton Keynes, England, and Philadelphia: Open University Press.

Huberman, Leo, and Paul Sweezy. (1969). *Socialism in Cuba.* New York: Monthly Review Press.

Hughes, Steven, and Kenneth Mijesky (Eds.). (1984). *Public Policy in Latin America.* Boulder, CO: Westview Press.

Huntington, Samuel. (1971). *Political Order in Changing Societies.* New Haven: Yale University Press.

IDRC. (1978). *Literacy: A Summary Review.* IDRC-M81. Ottawa: IDRC.

Inkeles, Alex, and David Smith. (1974). *Becoming Modern.* Cambridge, MA: Harvard University Press.

Ireland, Timothy D. (1978). *Gelpi's View of Lifelong Education.* Manchester: University of Manchester, Department of Adult and Higher Education.

Jacobs, W. Richard, and Ian Jacobs. (1980). *Grenada: The Route to Revolution.* Havana: Casa de las Américas.

Jarvis, Peter. (1985). *The Sociology of Adult and Continuing Education.* London: Croom Helm.

Jelin, Elizabeth. (1987). "Movimientos Sociales en Argentina: Una Introdución a su Estudio." *Cuestion de Estado* 1, no. 1, September: 28–37.

Jencks, Christopher, et al. (1972). *Inequality. A Reassessment of the Effect of Family and Schooling in America.* New York: Harper and Row.

Jensen, B. (1987). "Educational Change in Revolutionary Grenada." M.Ed. dissertation. Edmonton: University of Alberta.

Jessop, Bob (1982). *The Capitalist State.* New York: Academic Press.

Judson, Fred. (1987). "Nicaragua 1987: Revolution, War and Daily Life." *The Gateway.* Edmonton: University of Alberta, November 19.

Karabel, J. (1976). "Revolutionary Contradictions: Antonio Gramsci and the Problem of Intellectuals." *Politics and Society* 6, no. 2: 123–72.

Kenner, Martin, and James Petras. (Ed.). (1969). *Fidel Castro Speaks.* New York: Grove Press.

Knowles, Malcom. (1980). *The Modern Practice of Adult Education: From Pedagogy to Andragogy.* Wilton, CT: Association Press.

Kozol, Jonathan. (1978). *Children of the Revolution: A Yankee Teacher in the Cuban Schools.* New York: Delacorte Press.

———. (1985). *Illiterate America.* New York and Scarborough, England: Plume.

Kruss, Glenda. (1988). *People's Education. An Examination of the Concept.* University of Western Cape, Bellville: Centre for Adult and Continuing Education.

Kulich, Jindra. (1982). *Adult Education in Continental Europe: An Annotated Bibliography of English Language Materials.* Vancouver: University of British Columbia Press.

Labarca, Guillermo. (1979a). "Crisis de la universidad, alianzas de clases y pensamiento crítico en América Latina." *Revista del Centro de estudios educativos* 4, no. 2: 115–26.

———. (1979b). *Para una teoría de la acumulación capitalista en América Latina.* México, DF: Nueva Imagen.

Labarca, Guillermo, Tomás A. Vasconi, et al. (1978). *La educación burguesa.* México, DF: Nueva Imagen.

La Belle, Thomas. (1980). *Educación no-formal y cambio social en América Latina.* México, DF: Nueva Imagen.

———. (1986). *Nonformal Education in Latin American and the Caribbean. Stability, Reform or Revolution?* New York: Praeger.

La Belle, Thomas, and Robert Verhine. (1978). "Educación no-formal y estratificación ocupacional: Implicaciones para América Latina." *La universidad en el mundo* 3, no. 14 (January–February): 7–27.

Lacayo, Francisco. (1982). "La alfabetización: Un proyecto prioritario en Nicaragua." In Carlos A. Torres (ed.), *Ensayos sobre la educación de los adultos en América Latina,* pp. 555–80. México, DF: Centro de Estudios Educativos.

Lagrange, Henri A., et al. (1974). "A propósito de la escuela." In Michael Lowy (ed.), *Sobre el método marxista.* México, DF: Grijalbo.

Latapí, Pablo. (1984). *Tendencias de la educación de adultos en América Latina: Una tipología orientada a su evaluación cualitativa.* Pátzcuaro, Mexico: CREFAL.

———. (1987). "Poverty and Adult Education in Latin America. Prospects for Year 2,000." Edmonton: University of Alberta. Mimeographed.

———. (1988). "Participatory Research: A New Paradigm?" *Alberta Journal of Educational Research* 34, no. 3 (September): 310–19.

Latin American Bureau. (1984). *Grenada: Whose Freedom?* London: LAB.

Lechner, N. (Ed.). (1981). *Estado y política en América Latina.* México, DF: Siglo XXI.

Lenhardt, Gero. (1981). "School and Wage Labor." In *Economic and Industrial Democracy,* Vol. 2, pp. 191–221. London and Beverly Hills: Sage.

Lerner, Daniel. (1958). *The Passing of Traditional Society.* Glencoe, IL: The Free Press.

Levin, H. (1980). "The Limits of Educational Planning." In H. N. Weiler (ed.), *Educational Planning and Social Change,* pp. 15–47. Paris: UNESCO, International Institute of Educational Planning.

Levine, K. (1982). "Functional Literacy: Found Illusions and False Economics." *Harvard Educational Review* 52, no. 3: 249–66.

Llanusa, J. (1969). "Creando una nueva conciencia." *Bohemia* (January 24).

Lind, Agñeta, and Anton Johnston. (1986). "Adult Literacy in the Third World. A Review of Objectives and Strategies." Institute of International Education, SIDA, Education Division, document no. 32. Stockholm: University of Stockholm, SIDA.

Lindblon, C. (1968). *The Policy-Making Process.* Englewood Cliffs, NJ: Prentice-Hall.

Lowe, J. (1975). *The Education of Adults: A World Perspective.* Toronto: UNESCO Press–OISE.

Mackie, R. (Ed.). (1981). *Literacy and Revolution: The Pedagogy of Paulo Freire.* New York: Continuum.

Manitzas, Nita, and David Barkin. (1973). *Cuba: The Logic of the Revolution.* Andover, MA: Warner Modular Publications.

Marcus, B., and M. Taber (Eds.). (1983). *Maurice Bishop Speaks: The Grenadian Revolution 1979–83.* New York: Pathfinder Press.

Marin, A., and Psacharopoulos, G. (1976). "Schooling and Income Distribution." *Review of Economics and Statistics* 58: 332–38.

Martin, D'Arcy. (1971). "Pedagogía y política: La educación de adultos en América Latina." *Convergence* 4, no. 18: 54–60.

Mbilinyi, Marjorie. (1977). "Basic Education: Tool of Liberation or Exploitation?" *Prospects* 7, no. 4: 489–503.

McGinn, N., and S. Street. (1982). "The Political Rationality of Resource Allocation in Mexican Public Education." *Comparative Education Review* 26, no. 2 (June): 178–98.

MED. (1980). *Ya es nuestro. Cuaderno de educación sandinista para capacitadores.* Managua: Ministerio de Educación de Nicaragua.

Mezirow, Jack. (1979). "Perspective Transformation—Toward a Critical Theory of Adult Education." Paper presented as a public lecture at the University of Northern Illinois. September 27, 1979. Sponsored by the Department of leadership and Policy Studies, Graduate Colloquium Committee.

————. (1981). "A Critical Theory of Adult Learning and Education." *Adult Education* 32, no. 1, Fall: 3–24.

————. (1985). "Critical Transformation Theory and the Self-Directed Learner." in Stephen Brookfield (Ed.) *Self-Directed Learning: From Theory to Practice.* San Francisco: Dossey Bass.

Miles, M., and M. Huberman. (1984). *Qualitative Data Analysis.* Beverly Hills and London: Sage.

Miliband, R. (1977). "Réplica a Nicos Poulantzas." In Robin Blackborn (ed.), *Ideología y ciencias sociales.* Barcelona: Grijalbo.

Minnis, J. (1984). "The Influence of Progressive Thought on the Theory and Practice of Adult Education." *Progressive Education. Past, Present and Future*, pp. 117–52. Proceedings of the Alberta Universities Educational Foundations Conference, Edmonton: The University of Alberta, April 26–28.

Montoya, Alberto, and Rebeil, María Antonieta. (1981). "Televisión educativa en México." México, DF: Consejo Nacional Técnico de la Educación. Mimeographed.

Moore, S. N. (1957). *The Critique of Capitalist Democracy.* New York: Paine Whitman.

Morales, Abel. (1981). "The Literacy Campaign in Cuba." *Harvard Educational Review* 51, no. 1 (February).

Morales-Gómez, Daniel A. (1979). "Educación y gobierno militar en Brasil." In D. A. Morales-Gómez (ed.), *La educación y el desarrollo dependiente en América Latina*, pp. 257–87. México, DF: Gernika.

————. (1981). "Understanding Education and Work. A Review of the Main Theoretical Streams." Ottawa: IDRC. Mimeographed.

————. (1989). "Seeking New Paradigms to Plan Education for Development: The Role of Educational Research." *Prospects* XIX, no. 2: pp. 191–204.

Morales-Gómez, Daniel, and C. A. Torres. (1990). "The State, Corporatist Policies, and Educational Policy Making in Mexico (1970–1988)." New York: Praeger.

Morales Jeldes, Marcelo. (1986). "Educación popular e investigación participativa en México: Un estudio comparado de casos." México, DF: FLACSO. Mimeographed.

Morrow, Raymond. (1983). "Habermas on Rationalization. Reification and the Colonialization of the Life-World." Paper presented at the joint session of the Canadian Association of Sociology and Anthropology and the International Sociological Association Research Committee on Alienation Theory and Research, Vancouver, June 1–3.

————. (1989). "Habermas and Freire as Critical Social Psychologists: A Dialogue." Paper presented to the Critical Preconference of the 30th Annual Adult Education Research Conference. Madison: University of Wisconsin, April 26–27. Mimeographed.

Morrow, Raymond, and Carlos Alberto Torres. (1987). "Social Theory, Social Reproduction and Education's Everyday Life." Paper presented to the Western Anthropology and Sociology Association annual meeting, Edmonton, Alberta, February.

Muñoz Izquierdo, Carlos. (1979). *El problema de la educación de México: Laberinto sin salida?* México, DF: CEE.

———. (1982a). "Efectos económicos de la educación de adultos." In C. A. Torres (ed.), *Ensayos sobre la educación de los adultos en América Latina*, pp. 91–110. México, DF: CEE.

———. (1982b). "Educación y cambio social: Resultados obtenidos, su explicación y posibles alternativas." In Centro de Estudios Educativos, *Educación popular en América Latina: Avance o retroceso?*, pp. 363–84. México, DF: CEE.

———. (1982c). "Respuesta a los comentarios del maestro Carlos Alberto Torres." In Centro de Estudios Educativos, *Educación popular en América Latina: Avance o retroceso?*, pp. 403–11. México, DF: CEE.

Myers, Robert G. (1980). *Connecting Worlds: A Survey of Developments in Educational Research.* IDRC-TS35s. Ottawa: IDRC.

National Press of Cuba. (1960). *Revolutionary Works.* Havana.

Nun, José. (1969). "Superpoblación relativa, ejército industrial de reserva y masa marginal." *Revista latinoamericana de sociología* no. 69/2: 178–237.

———. (1982). "El otro reduccionismo." Paper presented to the XII Congress of the International Political Science Association, Rio de Janeiro, August 9–14. Mimeographed.

O'Connor, James. (1973). *The Fiscal Crisis of the State.* New York: St. Martins Press.

———. (1981). "The Fiscal Crisis of the State Revisited: A Look at Economic Crisis and Reagan's Budget Policy." *Kapitalistate*, 41–46.

O'Donnell, Guillermo. (1978a). "Apuntes para una teoría del estado." *Revista mexicana de sociología* 40, no. 4 (October–December): 1157–99.

———. (1978b). "Reflections on the Patterns of Change in the Bureaucratic-Authoritarian State." *Latin American Research Review* 12, no. 1 (Winter): 3–38.

———. (1982). *El estado burocrático-autoritario.* Buenos Aires: Editorial de Belgrano.

Ochoa, Jorge, and Juan E. García-Huidobro. (1982). "Tendencias de la investigación sobre educación de adultos y educación noformal en América Latina." In Carlos A. Torres (ed.), *Ensayos sobre la educación de los adultos en América Latina*, pp. 427–62. México, DF: CEE.

Offe, Claus. (1972a). "Political Authority and Class Structures—An Analysis of Late Capitalist Societies." *International Journal of Sociology* 2, no. 1 (Spring): 73–108.

———. (1972b). "Advance Capitalism and the Welfare State" in *Politics and Society* 2, no. 4. Summer: 488–97.

———. (1973). "The Abolition of Market Control and the Problem of Legitimacy." (I and II). *Working Papers of the Kapitalistate* 1:109–16, 2:73–75.

———. (1974). "Structural Problems of the Capitalist State." In K. V. von Beyme (ed.), *German Political Studies*, Vol. 1, pp. 31–56. Beverly Hills, CA: Sage.

———. (1975a). "The Theory of the Capitalist State and the Problem of Policy Formation." In Leon N. Lindberg et al. (eds.), *Stress and Contradiction in Modern Capitalism*, pp. 125–44. Toronto: Lexington Books.

Offe, Claus. (1975b [n.d.]). "Notes on the Laws of Motion of Reformist State Policies." Frankfurt: Suhrkamp. Mimeographed.

————. (1976). *Industry and Inequality.* London: Edward Arnold.

————. (1984). *Contradictions of the Welfare State* (ed. John Keane). London: Hutchinson.

————. (1985). *Disorganized Capitalism.* Cambridge: Polity Press.

Offe, Claus, and V. Ronge. (1975). "Theses on the Theory of the State." *New German Critique* 6 (Fall): 137–47.

Offe, Claus, and Helmut Wiesenthal. (1980). "Two Logics of Collective Action: Theoretical Notes on Social Class and Organizational Form." In M. Zeitlin (ed.), *Political Power and Social Theory,* pp. 67–116. Greenwich, CT: JAI Press.

Oszlak, Oscar. (1980). "Políticas públicas y regímenes políticos: Reflexiones a partir de algunas experiencias latinoamericanas." *Estudios CEDES* 3, no. 2.

————. (1981). "The Historical Formation of the State in Latin America: Some Theoretical and Methodological Guidelines for Its Study." *Latin American Research Review* 16, no. 2: 3–32.

Oszlak, Oscar, and Guillermo O'Donnell. (1976). *Estado y políticas estatales en América Latina. Hacia una estrategia de investigación.* Documento CEDES/G.E. CLACSO, no. 4. Buenos Aires: CEDES.

Pannu, R. S. (1988). "Adult Education, Economy and the State in Canada." *Alberta Journal of Educational Research* 34, no. 3: 203–45.

Parsons, Talcott, and Gerald M. Platt. (1973). *The American University.* Cambridge, MA: Harvard University Press.

Payne, Anthony, et al. (1984). *Grenada: Revolution and Invasion.* London: Croom Helm.

Paz, Octavio. (1982). "Latin America and Democracy." In *Democracy and Dictatorship in Latin America.* New York: Foundation for the Study of Independent Social Ideas.

Pescador, José A. (1981). "Alfabetización y desarrollo económico." *Revista territorios* 11–18.

————. (1982). "Una aproximación a la experiencia educativa en Cuba." *Revista latinoamericana de estudios educativos* 12, sem. 2, no. 2: 97–111.

————. (1983). "Evaluación del personal directivo del PRONALF." México, DF: Consejo Nacional Tecnico de la Educación. Mimeographed.

Pescador, José Angel, and Carlos Alberto Torres. (1985). *Poder político y educación en México.* México, DF: UTHEA.

Peterson, E., et al. (1982). *Adult Education and Training in Industrialized Countries.* New York: Praeger.

Phillips, H. M. (1970). *Literacy and Development.* Paris: UNESCO.

Portantiero, Juan Carlos. (1981). "Gramsci y la educación." In G. Gonzáles R. and Carlos A. Torres (eds.), *Sociología de la educación: Corrientes contemporáneas,* pp. 221–28. México, DF: Centro de Estudios Educativos.

Portes, Alejandro, and John Walton. (1981). *Labour, Class, and the International System.* New York: Academic Press.

Poulantzas, Nicos. (1969). *Poder político y clases sociales en el estado capitalista.* México, DF: Siglo XXI.

————. (1978). "The State and Transition to Socialism." *Socialist Review* 8, no. 1 (January–February): 9–36.

————. (1980). *State, Power and Socialism.* London: Verso.

Price, Ronald F. (1977). *Marx and Education in Russia and China.* London: Croom Helm.

Przeworski, Adam. (1981). "Material Bases of Consent: Economics and Politics in a Hegemonic System." In M. Zeitlin (ed.), *Political Power and Social Theory,* pp. 21–26. Greenwich, CT: JAI Press.

Psacharopoulos, George. (1988). "Critical Issues in Education and Development: A World Agenda." *International Journal of Educational Development* 8, no. 1: 1–7.

Puiggrós, Adriana. (1984). *La educación popular en América Latina.* México, DF: Nueva Imagen.

Puiggrós, Adriana, et al. (1987). "Hacia una pedagogía de la imaginación en América Latina." Manuscript.

Quijano Obregón, A., and Francisco Weffort. (1973). *Populismo, marginalización y dependencia.* San José, Costa Rica: EDUCA.

Rama, Germán (Ed.). (1980). "Introducción." In *Educación y sociedad en América y el Caribe.* Santiago de Chile: UNESCO-CEPAL-PNUD-UNICEF.

Ramirez Castañeda, S. (1981). "Althusser en México." In G. González R. and Carlos A. Torres (eds.), *Sociología de la educación,* pp. 247–52. México, DF: Centro de Estudios Educativos.

Read, G. (1970). "The Cuban Revolutionary Offensive in Education." *Comparative Educational Review* 14, no. 2. pp. 131–43.

Rebeil, M. A., and Carlos A. Torres. (1980). *Elementos que constituyen el sistema nacional de educación de adultos.* Cuadernos de Trabajo en Educación de Adultos no. 2. México, DF: DGEA-SEP.

Reich, M., et al. (1975). "A Theory of Labor Market Segmentation." In M. Carnoy (ed.), *Schooling in a Corporate Society,* 2nd ed., pp. 69–79. New York: David McKay.

Republica de Cuba. (1953). *Censo de Población.* Habana.

Rigal, Luis. (1978). "Sobre el Sentido y Uso de la Investigación-acción" Varios *Crítica y Política en Ciencias Sociales.* 1, Simposio Mundial de Cartegena. Bogotá: Editorial Punta de Lanza. pp. 379–94.

Rodriguez Brandão, Carlos (Ed.). (1979). *A questão política da educação popular.* São Paulo: Brasilense.

————. (1984). "Los caminos cruzados: Formas de pensar y realizar educación en América Latina." *Revista de educación de adultos* 2, no. 2 (April–June): 28–41.

Rogowsky, Ronald, and Lois Wasserspring. (1971). *Does Political Development Exist? Corporatism in Old and New Societies.* Beverly Hills, CA: Sage.

Roxborough, Ian. (1987). "Research." *London School of Economics Newsletter,* no. 1: pp. 4–5.

Rubin, Gayle. (1975). "The Traffic in Women: Notes on the Political Economy of Sex." In Rayna Reiter (ed.), *Toward an Anthropology of Women,* pp. 157–210. New York: Monthly Review Press.

Rubio, Maura. (1983). "El método de alfabetización de Paulo Freire y el programa nacional de educación para adultos" Licentiate thesis. México, DF: UAM-Xochimilco.

Russel, D., and R. Hudson. (1980). *Planning Education for Development.* Cambridge, MA: Harvard University Press.

Sanders, Thomas G. (1968). "The Paulo Freire Method. Literacy Training and Conscientization." American Universities Field Staff, Report, West Coast South America. 15, no. 1, Santiago de Chile.

Sardei-Bierman, J. C., and K. Dohse. (1973). "Class domination and the Political System. A Critical Interpretation of Recent contributions by Claud Offe." Working Paper of the Kapital state, 2, pp. 60–69.

Sartori, Giovanni. (1969). "From the Sociology of Politics to Political Sociology." In M. Lipset (ed.), *Politics and the Social Sciences*, pp. 65–100. New York: Oxford University Press.

Schmelkes, Sylvia. (1979). "La utilidad del alfabetismo en una zona rural de México." In Daniel A. Moralez-Gómez (ed.), *Educación y desarrollo dependiente en América Latina*, pp. 257–87. México, DF: Gernika-CEE.

———. (1982). "La investigación en educación de adultos en América Latina." In Carlos A. Torres (ed.), *Ensayos sobre la educación de los adultos en América Latina*, pp. 463–81. México, DF: CEE.

Schmelkes, Sylvia, and Luis Narro. (1988). "Adult Education in Mexico: An Overview." *Alberta Journal of Educational Research* 34, no. 5 (September): pp. 246–58.

Schugurensky, Daniel. (1987). "Adult Education and Policy-Making in Post-Revolutionary Regimes." Edmonton: University of Alberta. Mimeographed.

Schuman, H., A. Inkeles, and D. Smith. (1967). "Some Social Psychological Effects and Noneffects of Literacy in a New Nation." *Economic Development and Cultural Change* 16, no. 1: pp. 1–14.

Searle, Chris (Ed.). (1984). *In Nobody's Backyard: Maurice Bishop's Speeches 1979–83. A Memorial Volume.* London: Zed Books.

Shor, Ira, and Paulo Freire. (1987). *A Pedagogy for Liberation. Dialogues on Transforming Education.* Amherst, MA: Bergin & Garvey.

Simmons, John. (1980). *The Education Dilemma. Policy Issues for Developing Countries in the 1980s.* Oxford: Pergamon Press.

Sirvent, Carlos, and Regina Vergara. (1983). *El sistema nacional de educación para adultos. Una evaluación sociológica.* México, DF: UNAM.

Sklair, Leslie. (1988). "Transcending the Impasse: Metatheory, Theory, and Empirical Research in the Sociology of Development and Underdevelopment." *World Development* 16, no. 6: 697–709.

Skocpol, Theda. (1982). "Bringing the State Back in—False Leads and Promising Starts in Current Theories and Research." Paper presented at the meeting "States and Social Structures," Seven Spring Conference Center, Mount Kisco, NY, February 25–27. Mimeographed.

Snook, I. A. (1981). "The Concept of Conscientization in Paulo Freire's Philosophy of Education." *New Education* 2/3, 1: 35–40.

Solana, Fernando. (1980). *La política educativa de México en la UNESCO.* México, DF: SEP.

Solari, Aldo. (1977). "Desarrollo y política educacional en América Latina." *Revista de la CEPAL* sem. 1: 61–94.

———. (1982). "Desigualdad social y educación de adultos en América Latina." In C. A. Torres (ed.), *Ensayos sobre la educación de los adultos en América Latina*, pp. 21–34. México, DF: CEE.

Southam Report. (1987). *Illiteracy in Canada.* Ottawa: Southam News.

SPP-CONAPO-CELADE. (n.d.). *México: Estimaciones y proyecciones de población 1980–2000.* México, DF: SPP-CONAPO-CELADE.

SPP-DGE. (1978). "Proyecciones de la población Mexicana 1970–2000." *Evaluación y análisis* ser. 3, no. 8. Mimeographed.

Stepan, Alfred. (1978). *The State and Society: Peru in Comparative Perspective.* Princeton, NJ: Princeton University Press.

Sumra, Suleman, and Y. Bwatwa. (1988). "Adult Education, Literacy Training and Skill Upgrading Programs in Tanzania: An Overview and a Critical Assessment." *Alberta Journal of Educational Research* 34, no. 5 (September): 259–68.

Tedesco, Juan Carlos. (1980). "Educación y empleo industrial. Un análisis a partir de datos censados 1960–1970." In Germán Rama (ed.), *Educación y sociedad en América y el Caribe,* pp. 77–87. Santiago de Chile: UNESCO-CEPAL-PNUD-UNICEF.

———. (1985). "Reproductivismo educativo y sectores populares en América Latina." In F. R. Nadeira and G. Namo de Mello (coordinação). *Educação na América Latina. Os modelos teóvicos e a realidade social.* São Paulo: Cortez Editores-Editora Autores Associados, pp. 33–60.

Therborn, Göran. (1980). *What Does the Ruling Class Do When It Rules?* London: Verso.

———. (1988). "Does Corporatism Really Matter? The Economic Crisis and Issues of Political Theory." *Journal of Public Policy* 7, no. 3: 259–84.

Thompson, Jane L. (Ed.). (1980). *Adult Education for Change.* London: Hutchinson.

Thorndike, Tony. (1985). *Grenada: Politics, Economics and Society* London: Frances Pinter.

Titmus, Colin. (1976). "Proposed Theoretical Model for the Comparative Study of National Adult Education Systems in Europe." *Society and Leisure.* 8, no. 2: 39–54.

———. (1985). *Strategies for Adult Education. Practices in Western Europe.* Chicago: Follet.

Titmus, Colin, et al. (1979). *Terminology of Adult Education.* Paris: UNESCO.

Torrado, Susana. (1978). *Información e investigación socio-demográfica en América Latina.* Santiago de Chile: PISPAL-CLACSO.

Torres, Carlos A. (1980a). *La educación de adultos en México: Realidades y perspectivas.* Cuadernos de Trabajo en Educación de Adultos no. 1. México, DF: Dirección General de Educación de Adultos, Secretaría de Educación Pública.

———. (1980b). *Paulo Freire: Educación y concientización.* Salamanca, Spain: Ediciones Sigüeme.

———. (1981). "Materiales para una historia de la sociología de la educación en América Latina." In G. González R. and C. A. Torres (eds.), *Sociología de la Educación,* pp. 77–110. México, DF: CEE.

———. (1982a). "Introducción." In C. A. Torres (ed.), *Ensayos sobre la educación de los adultos en América Latina,* pp. 9–17. México, DF: CEE.

———. (1982b). "From the 'Pedagogy of the Oppressed' to 'A Luta Continua': An Essay on the Political Pedagogy of Paulo Freire." *Education with Production Review* 1 (Gaborone, Botswana) no. 2 (November): 76–97.

———. (1982c). "Alianzas de clase y educación de adultos en América Latina: Hipótesis para una investigación." In C. A. Torres (ed.), *Ensayos sobre la educación de los adultos en América Latina,* pp. 201–30. México, DF: CEE.

———. (1982d). "Reconstrucción económica, social y educativa: el límite de lo posible."

In CEE, *Educación popular en América Latina: ¿Avance o retroceso?*, pp. 385–402. México, DF: CEE.

———. (1983). "Adult Education Policy, Capitalist Development and Class Alliance: Latin America and Mexico." *International Journal of Political Education* 6: 157–73.

———. (1984a). "Public Policy Formation and the Mexican Corporatist State: A Study of Adult Education Policy and Planning in Mexico (1970–1982)." Ph.D. dissertation, Stanford University, School of Education, Stanford International Development Education Committee.

———. (1984b). "The Political Economy of Adult Education in Latin America." *Canadian and International Education* 13, no. 2: 22–36.

———. (1988a). "An Analytical Framework for Adult Education in Alberta." *Alberta Journal of Educational Research* 34, no. 3 (September): 269–86.

———. (1988b). "Adult Education as Public Policy: A Perspective from Latin America." *Prospects* 18, no. 3: 379–88.

———. (1989a). "The Capitalist State and Public Policy Formation. Framework for a Political Sociology of Educational Policy Making." *British Journal of Sociology of Education* 10, no. 1: 81–102.

———. (1989b). "Political Culture and State Bureaucracy in Mexico. The Case of Adult Education." *International Journal of Educational Development* 9, no. 1: 53–68.

———. (1989c). "The Mexican State and Democracy: The Ambiguities of Corporatism." *Politics, Culture, and Society* 2, no. 4 (Summer): 563–86.

Torres, Rosa María. (1984). *Educación y democracia en la Granada revolucionaria.* Managua: INIES-CRIES.

———. (1985). *Nicaragua. Revolución popular, educación popular.* México, DF: INIES-CRIES.

Tunnerman, Carlos. (1983). *El pensamiento pedagógico de Sandino.* Managua: Ministerio de Educación.

Turner, L. and N. McMullen. (1982). *The Newly Industrializing Countries: Trade and Adjustment.* London: George Allen & Unwin.

UNESCO. (1965). *Methods and Means Utilized in Cuba to Eliminate Illiteracy.* Havana: Cuban National Commission for UNESCO.

———. (1968a). "Literacy Work and School Education in Economic Development." In *Readings in the Economics of Education.* Paris: UNESCO.

———. (1968b). "The Conditions of a Return to Investment in Adult Literacy Development." In *Readings in the Economics of Education.* Paris: UNESCO

———. (1971). Conferencia de ministros de educación y ministros encargados de ciencia y tecnología en relación con el desarrollo de América Latina y el Caribe. Venezuela, December 6–15. Caracas, Venezuela: UNESCO.

———. (1974a). *Proposal for the Collection of Adult Education Statistics.* (COM/74/ISCED/5). Paris: UNESCO, Office of Statistics.

———. (1974b). "Evolución reciente de la educación en América Latina," 3 vols. Santiago de Chile: UNESCO. Mimeographed.

———. (1976). *Recommendation on the Development of Adult Education.* General Conference of UNESCO, 19th Session, Nairobi, November 26. Nairobi: UNESCO.

UNESCO/CEPAL/PNUD. (1981). *Desarrollo y educación en América Latina: Síntesis general,* 4 vols. Buenos Aires: Proyecto DEALC.

UNESCO, Misión de la. (1965). *Métodos y medios utilizados en Cuba para la superación de analfabetismo.* Havana: Editora Pedagógica.

United Nations. (1963). *Compendium of Social Statistics.* New York: United Nations.

Unsiker, Jeff. (1987). "Adult Education, Socialism and International Aid in Tanzania. The Political Economy of the Folk Development Colleges." Ph.D. dissertation, Stanford University.

Ureña, Enrique. (1978). *Teoría crítica de la sociedad de Habermas.* Madrid: Tecnos.

Valdés, Nelson. (1971). *The Cuban Revolution: A Research-Study Guide (1959–1969).* Albuquerque: University of New Mexico Press.

Van Waas, Michael. (1981). "The Multinational's Strategy for Labour: Foreign Assembly Plants in Mexico's Border Industrialization Program." Ph.D. dissertation, Stanford University.

Vandergeest, Peter, and Frederick H. Buttel. (1988). "Marx, Weber, and Development Sociology: Beyond the Impasse." *World Development* 16, no. 6: 683–95.

Vasconi, Tomás A. (1977). "Ideología, lucha de clases y aparatos educativos en el desarrollo de América Latina." In Guillermo Labarca et al., *La educación burguesa,* pp. 173–237. México, DF: Nueva Imagen.

———. (1981). "Etapas de un pensamiento." In G. González R. and C. A. Torres (eds.), *Sociología de la educación,* pp. 303–14. México, DF: CEE.

Vergara, Regina. (1981). "El sistema nacional de educación de adultos." Licentiate thesis, Universidad Iberoamericana, México, DF.

Vielle, Jean-Pierre. (1980). "Panorama de la investigación educativa en México, 1979." *Revista de ciencia y tecnología.*

Vio Grossi, Francisco. (1982). *Investigación en educación de adultos en América Latina: Evolución, estado y resultados.* Santiago de Chile: OREALC.

Waiser, Miriam. (1980). "An Alternative Theoretical Approach for the Study of Literacy and Its Role in Development." IFG Program Report no. 80-B21. Palo Alto, Stanford: Institute for Finance and Government.

Wallerstein, I. (1979). *The Capitalist World Economy.* Cambridge: Cambridge University Press.

Washburn, Philo C. (1982). *Political Sociology. Approaches, Concepts, Hypotheses.* Englewood Cliffs, NJ: Prentice-Hall.

Weffort, Francisco C. (1968). "L'education, praxis de la liberté—Une étude du mouvement d'alphabétisation et d'education de base au Brésil." *Communautés* (Paris) no. 23: 4–12.

Weiler, Hans. (1983). "Legalization, Expertise and Participation: Strategies of Compensatory Legitimation in Educational Policy." *Comparative Education Review* 27, no. 2: 259–77.

———. (Ed.). (1980). *Educational Planning and Social Change: Report on an IIEP Seminar.* Paris: UNESCO-IIEP.

Weinberg, Gregorio. (1984). *Modelos educativos en la historia de América Latina.* Buenos Aires: Kapeluz-UNESCO-CEPAL-PNUD.

Welton, Michael. (1986). "An Authentic Instrument of the Democratic Process: The Intellectual Origins of the Canadian Citizens' Forum." *Studies in the Education of Adults* 18, no. 1 (April): 35–49.

———. (Ed.). (1987). *Knowledge for the People.* Toronto: OISE.

Werlhof, Claudia von. (1981). "Las mujeres y la periferia: Los puntos ciegos de la economía política." Bielefeld: University of Bielefeld, Sociology Faculty. Mimeographed.

Whitty, Geoff. (1985). *Sociology and School Knowledge: Curriculum Theory, Research and Politics.* London: Methuen.

Willis, Paul. (1977). *Learning to Labour. How Working Class Kids Get Working Class Jobs.* Westmead, England: Saxon House.

World Bank. (1974). *Education Sector Working Paper.* Washington, DC: World Bank.

Wright, E. O. (1978). *Class, Crisis and the State.* London: NLB.

Yarnit, Martin. (1980a). "150 Hours: Italy's Experiment in Mass Working-Class Adult Education." In Jane L. Thompson (ed.), *Adult Education for Change*, pp. 192–218. London: Hutchinson.

———. (1980b). "Second Chance to Learn, Liverpool: Class and Adult Education." In Jane L. Thompson (ed.), *Adult Education for Change*, pp. 174–91. London: Hutchinson.

Yopo, Boris. (1983). "Investigación participativa y educación popular. Alcances y perspectivas." México, DF: UNICEF. Mimeographed.

Youngman, Frank. (1986). *Adult Education and Socialist Pedagogy.* London: Croom Helm.

Zachariah, Mathew. (1986). *Revolution Through Reform. A Comparison of Sarvodaya and Conscientization.* New York: Praeger.

INDEX

Adult education: approaches, 6–16, 22; as class-oriented practice, 2, 43, 100, 110, 114, 119, 123; definition, 44 n.1, 54, 111–12; and development, 6, 17, 20, 37, 41, 98, 116–18, 120; difference with school-based education, 113–14; goals and functions of, 49–50, 61, 74, 88, 97, 109–10, 111–13, 124, 150; the memory of the colonizer, 19, 110; national systems of, 48, 57, 61, 67, 79–81, 89–91, 101–2, 104, 107 n.18; and pedagogy of the oppressed, 8–9, 39, 40–41, 97, 110–11; and political education, 8, 18, 78, 123; and politics, 5, 9, 33, 35, 89, 93, 98, 120, 127–44; and popular education, 8–11, 15, 89; and social mobilization, 8, 14, 95, 98. *See also* Adult education clientele; Class; Development/underdevelopment; Illiteracy; Literacy; Nonformal education; Pedagogy of the oppressed; Policymaking; Political economy of education; Political sociology of education; Popular education; State

Adult education clientele, 33, 35, 38, 42–44, 49–50, 54, 57–59, 110, 112–13, 131, 133, 142; in advanced industrial societies, 113; definition of, 34, 113–14; in Latin American societies, 114–16; as political clientele, 14–15, 33, 147

Altvater, Elmar, 38, 44 n.5, 130

Apple, Michael W., 30, 35, 47

Argentina, 18, 22 n.2, 44 n.2, 48, 68–69, 105 n.3, 106, n.6, 144 n.

Arnove, Robert, 9–10, 50, 81, 83–84, 87–90, 97–99, 110, 128

Associate-dependent development, 42, 65, 68, 71, 78, 96, 100, 117, 129, 147. *See also* Dependency; Development/Underdevelopment; Latin America

Avalos, Beatrice, 22, 69, 71, 75, 105 n.3

Bacchus, M. Kazim, 92, 116–18

Basic education, 7, 48, 50–51, 54, 62, 64, 84, 89–91, 107 n.19, 109, 113. *See also* Adult education; Education; Nonformal education; Political sociology of education; Sociology of education

Bhola, Harban S., 22 n.2, 40, 49, 98–99, 107 n.21, 118

ABOUT THE AUTHOR

CARLOS ALBERTO TORRES was born in 1950 in Buenos Aires, Argentina. As an undergraduate he attended the Universidad del Salvador, in Buenos Aires; in 1974 he graduated with a Licentiate and a Teaching Credential in Sociology. He earned his Master of Arts in Political Science at the Facultad Latinoamericana de Ciencias Sociales, FLACSO, Mexico City, in 1978. He graduated and worked for several Mexican universities and the Secretariat of Public Education. He subsequently pursued graduate studies in international development education at Stanford University, obtaining a Master of Arts and a Ph.D. in Education in 1984. He conducted post-doctoral studies in educational foundations at the University of Alberta, in Edmonton, Alberta, Canada during 1986–1988. He has taught at the Universidad del Salvador, in Buenos Aires; Universidad Pedagógica Nacional, and FLACSO, in Mexico City; UCLA and World College West in the United States; and at the University of Alberta and the Ontario Institute for the Study of Education (OISE) in Canada. Presently he is an Assistant Professor with the Department of Educational Foundations, University of Alberta. His books relating to comparative and international education, nonformal education and sociology of education include *La Praxis Educativa de Paulo Freire; Entrevistas con Paulo Freire; Paulo Freire en América Latina* (published in Spanish and Portuguese); *Paulo Freire: Educación y Conscientización; Ensayos sobre la Educación de los Adultos en América Latina; Sociología de la Educación: Corrientes Contemporáneas* (with G. González); *Poder Político y Educación en México* (with J. A. Pescador); *La Economía Política del Financiamiento Educativo en Países en Vías de Desarrollo* (with Martin Carnoy et al.); and most recently *The State, Corporatist Politics and Educational Policies in Mexico* (with Daniel A. Morales-Gómez) also published by Praeger (1990). In addition, he has published a number of articles in reference journals, and chapters in books and encyclopedias.